Lavery Library

St. John Fisher
College
Rochester, New York

Hitler's Millennial Reich

*Apocalyptic Belief and
the Search for Salvation*

David Redles

NEW YORK UNIVERSITY PRESS
New York and London

Grateful acknowledgment is made for all quotations taken from the following:

From *Mein Kamp* by Adolf Hitler, translated by Ralph Manheim. Copyright © 1943, renewed 1971 by Houghton Mifflin Company. Reprinted by permission of Houghton Mifflin Company. All rights reserved.

From *Hitler: Memoirs of a Confidant* by Otto Wagener, edited by Henry Ashby Turner, translated by Ruth Hein. Copyright © 1985. By permission of Yale University Press.

NEW YORK UNIVERSITY PRESS
New York and London
www.nyupress.org

Library of Congress Cataloging-in-Publication Data
Redles, David.
Hitler's millennial Reich : apocalyptic belief
and the search for salvation / David Redles.
p. cm.
Includes bibliographical references and index.
ISBN–10: 0–8147–7524–1 (cloth : alk. paper)
ISBN–13: 978–0–8147–7524–0
1. Germany—Civilization—20th century. 2. Millenialism—
Germany—History—20th century. 3. Hitler, Adolf, 1889–1945—
Public opinion. 4. National socialism—Public opinion. I. Title.
DD256.5.R382   2005
943.086—dc22   2005009275

New York University Press books are printed on acid-free paper,
and their binding materials are chosen for strength and durability.

Manufactured in the United States of America
10 9 8 7 6 5 4 3 2 1

To Eileen,

    a shining light for one whose study

        too often takes him into darkness.

Contents

Acknowledgments

Writing a book is a strange mixture of exhilaration and frustration. While there were times over the years when various obstacles appeared to overwhelm me, there were many friends and colleagues whose advice and generosity kept me going, including Shawn Easley, Jon Lee, and Joel Tishkin. I would like to thank especially Richard Landes, of the Center for Millennial Studies at Boston University, whose belief in my work was manifested in many tangible and intangible ways, including a small grant that helped in the completion of this work. Thanks as well to the CMS staff, Beth Forrest and David Kessler, who always made my trips to Boston a pleasure. I spoke at a number of Center-sponsored events, including a series of annual conferences on all things millennial, as well as a symposium on the Holocaust as Millennial Moment. I would like to thank the many scholars and attendees for their support and criticism, including, but certainly not limited to, Chip Berlet, David Cook, Gershom Gorenberg, Andrew Gow, Robert Jay Lifton, Charles Strozier, and Robert Wistrich.

Others who invited me to their colleges to speak and to further refine my work include Howard Solomon, at Tufts University; Paul Elovitz, at Ramapo College; and Juanita Luna-Lawhn and Laurie Lopez Coleman, at San Antonio College. Thank you.

I would be remiss if I did not make a special thanks to my mentor at Pennsylvania State University, Jackson Spielvogel, whose advice and friendship early in my career got me started on this path. I would also like to thank the late George Mosse, not only for the body of his work, which continues to inspire me, but also for his kind words of encouragement when we met at the U.S. Holocaust Memorial Museum some years ago.

Too often forgotten are the many librarians and interlibrary loan staff who help scholars such as myself find often obscure materials. Thank you very much. Finally, I would like to thank a very special librarian, my wife, Eileen Oliver. Her academic efforts on my behalf have been many. I would like especially to thank her for her love and faith in me as this seemingly interminable project unfolded. Te amo mucho.

Introduction
Nazism, Myth, and Meaning

This is a book about myth. To be precise, it is a book about the myth of the millennium and the correlated myths of apocalypse and the anticipated coming of a world-saving messiah. While these terms originated in a specific Judeo-Christian tradition, it would be wrong to restrict them to that context, for variations have appeared throughout the world and throughout history. As they are narrowly defined, the millennium (from the Latin *mille*, meaning "thousand," and *annus*, meaning "year") is the thousand-year period after the Second Coming of the Christian messiah-figure Jesus, as prophesied by John of Patmos in the book of Revelation. In this version of the millennium myth, Satan (the epitome of what I term the Evil Other) is locked in chains for 1,000 years, only to break free for one final, eschatological battle. The Christian messiah, taken over from the Jewish apocalyptic Son of Man, finally and definitively defeats Satan, the ultimate force of evil and chaos.

The word "messiah" comes from the Hebrew word for "anointed," with Christ the Greek for "messiah." Being anointed signifies that an individual has been chosen, usually by supernatural forces, to bring order to a world fallen into chaos. This is typically done by defeating the forces of the Evil Other. The word "apocalypse" derives from the Greek for "unveiling," which reflects the idea that the prophecy of John of Patmos revealed the "gnosis," the secret knowledge of the world's end—thus the term "revelation." In more common parlance, "apocalypse" refers to the end of the world, the end of history, and the end of time as we know it. The apocalypse often entails visions of a final battle between the forces of good and the forces of evil (order and chaos, respectively), comprising upheavals of all kinds, from fiery conflagrations to great floods, earthquakes to pestilence and plague, all marked by signs that the world is unbalanced

1

and coming to an end. For this reason we also use the term "eschatology," meaning "thoughts on the end of things."

Scholars from a variety of fields have noted a number of different catalysts that often generate millenarian movements. That such different events, from natural disaster, war, and colonization to the process of rapid modernization, all elicit such strikingly similar millennial symbolic formations and behavioral responses, despite wide variations in time and place, culture and context, points to the existence of some underlying causal factor that these apocalyptic catalysts share. It is rarely *solely* natural disaster, war, colonialism, or rapid modernization that acts as the primary catalyst for millennial reactions, but rather that each generates a series of interconnected events that in their cumulative effect destroy the traditional order, in all its political, economic, social, and religious manifestations.[1]

The multiplicity of causality, the convergence of cataclysmic events, creates rapid, sudden, and irrevocable change in society and change within the psyches of those who experience it. Therefore, it is not the specific causal agent of change that is key but the degree and rapidity of the change itself—change so sudden and so severe that basic structural systems break down. While it can be argued that all people experience rapid and radical change at some time in their lives, they do not necessarily turn to apocalyptic beliefs for support. Yet for the millenarian, the perceived harmony or balance of the world, including such things as normal patterns of birth and death, of marriage, faith, leadership, and economic well-being, are severely skewed. The perception of a peaceful harmony degenerating into a chaos of apocalyptic proportions results, in part, from the breakdown of heretofore stable social-ordering factors, such as family bonds, faith, and governmental and economic stability. These social-ordering factors not only are essential for creating order (structure) in society but also are important for the psychic stability of individuals within that society. In times of personal trauma or chaos, such as the convergence of a loss of a job and a subsequent breakup of a marriage, an individual can fall back on family and faith to regain a sense of order and stability. However, if these social-ordering factors cannot provide the needed stability, that individual might seek out a millennial sect or messiah-figure to provide it. For small millennial groups, then, rapid social change is not needed, simply rapid change in the lives of enough individuals that they join together around a prophet, messiah, or guru.

During times of rapid social change, however, these societal-ordering factors are often weakened considerably. This increases the possibility that a mass millenarian movement will arise, rather than the smaller sects or cults that can arise during relatively stable periods. This can be seen in the case of colonized peoples in the nineteenth and early twentieth centuries whose religion, customs, leaders, and economies were suddenly rendered ineffectual or obsolete.[2] In some cases, apocalyptic movements arise in precisely those areas where the ordering factors are already weak.[3] Many individuals in such circumstances are left with a profound sense of being lost, of being cut off from others, of having no sense of direction or meaning in life. They experience an inner or psychic chaos that is then projected back on the society, which in turn is viewed as being in a state of utter chaos, approaching apocalypse. The idea that Weimar Germany exhibited the converging catalysts that led to an experience of rapid and radical change that was subsequently interpreted by many Germans who became Nazis as a time of apocalypse is the focus of chapter 1.

Interpreting the chaos of rapid and radical change as a sign of imminent apocalypse, millenarians believe that the world has reached a historic turning point and that it is at a time that will witness either the end of the world or the birth of a New Order—a New Age of millennial perfection. This New Age is usually described as a period of perfect order, a changeless and, for the most part, eternal world. It is typically portrayed as a time without hunger and crime, without want or need, without disease, and, often, without death. It is this sense of perfection, of timelessness and changelessness, that links millennial notions all around the world. From a comparative perspective, then, we should not fixate on the specific number 1,000 but should focus on the idea of a perfect order to come. As I discuss in chapter 2, the Nazi conception of the *tausendjährige Reich,* literally millennial kingdom, was taken to be just such a perfect world, one cleansed of racial degeneracy, among other things.[4]

The followers of apocalyptic movements usually believe that they are an integral part of this historic turning point. Millenarians believe that they are not only witnessing the birth of the New Age but actively taking part in its fruition. For example, the Chinese Buddhist White Lotus millennial sect believed, as most millenarians do, that their historic mission would result in a profound universal transformation of the nature of society and humankind itself.[5] This transformation means, in part, that society will be governed by a new system of values and human relationships. In other words, a new myth or world view will replace that of the dying contemporary society.

George Shepperson has pointed out that the use of the Judeo-Christian term "millennium," signifying a finality, the end of the world, is somewhat misleading, for it really describes a transitional period. The millennium marks a time of transformation to something new and better, a perfect order that is timeless and changeless. Time and change, therefore, come to an end, but existence, for the chosen in the coming New Age, goes on.[6] The apocalypse, therefore, means destruction and end for some but transformation and redemption for the chosen.

Millenarians usually believe that they have been divinely chosen not only to survive the apocalypse but also to witness and perhaps help create the millennial New Age, thereby living eternally in the transformed new order.[7] The psychologist George Atwood found that patients who felt themselves called by higher spiritual powers for sacred missions used imagery that bore a "striking parallelism" to "all those saviors and recurring heroes" in "fairy tales, myths, and the literature of religions."[8] This clearly reflects the archetypal nature of the apocalypse complex, a collection of symbols that generates a sense of order to replace the perception of chaos.

With the perception of a total collapse of order comes a deep insecurity brought on by fears that eternal instability will replace the sense of eternal order. The apocalypse complex, with its symbols of eternity and harmony, is an initially unconscious psychic response that alleviates this fear. The correlated myths of eternal paradise, the past Golden Age and the future New Age, are illusions. They never existed in the past and will never exist in the future. But, as a symbol, the New Age of millennial perfection restores a sense of order to a perception of chaos and gives the believers a heightened sense of self-worth as one of the chosen, imbued with a sense of meaning and purpose, rather than a sense of hopelessness, as they help bring the New Order to fruition through their faith and/or direct action. But who first envisions the coming New Age and leads the faithful to its realization? Prophets and messiahs are essential for the emergence and development of most millennial movements. The conversion experiences of the Nazi Old Guard, detailed in chapter 3, clearly betray this pattern.

The coming messiah-figure may first appear in the visions of prophets, individuals with a facility for nondirected thinking, a mode of comprehension that is highly symbolic and often experienced as coming not from within the thinker but from some external or supernatural force.[9] This type of thinking is contrasted with directed thinking, a mode of comprehension that involves a conscious focusing of one's thoughts on the external world. Directed thinking is used primarily in our conscious or waking lives. A proclivity for nondirected thinking can be rooted in the particular nature of the prophet's psyche or result from training in altering consciousness, whether from meditation, induced trance states, the use of mind-altering substances, or a period of profound physical or mental illness. The prophet, whether it is his personal life or that of his society that is in a state of chaos, elicits the apocalypse complex and the symbolic forms of messiah, savior, redeemer, returning king, or some other culture-hero. In whatever guise, the messiah-figure is seen as an ordering principle without parallel, bringing order (salvation, redemption, deliverance) to chaos, salvation from apocalypse. If the prophet's vision of the coming savior is prompted more by personal trauma (rapid and radical change in his life alone) than by social chaos (rapid and radical change in society at large), his voice may go unheeded.

If, however, those prophecies are passed down orally or in written form, as with the prophets of ancient Israel or the poet-prophets of the White Lotus sect in east Asia, then the visions and their symbolic power can reverberate even centuries later. Contemporary millennial visions, prompted by specific personal and occasionally collective experiences, are therefore associated with pre-existing millennial traditions, lending authority and adding depth to the new vision, often updated and tailored to reflect contemporary times.[10] It is not that the specific cultural millennial tradition prompts all later expressions but rather that new visions brought on by the apocalypse complex, usually highly symbolic and dreamlike in form, are subsequently explained and elaborated by pre-existing millennial traditions. Contemporary apocalyptic visions gain legitimacy through association with traditional correlates.[11]

In many traditions, the messiah/prophet (the roles often merge at some point) is viewed as having been sent from God or ancestral spirits to show the path to the new world that is emerging. The messiah/prophet knows all truth, knows exactly what must be done to achieve salvation. He often is a warrior figure who will lead the righteous into battle against the minions of evil and immorality. It is the messiah-figure, along with prophets, who has the vision of the "new way," or "new path," the new view of reality necessary to re-order society from chaos. The "new way" propagated by an apocalyptic movement therefore often is first perceived by a single individual, the messiah/prophet. The new way is usually made known by some means of divine intervention, such as revelation, ecstatic experience, dream, or vision. The suggestion that Hitler viewed himself as both prophet and messiah is the focus of chapter 4. How many Germans who became Nazis, and many others, came to accept Hitler in both roles is the subject of chapter 5.

For some millenarians, the signs of imminent apocalypse, and the promise of a coming, transformed, better world, is their signal to induce that apocalypse. Believing themselves chosen not only to witness the Endtime but also to help bring it to fruition, some true believers consciously or unconsciously induce the apocalypse, "forcing the end," as the ancient Hebrews termed the actions of impatient messianic movements.[12] These millenarians assume that, since the signs of the time tell them that now is the time and since they have been chosen for a special mission, then the apocalyptic event must occur in their lifetimes. The apocalyptic event is induced because the possibility that the prophesied apocalyptic event will fail to occur means that the believer's sense of being chosen, of having a special mission, of being immortal, indeed the entire new postconversion identity, is illusory. This cannot be tolerated. The idea that World War II and the Holocaust should be seen as examples of an induced apocalypse is the focus of the final chapter.[13]

The apocalypse complex, therefore, is a set of interrelated myths. By approaching our subject from the perspective of myth, of the symbolic formations constructed by the human mind to give meaning to the meaningless, to reconstruct a sense of order from a world perceived to have descended into chaos, we can come closer to understanding the millennialism, messianism, and apocalypticism that are at the heart of Nazism. But how best to understand such a myth?

Myth can be understood in two fundamental ways, seemingly contradictory, but ultimately complementary. One perspective defines myth by its unreality or falseness. A myth is something that, while generally accepted, is in fact untrue. The interrelated myths that encompass millennialism, apocalypticism, and messianism can in part be understood in this way. To give but one example, the idea of an imminent millennium, a dawning New Age of peace and harmony, is an archetypal image of perfection that can never and will never become real. Yet the very unreality of myth may be its most powerful attraction, surrounding the imagery that supports the myth with an aura of mystery and supernatural power. Moreover, in the attempt to realize the unrealizable, millenarians for thousands of years have in fact achieved wondrous personal and social transformations. Individuals lost in psychic darkness, adrift in meaningless and empty lives, have found themselves "reborn" into the "light," their weakened identities suddenly transformed with a much stronger sense of personal meaning and purpose. This conversion is often at the heart of the individual experience of the millennial myth, and so it is with the Nazi Old Guard. Societies also have been transformed by the myth of the millennium, from the transformations wrought by Christian apocalyptic belief in Roman times and again during the Renaissance (a collective rebirth of society through the myth of the perfecting of society) to the millennial impulse that helped shape the settling of the New World, giving deep symbolic meaning to the American Revolution and Civil War, as well as to the modern Fundamentalist awakening.

However, attempts to realize the unrealizable, fraught as they are with ultimate frustration, have led some millenarians to commit horrific examples of inhumanity on a grand scale. For, when the millennial New Age is not achieved (and as a state of perfection it cannot be), millenarians often resort to coercion in an effort to quickly and irrevocably bring it about. In other words, convinced that the New Age of millennial perfection is destined to be realized in their lifetimes, some true believers attempt to induce the apocalypse themselves, through mass suicide or mass murder or by consciously or unconsciously involving themselves in a scenario that brings about mass death, theirs or others'. The mass suicides by the cultists of Heaven's Gate, the Solar Temple, and Jonestown, the mass murders committed by the followers of Charles Manson and the Aum Shinrikyo cult, the mass deaths of the Branch Davidians and those of the Brazilian Canudos followers, and, finally, the mass killings of the Nazi Final Solution all must be seen in this light.[14] The road to millennial perfection is filled with possibilities, transformative and catastrophic.

Myth therefore has another meaning, and another more powerful relevance than simply being something that is not true. Myth can be a potent reality-shaping force. The myths of a coming millennium, apocalypse, and messiah, while unreal in the sense that they have never occurred and will never occur, have real power to shape reality, to transform human modes of conceptualizing reality, enabling us to literally change reality itself. Specifically, the millennial myth attempts to reconstruct a sense of order from a perception of chaos. The degree of chaos in a given society can determine how real the apocalypse is perceived and how large the millennial movement may become.

Both Hitlerism, which I consider the messianic aspect of the National Socialist movement, and Nazism, its millennial and apocalyptic aspect, can be understood in both the real and the unreal senses of myth. For the history of the rise of Hitler and National Socialism is full of myths that I explore in subsequent chapters, such as Hitler's role as savior of Germany, as its redeemer from economic depression and the alleged machinations of evil Jewish Bolsheviks. Interestingly, this version of the Hitler myth still resonates not only with contemporary neo-Nazis but also with many uncritical observers who still credit Hitler with saving Germany economically and with rescuing the West from Bolshevism, neither of which is true. Myths, real or not, never really die.

Not surprisingly, the magnitude of the horror that was National Socialist Germany has generated as much literature as any event in modern history. This too is a testament to the human construction of myth. Historians themselves, in attempting to understand this darkest period of human history, have encountered myth, in the archives, in memoirs, in Nazi propaganda, in the speeches and writings of Nazi elites and the confessional writings of the Old Guard, and, finally, in the construction of their own historical narrative. This historiography of what the novelist Don DeLillo sarcastically, but not inaccurately, terms "Hitler Studies," is as much about myth as it is about history. Therefore, it is essential to understand something of the mythography of Hitler Studies.[15]

Nazi Religiosity and the Millennial Third Reich

For many years, the literature on National Socialism stressed the relative lack of ideological commitment on the part of the Nazis. One of the first detailed examinations of Nazi ideology was undertaken by Hermann Rauschning, a one-time Nazi supporter turned vocal opponent. In a series of works, Rauschning emphasized what he termed Nazism's underlying nihilistic character.[16] However, while Rauschning hoped to warn the world of the nihilistic and thus destructive nature of Nazism, his own writings, especially his controversial *The Voice of Destruction,* point in an entirely different direction. From his view, the horrors of Nazi Germany resulted primarily from the monomaniacal power goals of a shallow Machiavellian figure. However, if Nazism, in its apocalypticism, and Hitler, in his role as prophet and messiah, are not unique in history but simply another variation of the apocalypse complex, then this perspective will not do. If ideology was of little importance in the formation and spread of the movement and, consequently, of little relevance for understanding it, what is left for the historian to grasp? Was it all a shell game? Did 60 million people die simply to gratify the aggrandizing appetites of a few historical anomalies? This oft-mentioned nihilism may reflect the existential cynicism of Nazi contemporaries and later historians more than the historical reality of the times.

The Nazi nihilist myth then, like most myths, never really died. Many leading historians, while they now accept that the Nazis *expressed* a more or less cogent world view, argue that this fact is largely irrelevant since the leaders, followers, and most Germans never really *believed* it. These historians are still operating under the spell of the nihilist myth, clinging to the notion that it was all, in the end, *only* propaganda, the great lie, well told. And, even if these historians agree that Hitler and his closest associates believed in Nazism as a coherent set of beliefs, they argue that, since most other Nazis and, more important, most Germans seemingly ignored it, it is therefore largely irrelevant. However, I demonstrate in the following chapters that many in the Nazi Old Guard, and significant numbers of other Germans (as the reports of contemporary journalists attest), were indeed attracted to the millennial and messianic beliefs of the Nazis.

A few early studies of the Nazi world view did take its ideas seriously. These writers noted its obvious debt to volkish thought, a German offshoot of Romantic nature mysticism.[17] This approach is sometimes referred to as "irrationalist," since it ultimately charges the Nazis with adopting irrationalism as an intellectual virtue. By extension, this "struggle for the irrational" is then used to explain the conspiratorial hatred of the Jews and Germany's descent into barbarism.[18] Implicit in this view is the belief that the triumph of the irrational helps explain the brutality and violence of Nazism, ignoring the brutally logical nature of Nazi racial hygiene measures and ultimately the Final Solution itself. As becomes clear in later chapters, within its own conception of the apocalyptic nature of the struggle between Aryans and Jews, the Nazis' attempt to exterminate the Jews once and for all was highly logical. The means to achieve this goal were often rationalized to the extreme.[19] This criticism aside, the irrationalist approach did acknowledge, if only indirectly, the centrality of millennial thinking, pointing out the imagery of rebirth and regeneration, the fears of a racial apocalypse, and the hope of a coming messianic *Führer* (leader). These works, however, rarely moved beyond implying an

influence of volkish thought on the Nazi inner circle and never fully ac-
knowledged that the concepts they were discussing were in fact millennial.[20]

Robert Pois, in keeping with the authors already mentioned, argued
that National Socialism must be seen from the perspective of its religiosity.[21] In this he follows a number of authors who have focused on religious aspects of Nazism, including Ackerman, Stern, Heer, Ach and Pentrop, Tal, and, most recently, Steigmann-Gall.[22] Most of their works have
noted the Christian or, conversely, anti-Christian nature of Nazi religiosity. While they are certainly correct in both regards, such approaches miss
the archetypal nature of Nazi millennialism. Perhaps for this reason, each
study finds in Nazi religiosity a different expression of the religious impulse. Pois, for instance, stresses the importance of nature worship in the
Nazi world view, while Friedrich Heer profiles the Nazis' use of Christian
symbolism and rhetoric. Nazi ritual and pageant, and their obvious religious content, have also been a focus of study.[23] More often than not,
however, Nazi ritual has been interpreted as insincere in performance, a
blatant attempt to manipulate mass psychology. Once again this makes
the mistake of projecting the historian's own cynicism onto the sincere,
albeit horrid, aims and beliefs of the Nazis. In the same way, propaganda,
one of the most successful Nazi tools for instilling (or, in their term,
"awakening") racial consciousness in the populace, is often wrongly interpreted as just another device for gaining and maintaining power. While
political expediency was important, the message promoted was also
widely held by its promoters and by many of its intended audience. Besides, the politically expedient and the fervently believed often are part of
the same propaganda effort. Moreover, both efforts had the same ends in
mind—the translation of a specific *Weltanschauung* (world view) into political and social reality. Therefore, while Joseph Goebbels could be the
epitome of calculated cynicism, he was a true believer, as well. Propaganda, whether operating as the great lie or as a vehicle of sincere belief,
had the same goal of awakening the racial soul and always was a means
to an end—racial salvation.

A few contemporary observers, most importantly Peter Viereck and
Eric Voegelin, likewise saw a neoreligious impulse in Nazism. Yet they,
too, were strongly influenced by the nihilism myth, interpreting Nazism
as a "political religion" centered around a total rejection of the world.
According to this view, Nazism was ultimately a form of secular gnosticism.[24] Therefore, while these scholars noted the relevance of Nazi reli-

gious beliefs, they still found the Nazi world view to be at heart nihilistic—the Nazis were simply modern-day gnostics who rejected the world and consequently attempted to destroy it. Such views at times betray a none too sophisticated knowledge of gnosticism, for the world-rejecting aspect of gnostic thought was not, and is not, universally held.[25] However, this approach does underscore a valuable and little understood aspect of Nazi thought—the connection between gnosis and prophecy, the perceived ability to foretell the flow of history and, therefore, to choose the correct course. Traditionally, millennial beliefs originate in prophetic gnosis attained via some magical, occult, or visionary experience. According to a few authors, the esoteric world view of the Nazi inner circle was based, at least in part, on modern occult thought and visionary experience.[26]

Most important for the topic under consideration here, a growing body of literature points to the importance of millennialism, messianism, and apocalypticism in the Nazi world view. Norman Cohn first noted the possible connection between millenarianism and Nazism in his classic study, *The Pursuit of the Millennium*.[27] Importantly, Cohn also argued that psychology may be an important means of understanding millennialism. In later editions, Cohn tended to de-emphasize both Nazi millennialism and the psychological analysis, but time and subsequent research have proven Cohn right on both scores.[28] It was not, however, until the 1980s that Cohn's line of inquiry was developed to any great extent. James Rhodes, in his important and underutilized study, *The Hitler Movement: A Modern Millenarian Revolution*, analyzed both elite and minor Nazis and found a consistent millenarian tone in their writings and speeches.[29] My research both confirms and extends this view. Robert Wistrich, in his equally significant but similarly ignored *Hitler's Apocalypse*, likewise returned to original Nazi literature and speeches, especially as they related to the Nazi construction of the Jewish Other, and found them to be thoroughly apocalyptic.[30]

A number of German scholars have recently returned to the original writings and speeches of the Nazi elite and, rather than interpret them solely as propaganda (in the sense of the great lie), have begun to take them seriously as accurate reflections of the Nazi world view. Michael Ley and Claus-Ekkehard Bärsch especially have stressed the apocalyptic, messianic, and millennial aspects of Nazism.[31] Allowing the Nazis to speak for themselves, both Ley and Bärsch have concluded that Nazi messianism and apocalypticism were central to the Nazi construction of reality. Their work, however, is heavily indebted to Eric Voegelin's notion of political religion, with its secularizing of spiritual experience, and are too Judeo-Christian oriented to fully explain the archetypal aspects of millennialism. Ley and Ekkehard-Bärsch also focus solely on the Nazi elites and do not extend the implications of their work to the rank and file.

Finally, a common element of all of these works, from the 1930s to the most recent German works, is that they stress the "secular" nature of Nazi religiosity. There is a constant refrain that speaks of Nazism as a "secular," "political," "pseudo," or "ersatz" religion, a "secular" or "political" faith, a "secular gnosticism," or a "secular millenarianism." Such an interpretation seems to take for granted that a modern political movement, almost by definition, must be secular. In fact, this need not be so.[32] The all too easy comparison to millennial aspects of Russian Marxism has something to do with this as well.[33] Most important, the contemporary literature and archival sources that make up the bulk of the documentation in this book all speak of National Socialism as a *spiritual* movement created to meet corresponding spiritual needs. It is for this reason that I have subtitled the present volume *Salvation and the Spiritual Power of Nazism*, for it was the profoundly held belief by many elite and minor Nazis that National Socialism, led by its messianic Führer, held the key to salvation, not simply an economic and social miracle but a genuine spiritual transformation of Germany and, eventually, the world. This is apparent in the conversion experiences of minor Nazis, discussed in chapter 3, which alone demonstrate that Nazism was perceived by its followers as a spiritual phenomenon. Again, the question of sincerity is important. It is abundantly clear from the original sources that Hitler, his inner circle, and many lesser party members were indeed sincere in their millenarian spiritual beliefs.

This book began with a number of specific goals. First, as was mentioned, I desired to verify that millennialism, messianism, and apocalypticism were indeed major aspects of the Nazi construction of reality. Second, if this was so, what if any influence did this millennial world view have on the creation of the movement, and, importantly, in its rise from obscurity to a mass movement? And, finally, what were the catalysts for the generation of Nazi millennialism? I have concluded that Nazi millennialism was a pervasive aspect of the movement and that it was rooted in the very real social changes that occurred in Weimar Germany, changes that affected not only the Nazi elite but also the populace at large. In other words, I ground the intellectual beliefs of this elite in its social and cultural environment and unite its chiliastic dreams and aspirations with those of the masses that supported it.

But how best to understand this Nazi millennialism? If secularizing theories, irrationalist views, or views centered solely on Judeo-Christian apocalyptic traditions fail to encompass the complexity and ubiquity of millennialism, a broader multidisciplinary understanding of this subject is required. An approach is needed that encompasses the diversity of millennial movements that have occurred throughout the world throughout recorded history. This tack is in fact now being undertaken in the nascent field of millennial studies, and it's hoped that the brave scholars associated with this somewhat renegade academic movement will help answer the ultimate question of the essential humanness of millennialism.[34]

To better understand the ubiquity of millennialism and associated phenomena, I turned to sociological and psychological insight. I have avoided the all too easy trap of resorting to psychopathological analysis, interpreting millennial movements as examples of mass psychosis, all constellated around messiahs who are no more than psychopaths. Rather, I have tried to focus on both the potentially positive and the negative outcomes of movements that I believe result from the same initially therapeutic attempt by the human psyche to reconstruct a sense of balance and order after an experience of rapid and radical change, whether in individual lives or collectively in society at large.

What follows, then, is a study of myth. In particular, it is a study of how the apocalypse complex helped shape Hitler's messianic self-perception, propelled the formation, growth, and success of the Nazi movement, and ultimately gave impetus to what the Nazis termed the Final War and the Final Solution—World War II and the Holocaust. To best understand the Nazi version of the apocalypse complex, I have resorted to a number of sources that have been simultaneously misused and misunderstood. To grasp the richly symbolic world of the millennial myth, I have looked at not only the published speeches and writings of the Nazi elites but also the confessional writings of the Old Guard. I have also utilized a number of accounts of Hitler's monologues, his prophecy sessions, written by men such as Eckart, Rauschning, and Wagener. Although controversial, they are essential for comprehending Nazi millennialism. Because of the controversy, I urge the specialist to read the appendix to better understand my use of these sources. For the general reader, we turn to the Weimar culture of apocalypse.

1

A World Turned Upside Down
*Weimar Chaos and
the Culture of Apocalypse*

Before his untimely passing, the historian Detlev Peukert noted perceptively that the Weimar period (1918–1933) should not be seen solely as
marking the end of one era (the Wilhelmian) or as the beginning of another (the Nazi). Rather, he pointed out, it should be studied as an era "in
its own right."[1] And, I would add, as an era, Weimar was a culture of
apocalypse. While certainly not beset by the natural disasters that have
generated millennial movements elsewhere, post–World War I Germany
nonetheless saw changes take place in political, economic, social, and cultural spheres that were pervasive, profound, and irreversible.[2] It is more
than ironic that the word "Weimar" has become synonymous with the
very concept of modernity, for it is the process of modernization, more
than any other factor, that wrought the severe structural changes in all aspects of German society that in turn sparked the chiliastic fires that
loosed the demons of Nazism. While most of the structural changes
brought on by modernization were rooted in the industrialization of the
nineteenth century (and the urbanization that it generated), and while the
significant cultural changes that mark modernity generally had begun
around the turn of the century, it was during the Weimar years that this
rapid change was most profoundly *experienced* by a broad mass of people.[3] Postwar German society, therefore, appeared as far removed culturally from the prewar times as the twentieth century was from the nineteenth.[4] The convergence of catalysts that generates the rapid and radical
change necessary to collapse perceptions of order and thereby elicit the
apocalypse complex was not only present in Weimar society, it all but defined it.[5]

Political Chaos

World War I was greeted in Germany with a feeling of national euphoria, much as it had been in other countries. The war was viewed by many individuals as a holy mandate. One veteran and future Nazi believed that "it signified a holy duty to be followed through until its consummation." Another man saw "the outbreak of war as salvation." It was a divine fate that necessitated for many the ultimate sacrifice—one's life. A popular war motto, later taken over by the Nazis, was "Germany must live and so we must die." Some men even felt chosen for this duty. Another soldier and future Nazi explained that "we were chosen by destiny so that we could experience the front."[6] It was an experience that many yearned for, as one young man described it,

> I felt in me the draw to the front. The desire to be permitted to actively participate finally in this holy struggle grew stronger and rose mightily to pathological proportions. Beginning in October 1914 my wish found its fulfillment. With thousands of young volunteers I left for Flanders. A great bloodbath and dying had begun. All misery and danger, however, could not possibly result in the destruction of young Germany's power and will.[7]

Many Germans believed that from the bloodshed and martyrdom a social regeneration or rebirth could occur, as all classes and social groups pulled together in a *Volksgemeinshaft*, or "people's community." Kaiser Wilhelm's call for a *Burgfrieden* (domestic or civil truce) whereby all political parties, and the class interests they represented, would join in a common cause for Greater Germany only bolstered this enthusiasm. Yet, the truce was short-lived and the utopian dream of a community of unified Germans left unfulfilled. By 1917–18, disenchantment and disillusionment had become the norm among the various groups involved in the *Burgfrieden*. As the war dragged on, class conflict escalated, and, with the war's abrupt end in November 1918, the threat of Russian-style civil war appeared more a certainty than a possibility. After the war, the soldiers, after experiencing the organized chaos of war, returned home from the front to a chaos of a different sort. Roman Pornschlegel, a veteran and an eventual Nazi, recalled of his return: "but what did I find before me? A poor, bled to death Germany—divided and fragmented."[8] It was a world that appeared to be in a chaos of apocalyptic proportions. Another veteran remembered that "when I came from the field at the end of 1918 the situation which dominated Germany made it completely clear to me that under this system our Fatherland must go to the abyss."[9]

For many Germans, the most significant event that marked this "collapse" was the "evil revolt of 1918."[10] In contrast to the euphoria that greeted the outbreak of war, the collapse of 1918 and the many revolts of 1919 were seen, in the words of one future Nazi, as the "the pure antithesis of August 1914."[11] Another Nazi, Hans Neff, remembered that "the World War had ended, there followed a horrible time in German history: betrayal, infamy and economic decline were the consequence of that gray November day in 1919."[12] The contrast of perceptions of postwar chaos with the euphoria of the prewar *Burgfrieden* was especially hard for returning veterans, many of whom looked for scapegoats. The recollections of the veteran and Nazi Friedrich Schott reflect this tendency, linking the loss of the war with the infamous "stab-in-the-back" myth:

> When I returned home to my family circle after the war in the winter of 1918/1919, I was filled with a profound bitterness. I had experienced the war from the first day, with all its horrors and suffering, participating in many engagements and massacres. But I had endured all of this gladly, as I always had the unwavering hope that Germany would emerge victorious from these frightful battles. And now I had to experience in these dark November days, as a band of traitors, led by Jews, snatched the fruit of victory from the hands of our Fatherland and delivered us to the caprice of our enemies. So it was natural that I fed from the beginning on a profound hatred for the unscrupulous December men.[13]

Workers' rebellions, mutinies, and outright communist revolution were commonplace immediately after the war. One Nazi remembered these events with obvious disgust, using typical metaphors of sexual depravity and filth:

> With a bleeding heart I lived through the circumstances of the day, saw the worthless traitors stir up masses of men to storm upon the streets, saw them plunder stores, rummage through occupied houses, saw this more and more bestial mass orgy celebrated as everything holy was dragged into the mud.[14]

Many veterans of the front experienced the revolt "back home" as a betrayal. They were hurt by the lack of a hero's welcome. They quickly looked for a scapegoat, as one Nazi remembered, "the revolution was rampaging, the front suffered from behind. The veteran was scoffed at and derided, the International triumphed, Jews and Jewish servants seized power in the state."[15] The rising importance of the *Räte* (worker's councils) movement, the Syndicalists, and the Communist party frightened and confused many Germans. Similarly, Spartacist uprisings presented a threat of a Russian- or Hungarian-type revolution from the extreme left. The Nazi Heinrich Völker interpreted the lack of civil peace as a result of class conflict rather than the social unity that he believed would bring peace:

> I felt sad and disheartened when I saw the revolutionaries with their arm bands roaming about the streets. In my circle of comrades I searched with all my power to make clear that one cannot promise a people bread when in Germany itself none was on hand. Peace could not come if men and families inside Germany could not be as one.[16]

Another veteran and future Nazi described his experience similarly. His use of metaphors of darkness and light and his sense of an inversion of order, as well as the localizing of blame for the chaos on a perceived Evil Other, in this case the Jews, are typical of the Nazi apocalyptic mentality. He wrote:

> Barely 18 years old, I went to the field to defend our homeland against a world of instigating enemies. Twice I was wounded. Then in November 1918 the Marxist revolution broke out—dark thunderclouds descended over Germany that for fifteen years allowed no rays of light and no sunshine upon the earth. In Germany everything went upside down. The Spartacists, clothed in sailor's uniforms, devastated and destroyed everything they could lay a finger on. The Jew rose to the pinnacle.[17]

The German Revolution of November 1918 therefore made the specter of communist revolution seem all too real. Street violence was rampant as the extreme left and right battled over the fate of the nation. One Nazi remembered the times in vivid fashion. His reference to "unknown forces," most likely referring to Jews, working against the Volk hints at the conspiratorial mentality so typical of the apocalyptic movements in general, and Nazism, in particular:

> In March of the year 1919 there dawned in Germany the freest republic in the world, and yet unknown forces did not permit the Volk to rest. Spartacists marched through the streets with blood red flags and murdered and plundered. Civil forces and Noske-troops stood powerless against the goings on and were set upon and slaughtered.[18]

To battle the rising communist threat, right-wing paramilitary groups, called *Freikorps,* formed to battle the leftists. One *Freikorps* member and future Nazi, Josef Schulz, explained his decision to join:

> 1918—collapse. Instant unemployment. There was no assistance. The "victor" marched in. The Rhineland occupied. Americans in Linz. In unoccupied Germany Spartacists raged. I came as a volunteer orderly with a medical transport to Stettin in early 1919. Upon the return journey I saw on a placard in Berlin a proclamation: "Who will save the Fatherland? *Freikorps* Lützow! Join *Freikorps* Lützow!" Rootless and jobless, without even returning home, I joined *Freikorps* Lützow in Berlin.[19]

This man, having lost the sense of meaning and direction he had had during the war, found it anew in the paramilitary group. He would find it again with the Nazis.

The Kapp and Hitler *putsches,* or coups, which proposed to "save" the Fatherland from the leftists, were supported by many Germans (including many civil servants). Whereas the "revolts" from the left were seen as "betrayals," the putsches, though no less divisive and revolutionary, were viewed by many as a sign of hope. As Hans Haster interpreted the putsch, "Kapp is in Berlin, the Red government flees to Stüttgart. Anxiously I hope: has the turning point finally come?"[20] Similarly, another man said of the Hitler putsch, "Yet in Berlin one knew little of the Hitler movement. As with the Kapp putsch in 1920, so were the happenings in Munich a cause for my heart to rise higher—hope awakened. Yet also in this case it was again not fulfilled. It was again still."[21] Others, however, were more optimistic. Wilhelm Schuchman explained that while he had studied politics a good deal in the early 1920s, he had found that "nothing could inwardly liberate me. Then information of the Hitler putsch penetrated our region and caused me to prick up my ears."[22] Yet, despite this support, the putsches had the effect of making the threat of all-out civil war seem a very real possibility. As one man recalled, "the year 1920 was character-ized by the Kapp putsch and the communistic Ruhr revolts. It was a year of domestic chaos, a year of civil war. All of Germany stood opposing one another in two armed encampments."[23] Another man concluded, as many others did as well, that "all the difficult sacrifices at the front were done for nothing, and the camaraderie of the front was replaced in our Volk with fraternal strife and civil war."[24] The dream of the *Burgfrieden* was dead, but it would be resurrected in Hitler's National Socialism.

The political situation, therefore, was anything but stable. Decisions made at the Paris Peace Conference only made Germany's fragile condi-tion worse. In an effort to weaken Germany and to provide buffer zones in the east and the west, the Allies decided that Germany should lose ter-ritories on the continent and abroad. For many Germans, this territorial reduction was a ghoulish dismembering of the Volk body, designed to fur-ther weaken an already sick nation. The Allies further decided that the German military should be dramatically weakened in arms and people. While this was supposed to be the first step in a general European reduc-tion of arms, it was, for many Germans, a needless emasculation. The in-famous war-guilt clause, which forced Weimar leaders to accept German responsibility for the war, was another point of national humiliation. Not only did this indict the leaders of the fledgling democracy, but also it flew in the face of the opinion held by most Germans that their country had been forced to defend itself against "a world of enemies." It is perhaps not surprising, then, that the "insane dictate of Versailles," as one Nazi referred to it, became the focus of grievance.[25] Roman Pornschlegel re-counted with bitterness,

> The unholy Peace Treaty and the inflation squeezed us like a lemon. Many people had to live out their lives in the postwar time poor and hopeless. The promised silver lining remained out on the horizon. The former enemies were ever insolent and thoughtlessly used German land and exploited us yet more.[26]

This linking of Versailles to the perceived apocalyptic chaos of the post-war years was common, as one Old Guard Nazi recalled,

> The nightmare of the degradation of our Fatherland, which through the Versailles Treaty nearly had its breath stolen, hindered the free develop-

ment of industrious German working men. Everything that was created by hand was stolen by the Versailles Treaty. Hunger and deprivation swept over Germany like an epidemic. It appeared to us nearly unthinkable that such a treaty, one that led an entire nation to the edge of an abyss of destruction, could be created in a civilized world.[27]

Any political system that arose from such a hated treaty was faced with the near impossible task of winning supporters from a suspicious and frightened populace. The Weimar democracy encountered such a challenge.

Perhaps most important, in the view of many of its citizens, Germany was forced to yield a say in its political determination. Deeming German monarchism one of the prime agents responsible for the war, the Allies believed, rather naively, that the institution of true parliamentary democracy in Germany would prevent a recurrence of such a conflict. Unfortunately, the democracy that developed, the Weimar Republic, was viewed by many as an un-German, "Judaized" system forced on the German people. Many dedicated their lives to its destruction, such as Jakob Buscher, who explained that "now more than ever my solution was to fix everything upon the destruction of this murder-state, this Jewish-Republic."[28]

The confusion and indecision that parliamentary democracy can create, particularly in a society unfamiliar with it, led to the perception of a "parliamentary quagmire" at exactly the time when a clear and decisive policy appeared sorely needed.[29] The proliferation of competing parties created what many termed pejoratively the "Parteisystem." This "system" became a symbol of the disunity and chaos that were bringing Germany to the verge of apocalypse. It was a common complaint that "party quarrels and squabbles splintered the Volk."[30] Hans Otto observed that parties "grew like a fungus upon the earth."[31] Another Nazi agreed:

one government alternated with another. Marxist mass gatherings! The citizenry was splintered into smaller and smaller parties. Program upon program swirled through the air. A completely uniform and clear direction was lacking. It appeared impossible in this witch's temple to find one's way from one slogan or another. The Volk was fissured in interests and opinions, in classes and estates—a plaything of enemy powers and nations.[32]

Once again, metaphors of filth, depravity, and decomposition are associated with the disunity that was bringing Germany to the abyss. What they called for were purity and a regeneration of society, something the Nazis would make a fundamental tenet of their beliefs.

Economic Chaos

If the political situation seemed chaotic, economic conditions during most of the Weimar years were nothing less than catastrophic. Prior to the war, the German economy, powered by rapid industrialization, had been marked by almost continuous growth. It was this expansion that, in many ways, made modernity possible. It raised the possibility of a broad spectrum of social welfare reforms while simultaneously providing the monies necessary to fund them. Yet, thirty years of industrial expansion ended abruptly with the beginning of World War I. The war itself played a large role in the sudden change in economic good fortune. Germany's first real inflation began during the wartime economy, as the government financed the war through deficit spending. Following the war, the transition from wartime to peacetime economy was difficult. The new socialist government desired to fulfill the prewar promise of a modern welfare state and a more cooperative relationship between trade unions and employers. The *Burgfrieden,* which held out the dream of employers and employees working hand in hand for the betterment of society, now seemed attainable. With the revolution of 1918–19, the opportunity of realizing these dreams was seized by the reformers from the left. Unfortunately, the postwar economy was such that these generally humanitarian (and costly) aims were attempted at the worst possible time. The rapid and radical change wrought by modernity, combined with the general chaos of postwar Weimar, eroded the social-ordering factors that had made that change at least bearable, creating exactly the scenario necessary for the appearance of a millenarian movement.

Like the other participants in the war, Germany was burdened by massive debts. This was greatly exacerbated by the Allies' decision to demand reparations from Germany to pay for their material losses. These included not merely those damages caused directly by Germany but the cost of the war as a whole. At the Paris Conference in January 1921, a sum was fixed at a seemingly astronomical 226,000 million gold marks. While this figure was later reduced to 132,000 million, it was no less staggering.

The main cause for the enormity of the debt figure were the loans owed by Belgium, France, and Britain to the United States, which had greatly financed their war efforts as the war dragged on. When the United States demanded repayment of the loans, the Allies in turn required fulfillment of the reparations. As a number of historians have noted, the actual burden was not as dramatic as it first seemed, for it is not the size of the debt but the method of payment that matters. It was, over time, a workable plan. However, what matters for the present study is how the average German experienced and interpreted the imposition of reparations, not the economic reality. For most Germans, the reparations appeared to mean that generations of Germans would live out their lives in what was often termed "debt slavery." It also seemed to be a tacit acknowledgment of German war guilt. Reparations, then, came to be important not so much for economic reasons but for symbolic and psychological ones.

When Germany was late in making a payment toward the end of 1922 and asked for a temporary suspension of payments, France marched into the Ruhr. While officially the occupation was meant to guarantee payments by assuming control of Germany's industrial heartland, French leaders also hoped to separate the region from the rest of the Republic. The German populace understandably was enraged. For many, it was this incident above all that led to an acceptance of Nazi thought. One man noted that "first the Ruhr march, with all its hardships, brought me nearer to this way of thinking, and with a feverish heart I followed the goings on and great deeds of our German freedom fight in the homeland."[33] The Republic used this outrage by declaring a policy of passive resistance. A general strike was called in an effort to eliminate France's "guarantee" by paralyzing industrial production in the Ruhr. The wages and salaries of all workers and public employees were paid by the state. Not surprisingly, violence in the region increased dramatically, with various acts of terrorism, as well as struggles for, and against, the so-called separatist movements. Paramilitary groups sprang up to meet the challenge. As one Nazi explained, perhaps with some justification:

> The year 1923 will be predominately characterized by the Ruhr invasion and the foreign crisis. 1922–1923 found the state in its highest misery. In this highest misery the Black *Reichswehr* was created. If it had not been for Versailles, if the French imperialistic policy had not triumphed and reached its hand toward the Rhine and the Ruhr to split Germany, then the Black *Reichswehr* would not have been created.[34]

This resistance separated the residents of the Rhine region into what another Nazi, Heinrich Wick, designated "patriots" and "Volk traitors."[35] Once again, the "traitors" were linked symbolically with Jews as Evil Others, forces deliberately creating apocalyptic chaos. As Ludwig Nöll attempted to explain, "the Jews were for me, from purely instinctive foundations, already an atrocity, as were the Separatists who succeeded in their domination of the Rhine. I assisted in bringing this 'domination' to an end." Gustav Bonn recalled that "Rhineland Separatism raised its head already here in Wiesbaden, bringing great disorder and terror to the city and promoting the ruin of broad masses of people." Dr. Daum, another future Nazi, remembered that "the shame of the November criminals of 1918, the occupation of the French and the activities of the Separatist rabble oppressed the Rhinehessen in intolerable ways."[36] The Separatist movement split workers, creating further disunity. One man noted that "my boss at that time, Hecker, confessed finally one day to bearing a membership card to the Free Rhineland Movement [a Separatist movement]; whereupon a violent argument between him and me ensued. Result: jobless!"[37]

Those who died in this resistance, such as Albert Leo Schlageter, became the first martyrs in the Nazi pantheon. The description of one man who participated in Schlageter's funeral demonstrates the unifying effect martyrdom can have for those searching for a sense of community. The implicit notion of martyrdom, the ultimate self-sacrifice, leading to the resurrection of the Volk from an abyss to a paradisiacal New Age reflects the millennialism found throughout the autobiographies of minor Nazis. He wrote,

> The flag-draped coffin and the serious eyes of the honor guard left behind a profound impression for me. With the song of the fallen comrade the old banner of the student union was presented as a final salute. A holy vibration seized the multitude from the great love of Volk and Fatherland as it had this quiet hero. As this moment slowly vanished the multitude voiced the song *The Watch over the Rhine,* and there I felt that this must be the spirit of this hero, this spirit of the final submission, which alone is fit to return our Volk from the abyss and to lead it to a new, better future.[38]

Constanz Heinersdorf, in his eulogy for Schlageter, likewise spoke of sacrifice, rebirth, and immortality:

you were inspired solely by a glowing love for our fatherland. . . . You believed in Germany's future and longed for its rebirth. . . . Through your manliness you knew how to gain even the great respect of your enemies. . . . Yours was a moving, exemplary character. . . . Live on, comrade.

A memorial rally was held on the first anniversary of Schlageter's death in Nuremberg, complete with torchlit parade. At the rally, Rudolf Kötter also spoke of redemption and resurrection to eternal life:

> You have redeemed us like that other hero who died on the cross at Golgotha, and you have given us the strength to live and to die just as you did, for your belief in freedom and greatness for our Volk and Fatherland. Albert Leo Schlageter lives![39]

To pay the wages and salaries of the passive resisters, the government simply printed more money, for which it had no real backing. This sent the already steadily rising inflation soaring. The decade from 1914 to 1924 was one of constant inflation. In 1914, 4.2 marks equaled one U.S. dollar, soon after the war, in 1919, it took 8.9 marks to buy one dollar. However, by November 1, 1923, the ratio had reached 130 billion to one, and by the twentieth of the same month it had peaked at 4 trillion, 200 billion to one.[40] With money essentially worthless, life savings, pensions, and salaries became meaningless. The stories of loss are sad and many. One Nazi recalled his parent's experience:

> My parents' house, which had a peace value of Rm. [Reichsmark] 38,000, was sold by them for the price of a pound of butter. Bank savings shortly disintegrated to almost nothing. From this [it] occurred that the life-long property of my parents went over to foreign hands and they were simply put out on the streets. This experience, to have lost everything that my father had worked for during his entire life, brought my parents to an early grave. It was simply inconceivable for the old people that this bale of banknotes in their hands was simply worthless.[41]

Heinrich Wilkenlon, describing 1923, recalled that "we stood in the midst of the chaos of inflation. My first apprenticeship compensation cost me Rm. 40,000."[42] Previously, that sum would have bought him a house.

It is important to remember that, before the war, Germans had known little inflation. Consequently, the fall in the mark's purchasing power at home and its rapid decline in foreign-exchange markets hit especially hard. With money worthless, unemployment increased, and hunger riots occurred with increasing frequency. One future Nazi recalled that "many times I had hunger—I received for my millions of marks not even a breakfast roll." According to Willi Martin, "then came the eventful and fateful year 1923. The inflation wave rose immeasurably, the Reds pursued the Volk with one demonstration after another. Nothing remained of the German Volk save hunger and misery." Another future Nazi, Werner Goerendt, remarked that "the madness of the inflation was celebrated like an orgy."[43] The inflation further increased the sense of division within German society. The story of one young man bears this out:

> The inflation incited, to a large degree, the small against the great. Conceptions of "mine and yours" became arbitrarily exchanged. Foreign currency here and there and then another election. Only the strongest, with great hearts and deep souls, could withstand such a crash.[44]

The social effects of inflation, therefore, were complex and profound. While the introduction of the *Rentenmark,* equivalent to 3 trillion marks, in combination with American loans, stabilized the inflation, the psychological effects of this period would continue to reverberate throughout the relatively tranquil period to follow. The word "relative," however, is important. In fact, historians often refer to this period from the end of the hyperinflation to the Great Depression as one of "deceptive" or "illusive" stability, with the "appearance" or "semblance" of normality.[45] Detlev Peukert noted that neither the deeper structural tensions caused by the peace treaty and the establishment of the Republic nor the profound tensions generation by the inflation were alleviated by the end of the inflation, in 1924. In fact, it can be argued that these very tensions gathered strength during the years of so-called stabilization and were ultimately responsible for the collapse of the Republic from 1930 to 1933, when the final catalyst, the depression, proved too much.

The collapse of Wall Street reverberated around the world, striking Germany particularly hard, for it was overly dependent on foreign credits. With the fall of the last parliamentary government under the Social Democrat Hermann Müller, Germany entered a period of renewed chaos.

The economic effects of the depression in Germany were particularly harsh. Production fell so precipitously that capitalism itself seemed to have run its course. From 1929 to 1930, the capital-goods production index fell from 103 to 81; from 1913 to 1932, it sank to a level below that of the prewar years, from 61 to 46. Consumer-goods production and prices also dropped, although not as dramatically. At the same time, wages were extremely depressed, with real wages dropping to 87 percent of the 1928 level. Most significant, mass unemployment ravaged Germany with plaguelike horror. Unemployment, at 8.5 percent when the depression hit in 1929, rose to 14 percent in 1930, 21.9 percent in 1931, and 29.9 percent in 1932. The rate was even higher among unionized workers, reaching 43.7 percent in 1932. Of course, unemployment affects not only workers but their dependents, as well. To grasp the effects of unemployment it is essential to understand that numbers tell only a part of the story. Even white-collar workers who kept their jobs faced huge salary cuts, while shopkeepers and tradesmen were struck by falling prices and equally dwindling purchasing power. Farmers were not immune to the catastrophe, either. The situation in Germany, then, was bleak and seemingly spiraling downward. As one Nazi remembered, "the economic misery was daily greater, the mood in the Volk daily embittered."[46]

Importantly, the phenomenon of long-term unemployment (lasting up to five years) became increasingly common. Besides the obvious catastrophic financial difficulties long-term unemployment engendered, it also increased the sense of loss of status, self-worth, and, consequently, self-respect. Living year after year at bare subsistence level, without any means of contributing productively to society, made poor self-perceptions even more acute. Morever, the fact that unemployment insurance and emergency relief benefits were meant for only short-term situations exacerbated the crisis. That the much-hyped welfare state of Weimar could not help these people (in fact, it was not structurally designed to do so) only made its claims to legitimacy seem all the more fallacious. Consequently, the depression meant more than economic hardship; it legitimated the desire for a messianic Führer who would take the reigns of power in his hands, demolish the ineffectual and much hated "system-state," and usher in a millennial New Age of peace and prosperity, bread and work.

Social Chaos

The experience of social change during the Weimar years was as radical for many Germans as the political and economic changes. Most of this change resulted from the fundamental demographic shifts that accompanied industrialization (and its offspring, urbanization and modernization). The demographic revolution did not occur unnoticed. Many Germans feared a *Volkstod,* the literal extinction of the German people through a decline in the birthrate. The German population had experienced a high annual growth rate for decades as industrialization, with its concomitant improvements in health and welfare, led to a surplus of births over deaths. That this population surge was accompanied by a migration to the cities, particularly by the young, made the growth rate seem all the more vital and impressive. However, a closer look at the numbers reveals significant changes, particularly apparent for the years 1910–1925.[47] Statistics show prewar growth in population with a baby-boom generation, born around the turn of the century flooding the job market as never before. Indeed, by 1925, the active work force (ages 14–65) was at its highest level ever. Moreover, all age groups age 12 and up were larger in 1925 than in 1910. But within this growth there were significant changes, with the war being the most precipitous cause. The number of thirty- to thirty-five-year-old men in 1925 was below the 1910 level, with a corresponding surplus of women, many forced to remain single, creating a large reservoir of working women. The fifteen- to twenty-five-year-old baby-boom group, most of whom had missed the war, now faced a saturated and declining job market.

These demographic shifts and other changes brought on by industrialization generated fissures and tensions between the sexes, between generations, and among social classes. The result was a growing perception that society was becoming increasingly fragmented, a fragmentation that mirrored the psychic condition of many Germans who longed more and more for a community of blood, a unified nation miraculously healed of its many traumas. The Nazis' notion of a *Volksgemeinschaft* (racial community) appealed to this need. A deeper look at how profound these fissures were is warranted.

For the younger generation, these demographic changes were particularly frustrating as they faced a saturated and virtually frozen job market. This only exacerbated the traditional conflicts that occur when a younger generation attempts to make its place in society. This "redundant" or "superfluous" younger generation, as it was sometimes termed, responded with a cult of youth, attempting to replace self-perceptions of nullity with a heightened sense of self-importance, one that manifested as a sense of mission encouraged by an atmosphere of "apocalyptic expectation."[48] While these efforts to elevate the status of youth (and, for the older generation, to solve the problem of youth) had begun in the nineteenth century, they, like so many other aspects of Weimar, were most significantly felt and noticed in the 1920s. Since the youth movement was essentially an urbanized and industrial phenomenon, it manifested a dynamic and progressive sheen, yet simultaneously frightened an older generation that viewed the young as potentially dangerous if left uncontrolled.

Just how to socialize these wayward youths into the old order during times of rapid change was hotly debated. Youth were funneled into various sports clubs and other youth organizations, such as the relatively small but vocal *Bund* elite groups (including the *Wandervögel,* a hiking group that evolved into a highly nationalistic entity). This "constructive" use of youths' free time was considered extremely important, for it was believed that too much freedom (or lack of authority, as it was often construed) was the main cause of youthful excesses. Although it was meant for everyone, free time became synonymous with the young. Group leisure activities, such as listening to the radio and to records, going to movies and dance halls, hiking and journeying cross-country from youth hostel to youth hostel (part of the emerging culture of tourism), all were products of modern life. The marginalist wild clique, predominately working-class youth who thumbed their collective noses at social conventions, deliberately shocked the staid older generation. That the model for the new youth subculture was deemed "American" alarmed many Germans (old and young), who found it "un-German" and polluting. The fear of an "Americanization" of Germany was largely specious, but, as Americanism was equated with the hated values of modernity, German youth found themselves divided. They were either supporters of a new, exciting culture or defenders of a embattled traditional one (a group to which many young Nazis belonged). The sudden growth and popularity of youth movements, sports clubs, and other such age-specific group activities provided dynamic groups like the Nazis with ready-made fodder for the coming battle for the Third Reich.

The changing role of women in the Republic was somewhat similar to that of youth. There was a conflict between new opportunities and freedoms on one hand and an unfortunate (and specious) association with what many saw as the shadow side of modernity on the other. Detlev Peukert delineated three main areas of change regarding women—the role of women in the workforce, the significance of the women's movement, and the largely mythic appearance of the "new woman."[49] In the workforce, the change was not so much in the total number of women working, which rose only slightly, but in the declining number in traditional "woman's" work and the concomitant rise in the number in new "modern" jobs. From 1907 to 1925, the proportion of women working as domestics and farm laborers declined (from, respectively, 16.1 to 11.4 percent and 14.5 to 9.2 percent). However, in the industrial sector, the proportion of female workers rose from 18.3 to 23 percent; among white-collar workers, women constituted 12.6 percent, where they had been only 6.5 percent.[50] Besides these changing patterns of employment for women, the most significant change, and the one that engendered the most heated debate, was in the gender-based division of labor. Women were predominant in modern jobs, many of which had been dominated by male workers but which now were becoming the new "women's work" (e.g., shorthand typist, assembly-line worker, shop assistant, primary-school teacher, and social worker). These occupations were considered appropriate for single or widowed women, while a married woman with a job was considered a *Doppelverdeiner* (double earner), and a threat to the earning capabilities of men.

The organized women's movement in Germany had begun, like other developments in question here, during the Wilhelmian age. German feminism pushed for a greater role for women in society by arguing that women could bring a special "motherliness" to the heretofore manly society. Great strides were made, and the war provided many women with new opportunities to contribute to a variety of social services. With the creation of the Republic came the right to vote and to run for office. Educational opportunities, especially in universities, were likewise expanded (though traditional male exclusivity, particularly in fraternities and social clubs, limited those opportunities). These significant advances for women alarmed more conservative men and women. The fact that the new modern woman had taken on an image as the American flapper (more a male fantasy drawn from Hollywood films than a reality) did not help matters. The rejection of modernity and the rejection of the mythic new woman often went hand in hand.[51]

These changing definitions and perceptions of youth and women were often tied to changing perceptions of sexuality. Such perceptions—

including changing gender roles (in work, marriage, and child-rearing), fears of increasing sexual freedom (and the concomitant rise of venereal disease), falling birthrates (and the alleged duty of women to halt it), and the need to deal rationally with these issues of sexuality—were fiercely debated. Attempts to provide clear, concise, and much-needed information on safe sexual practices (including contraception and the prevention of venereal disease) were contrasted with fears of falling birth rates and the pollution of the Volk body, once again making fears of an imminent racial apocalypse seem legitimate. Progressive thinking on safe sex, then, became mixed with the new eugenic movements, inspired by U.S. models, which were more concerned with natural selection than with healthy sexual relations. New ideas on sexuality gained some acceptance but were as often condemned by traditional views of church and of middle-class and provincial society.

Many Germans viewed these changes in sexuality as marking the decline of the family, of family values, and of morality in general. The openness of sexuality was also a startling change. Nude and homosexual theater abounded, particularly in the cabarets of Berlin. The free-love movement grew, and hard-core pornography and prostitution proliferated. Berlin became the symbol of the new Sodom and Gomorrah, much as New York still commands that image in present U.S. society. Once again, this "new society" seemed particularly shocking to the returning veteran. One Nazi felt that "immorality, brutalization, assaults were the order of the day and there were yet few men who looked upon these goings on with disgust."[52] However, the most hated "development" in postwar German society was the hardening of class divisions that seemed to bring the nation to the verge of civil war.

Tensions between the generations and between the sexes, as strong as they were, were overshadowed by those among classes. Many a future Nazi complained that "the Volk was fissured into interests and opinions, in classes and estates," and bemoaned the "madness of class hatred." For these individuals, the Volk's "greatest misfortune was the splintering into parties and classes."[53] The use of words such as "fissure," "fragmentation," and "splintering" occur throughout the autobiographies of Old Guard Nazis, reflecting a perception that society was breaking apart at the seams. While this social disintegration was never as real as these Nazis believed it to be, it was real enough to be believed. And, once again, this sense of fragmentation in society reflected, at least in part, a projection of the psychic fragmentation that occurs when a perception of order is destroyed by rapid and radical change.

Modernization played a large role in this developing sense of social fragmentation. Class structures were shifting perceptibly, with the self-employed dropping from 19.6 percent of the workforce in 1907 to 15.6 percent in 1925, while white-collar workers and civil servants increased from 10.3 to 17.3 percent, and manual workers decreased from 54.9 to 50.1 percent. The migration from country to city, which fostered an intense debate on whether Germany was to be an agrarian or an industrial country, also affected social classes. The social, religious, and regional segmentation of society was experienced as a fragmentation, or "splintering," of the German Volk.

The splintering within social groups can be seen most clearly within the socialist working-class society. The years of revolution, 1919–1920, saw a seemingly irreparable split occur within the socialist working class. The impetus for fissure, the revolution itself notwithstanding, included increasing tensions between skilled and unskilled workers, young and old, and large firms and small ones. The revolution created a huge gulf between Communists and Social Democrats over just how far the revolution should go. Differences in party memberships clearly show the social differences, with the Communist party members much younger, less skilled, and more unemployed. There was little common experience between the social groups that constituted the two parties. Labor groups developed into increasingly insular worker's associations that, although they were designed to foster solidarity, had the effect of increasing social segmentation among laborers. The experience of one worker who would turn to Nazism for salvation from this division is relevant here, for it displays the fraternal strife within the working class as well as the tendency to look for conspiratorial forces manipulating workers from without:

I took an active part politically, for I could not see how good German colleagues of mine could see me as a class-man and not as a worker because I was a baker's son—that knocked me over. These people were goaded on, for nothing came from their hearts. Rather one perceived in them that they were incited from without. It must be those circles who truly felt that if brother struggled against brother than they could dispose of peaceful shops. I had severe arguments with my colleagues in the trade union, as I often said to them that any German who works was an equally entitled *Volksgenossen* (racial comrades) and there should be no class distinctions. I must work like any other.[54]

Emil Hofmann was more direct in laying the blame for the class division. His interpretation that class conflict was a deliberate ploy of the Jews within and without Germany, and his belief that such divisions were the primary cause of Germany's impending apocalypse, avoided only because of the intervention of the Führer, is typical of the Nazi millennial mentality. He wrote,

> It was clear to me what had brought the war and the revolt of 1918, namely a class state: here peasant, here city person, there worker and the laughing third, the Jew. Each party believed itself to be right. They went after, however, the final goal which was not the welfare of the Volk, rather each was concerned solely for itself. No wonder the German Volk had lost the faith and will to live. In its place tread shame, disgrace and baseness. The Versailles Dictate robbed us of our colonies and we had to surrender entire districts to the enemies. Our beloved Fatherland appeared heading for its complete ruin. Jews governed with their helpers, the Marxists and the bourgeoisies. Only one man understood these politics and that was Adolf Hitler, who opposed this madness.[55]

As industrialization and modernity brought changes and divisions within worker's culture, it did much the same with the many new white-collar workers and the old middle class. This old middle class, the so-called *Mittelstand*, centered around craftsmen and shopkeepers and maintained its identity through a mythic and decidedly antimodern idolization of *Stand* (estate). However, war and inflation hurt the *Mittelstand* considerably. Income decreased precipitously and perhaps, more important, the privileged position the *Mittelstand* had enjoyed during the Imperial age had largely vanished. The new economic world meant big business and trade union corporatism—not estate privilege. This decline in social status led, in part, to the erosion of the liberal middle-class vote. Many turned to the far right, while many more simply became politically apathetic. Georg Witt, a justice inspector and a future Nazi, went so far as to blame his own middle class for not standing up against the Spartacist communist revolts:

The year 1919 followed with all its unpleasant happenings. *Spartakus* rose up its menacing head. Rifle shots cracked, machine guns rattled and gunfire roared through the streets of our residential district. German blood was shed by Germans. I found nowhere something to which I could cling onto in my concern for Germany. The Spartacists were for me criminals. The Social Democrats I came to assess differently: they contained perhaps many courageous idealists. However, they did not have the power to master the situation. One thing, however, I understood ever more and more and that was the cowardice and complete lack of resistance of the middle class which allowed these criminals in our Volk.[56]

As divisions existed within the working classes, the middle classes were divided between *Mittelstand* (middle estate) and *Angestellten* (white-collar workers). Whereas the *Mittelstand* were generally self-employed, white-collar workers were employees (as were blue-collar workers). Yet, white-collar workers, with greater status and income, perceived themselves to be distinct from the working classes. Consequently, they existed somewhere between the *Mittelstand* and the working class. Reflecting this fact, white-collar workers generally supported the new Republic and trade unions. But the effects of modernization quickly eroded this support. Mechanization, anonymity in a mass culture, and a loss of individuality as workers became facts of the new modern economic life; all tended to subsume white-collar workers in the morass of rampant (and vapid) consumerism.

The demographic shifts brought on by industrialization, urbanization, and modernization generated numerous profound and unsettling tensions and divisions. Relations among age groups, sexes, and social classes became increasingly strained. Social classes especially became radicalized, as tensions created divisions not only among classes but also within them. Germany, therefore, was a country bitterly divided at a time when only absolute unity appeared capable of bringing salvation. The very social-ordering factors that individuals normally fall back on during times of personal trauma were themselves greatly weakened. Economic collapse weakened social supports, such as relief programs, while social divisions strained traditional relationships between elders and youth, parents and children, and men and women and among workers of all classes. If that were not enough, one other important area of Weimar life was in a state of rapid and radical change—culture. In culture, further divisions, this time between proponents of modernism and its many detractors, only made this disunity all the more noticeable.

Cultural Chaos

Although often underestimated in its importance regarding the rise of Nazism, the cultural change manifested in Weimar Germany was as dramatic and, perhaps, as consequential as the political, economic, and social factors. The very concept of modernity is borrowed from art history, and it was during the Weimar years that modern art made its most profound impact on the psyches of the masses. For, while modern art had begun around the turn of the century, it was during Weimar that it began to move from the margins to the masses, at least in terms of awareness, if not taste, for most Germans remained attached to traditional styles. Many conservative voices condemned the new art as un-German and decadent (it was often viewed pejoratively as "American," "Bolshevik," or "Jewish"). This was particularly true of those who turned to Nazism for salvation from the seeming decay of modern culture. This tendency can be seen in the cultural impressions of one minor Nazi who portrayed Weimar culture as a decadent world ripe for apocalyptic cleansing, with the usual blaming of the Jewish Evil Other:

> Meanwhile Germany further decayed. In unpleasant ways an entire Volk was alienated from itself. A new society spread out which only recognized the majesty of one's own ego. Sinister poison gushed forth into the brains and blood of German men in theaters and cinemas, in varieties and in dance halls. German youth, often still children carried in one's arms, moved about this hideous depravity, as all that was great and holy in our Volk drifted away. An unbelievable sensual orgy had seized Germany and a Volk danced a death dance to the rhythm of foreign music—and the Jew held the baton.[57]

This situation created a divided culture—with one side embracing modernity, while the other rejected and feared it. One promoted art as a utopian enterprise, while the other remained highly pessimistic and sought salvation elsewhere. The modernist culture and the traditionalist culture coexisted in Weimar, each viewing the other as "mutually alien and hostile, each denying (though with very different degrees of justification) that the other was a culture at all."[58]

The avant-garde was first represented in painting around the turn of the century. Expressionists, cubists, and futurists broke with tradition, freeing color, form, and perspective from their basis in observational reality. This detachment from objective reality, and the retreat to an inner subjective and highly emotional reality, culminated in abstractionism. The avant-garde prided itself on its alleged, or at least desired, connection with the masses (in the hope of leading society to new spiritual heights via art). Dadaism responded with a mockery of these utopian desires, putting forward everyday objects, such as commodes, as works of art. And yet, the use of utilitarian objects for artistic expression, such as John Heartfield's photomontages, ironically led to mass artistic reproduction. The merging of art, utilitarian craftsmanship, and consumerism, now a hallmark of the twentieth century, had begun. For some artists, however, seeing expressionist cigarette billboards marked the death of expressionism as an art form and, perhaps more pointedly, reflected the apocalyptic chaos in Weimar society. The art critic and Social Democrat Wilhelm Hausenstein found this commercialization of expressionism "disgusting," saying that

> those responsible really ought to have their skulls fractured. They are playing fast and loose with catastrophe. With the catastrophe—with our catastrophe. Expressionism is the ideal realm of the catastrophe; the fanciful flight of the catastrophe; its attempt to be positive, indeed optimistic. It has, however, secretly become the catastrophe of the catastrophe.[59]

While expressionism, abstractionism, and Dadaism (as well as purism, verism, futurism, and constructivism) all are often seen as being definitive of Weimar art, it was the so-called *neue Sachlichkeit* (New Objectivity, or Matter-of-Factness) that may have been Weimar's true original contribution. The *neue Sachlichkeit* stressed a return to reality-based representation, albeit in a still somewhat abstract and stylized way. It emphasized pragmatic, sober reflection of everyday life. Otto Dix's paintings of poverty-stricken street people were meant to awaken socialist passions of righteous indignation against the callowness of the modern capitalist city. The new objectivity was, in comparison to the utopian salvationism of the early expressionists, highly pessimistic. It acted through reportage, attempting to show modern life in all its hollow glory. One contemporary critic summed up this pessimism in a review published in *Die schöne Literatur:*

> But what if [artistic] form—that is, all known and familiar forms—has become a lie, because the present age, as a cultural epoch, has no form—creates no forms other than steel structures, machines and other technical marvels? What if the present age, both in its material externals and in spiritual, cultural and artistic terms, is itself a formless, disintegrated mishmash—it is as God-forsaken and futile as any age has ever been? . . . Who can doubt that a casualty of this age will want to vent his cries of despair?[60]

Yet, for conservatives, representing such a formless, chaotic world where beggars and prostitutes reigned supreme could only but hasten the coming collapse. Paul Schultze-Naumberg, an architect, art critic, and later favorite of the Nazis, rejected a contemporary art where "were one to name the symbols that find expression in the majority of the paintings and sculptures of our period, they would be the idiot, the prostitute, and the sagging breast. One has to call things by their right name. Spreading out here before us is a genuine hell of inferior human beings." His "overall impression" of contemporary art was "of utter chaos, of a planless and rootless mess, of an uncreative groping for sensations, of an utter lack of genuine, unpretentious humanity, and the absence of truthfulness of any kind." Hitler simply found in modern art the "mental excrement of diseased brains."[61] Critics, and many Germans, were divided between those who saw in the new art an honesty that could lead to social reform and those who saw it as being just another sign of approaching apocalypse.[62]

In classical music, twelve-tone composers such as Arnold Schoenberg, Anton Webern, and Alban Berg created radically new forms of musical expression, although the atonality of their work offended many listeners. Performances of Berg's 1925 opera *Wozzeck* caused near-riots because of the subject matter and the new musical forms. Critics were largely hostile to the new music, and the masses never really warmed to it, either. Other composers, however, such as Paul Hindemith, Kurt Weill, Hans Eisler, and Ernst Krenek, attempted to translate the new music to a wider audience through the use of film, radio, the gramophone, and the popular theater.

In popular music, jazz was the rage. For some critics, jazz had the power to revitalize and renew a Germany grown staid and ossified. The speed and rhythm of jazz seemed a perfect music to accompany the rapid staccato of a world increasingly ruled by the repetitive movement of pistons and gears. Alice Gerstel, writing in 1922, found in jazz the expression of all the chaos that was Weimar and, ultimately, a clarion call for the masses to rise up and revolt. Describing jazz as the sound of the times, she wrote,

> It unifies within itself everything that remains from the great collapse of the world and humanity, dances with it over the abyss. . . . It has that "rat-a-tat" of the cannons they have been firing at the "enemy" for five long years. . . . It has the trumpets that called the coal miners in Ostrau to arms, the drums that called exploited humanity to its last revolt.[63]

That jazz was the music of African Americans attracted some and horrified others. Both groups used racial stereotypes in their praise or condemnation. Ivan Goll, in a piece titled "The Negro Conquers Europe," wrote, "the Negroes are here. All of Europe is dancing to their banjo. It cannot help itself. Some say it is the rhythm of Sodom and Gomorrah. . . . Why should it not be from paradise? In this case, rise and fall are one."[64] Other, more conservative individuals vilified jazz exactly because of its primitivism and dangerous sexuality. There was no redemption to be found in humanity's baser nature, only in its highest spiritual virtues. The infiltration of jazz into German culture, whether in popular form or in the music of Weill and Krenek, was interpreted as a poison. For some, this new music reflected a deliberate attempt to destroy the older forms. One music student, who would later become a Nazi, believed that "Jewish-Marxists" wanted to annihilate "Germany's highest spiritual good, its music."[65] While all this new music stimulated many adventurous listeners, for others it simply reflected the divisive and fractured state of modern life, providing a cacophonous soundtrack to the approaching apocalypse.

In popular theater, the use of new forms to reach a mass audience made strides. Revues, many featuring near-nude American dancers, were popular with the general public but scandalized just as many others.[66] Deliberately chaotic and fragmented like the world in which they were born, these revues, with colorful sets, new music, and precisely timed dance routines, provided light entertainment for the masses. Cabaret was another attempt to lampoon modern life, albeit with a sharper tongue and a more biting wit than the revue. Beginning around the turn of the century, cabaret mixed entertainment with nonconformist attitudes such as Dadaism. Especially popular in Berlin and among homosexuals, cabaret continued throughout Weimar as a center of nonconformist (or, more properly, nontraditionalist) expression. For some critics, it was precisely cabaret's satirical sadism that justified its existence. Not all cabaret had such highbrow aspirations. The Cabaret of the Nameless, where no-talent wannabes performed nightly to the derisive jeers of jaded audiences, was part Roman spectacle, part Gong Show. But even here critics found refuge from the horrors of contemporary existence. For the lyricist Erich Kästner, the Cabaret of the Nameless acted as an outlet for the darker side of human nature. It was better that people express their sadism here than on the streets of Berlin:

> The metropolis in its natural form is an inhumane place to be and inhumane means are required for it to be endured. The main thing is that the nameless are as invulnerable as a sword swallower. So it is probably possible after all to absolve this cabaret, just like one excuses dreams in which murderous and shameful acts occur. Such dreams purify people for their doings by the light of day.[67]

For many other Germans, however, cabaret simply marked how far society had fallen—Sodom and Gommorah as sideshow. Topical theater, socialist multimedia spectacle, bawdy revues and cabarets were seen as reflections of a nation collapsing from within and without. This perspective was especially prevalent among those who became Nazis, many of whom viewed this "immorality" as a deliberate "weapon" of the Jews. One Old Guard Nazi, Robert Rohde, an actor/playwright and a friend of Goebbels, described his perceptions of the Berlin theater scene in this way:

> During my activity on the Berlin stage I acquired deep insight into the judaization of German theater arts and of the absolute dominance of Jewry. Reinhardt, Rosa Valetti, Gilbert, Rottus were my superiors! The German actor was merely put up with. Fifty-one Jewish theater directors were in Berlin.[68]

Perceptions of degenerate art forms were interpreted as a rising immorality that itself betrayed the evil machinations of sinister forces. Joseph Goebbels, not surprisingly, felt much the same way as his disgruntled friend. Writing in 1928, he described the Berlin theater district in words as salvational and millennial as they are xenophobic and anti-Semitic:

> The eternal repetition of putrefaction and decay, of wanting originality and genuine creative power, of inner emptiness and despondency, with the patina of a Zeitgeist sunk to the level of the most repulsive sham-culture. . . . Here the German people is alien and superfluous. You attract attention if you speak the language of the country. Pan-Europe, the *Internationale*, jazz, France and Piscator—those are the catchwords. . . . This is not the true Berlin. It remains elsewhere and waits and hopes and struggles. It begins to recognize the Judas who sells and disposes of our people for thirty pieces of silver. The other Berlin lies in wait, ready to pounce. Several thousand work days and nights on end so that one day the day will come. And this day will shatter the abodes of putrefaction all around the *Gedächtniskirche* [memorial church]; it will transform them and give them over to an arisen people. The day of judgment! It will be the day of freedom![69]

Weimar culture was noted for its innovations—its radical departures from traditional forms, whether in a modernist abstract sense or in the New Objectivity's emphasis on the harsh and often seamy reality of modern life. While most of the modernist innovations were in fact pre-Weimar in origin, it is the general perception of radical change *during* the Weimar period that is important here. And when that change is perceived as being one from order to chaos, form to formlessness, purity to impurity, then the sense of a coming apocalyptic end becomes more understandable. The emphasis of the New Objectivity on exposing the existential horror of Weimar, while designed to foster positive social change, for many only reinforced their perception of imminent social collapse. However, perceptions of cultural decay are usually not sufficient to elicit apocalyptic fears; nor is a sense of chaos in political, social, or economic spheres alone. It is the combined and convergent nature of the chaos, the sense of total chaos, that is most significant.

Total Chaos and the Perception of Apocalypse

The sense of apocalypse was generated by two intertwined factors. First, the four areas of chaos (rapid change) did not occur separately but were inherently and inextricably linked. For political, economic, social, and cultural changes do not occur in isolation from one another. Second, it is the accumulated and convergent nature of the chaos, the total chaos, that makes apocalyptic fears and millennial and messianic hopes attractive. Both of these factors are tied to structural aspects inherent in modernity, for if modern life is characterized by anything, it is the ubiquitousness of change. Technology breeds change, and change necessitates further technological innovation. Moreover, in modern life, all aspects of existence (political, social, economic, and cultural) have become, more than in any other time in history, linked in a web of causality. What occurs in one sphere, almost without derivation, affects other spheres.

Some Germans who experienced the various areas of rapid and radical change tended to blend them into one general perception of chaos. The Nazi Georg Heinzebecker recalled that "soon after the revolts began the misery: unemployment, relief works, then the inflation. Parties formed like sand in the sea. Then the year 1923 came upon us. Misery stood at its height."[70] Another Nazi, Hans Neff, had a similar impression of the early 1920s. Characteristically, he blamed the usual Evil Other—Jews:

> Then followed strikes, lock-outs one after the other, wage increases and price inflation alternated reciprocally, ever more class struggle was preached and exhorted by International Jewry. Civil war raged in German districts and completely overwhelming was the degree of want and misery as the inflation overtook our Germany.[71]

A review of a few of the cataclysmic events discussed earlier in this chapter should suffice to make clear the degree of intertwined change and its pervasive effects. For instance, the hyperinflation of 1923–24 was decidedly more than an economic catastrophe. The Republic, which was hardly basking in the glow of public support, lost much of what little respect it retained. When the salaries of the civil servants failed to keep up with inflation, and when the recession of 1926 caused job reductions and salary cuts, any support the government enjoyed quickly evaporated. This can be seen in the story of a former supporter of the Social Democratic Party (SPD) and later Nazi Party, who worked at the Hüttenwerks factory in the Ruhr district. In his case, fear of an imminent racial apocalypse overrode any advances in social reform for the working class:

The achievements of the glorious revolution, with its eight-hour day, vacation and so on, allowed me soon enough to become a trusted council of approximately two hundred apprentice members of the Free Trade Union and a follower of the SPD. Prudently one said in a whisper the maxim, "I know no Fatherland called Germany." And yet a day had to come when I understood that faith alone in the power of Germans who had pride of race-consciousness must get my vote. For the existence or non-existence of my Fatherland, indeed the entire world, was at stake.[72]

An erosion of support likewise occurred among many young students who soon realized that their futures were decidedly bleak. The inflation heightened the animosity toward the state as employment opportunities in the civil service and in higher education were found wanting. One young man, who later turned to Nazism, found in radical youth groups that "for me only one thing was clear: the limp government could at no time bring a salvation from the misery."[73]

Besides the political effect of inflation, the psychological consequences deserve mention. The inflation caused many to lose their accustomed way of life, as well as their position in society (and the self-worth that went along with it). Consequently, many people turned to profiteering and crime motivated by poverty in a desperate effort to maintain status and, ironically, to achieve some semblance of the old social order. According to Detlev Peukert, an "inversion of value" had occurred, with the drive for money and success justifying breaking the law, while honesty became a useless luxury in times of runaway inflation.[74] The war, revolution, and inflation led to a weakening of traditional social and moral ties, evident in the rise in crime, especially among the youth who saw their futures fading away. Not surprisingly, mass crime mushroomed during the inflation of 1922–23. The sense of inversion, its apocalyptic rendering, and the explanation of its occurrence by blaming the Jewish Evil Other can be clearly seen in the following description of postwar Berlin by another future Nazi:

All the great buyers were mostly cheap Jews. Central sales in Berlin: profiteering and corruption on a large scale. Jews and the white profiteers became rich, feasting and living at the cost of the Volk as if in a "Promised Land." The newspapers agitated against any national awakening. Germany appeared lost. Resigned, the Front soldier attempted to safeguard his family from ruin and hunger. The German housewife and mother stood shoulder to shoulder next to her husband in this struggle against a difficult fate. Strikes and revolts in all districts. Germany's fate appeared sealed. A temporary false boom after the inflation, the greatest fraud of all time perpetuated on a thrifty, industrious and decent Volk. A world turned upside down! Work was punished, the profiteer became rich. Public houses with prostitutes worked and sprouted up all over the earth. All the sluices of vulgarity appeared open. The Front soldier and the decent part of the population led a nearly hopeless struggle against this epidemic. Parliamentarianism was celebrated like an orgy. Roughly 35 parties and factions arose and confused the Volk. A pure witch's Sabbath! The German Volk, devoid of political acumen, staggered toward the diverse will-o'-the wisps, sick in body and soul.[75]

German society was, in many real ways, profoundly divided. This division was reflected in the shattered psyches of many Germans. Here social division was seen as reflecting moral decline, which in turn generated a search for a messianic leader to bring unity and, therefore, salvation. The following description of postwar Germany by a returning veteran exhibits this tendency:

A new Germany appeared before the eyes and one felt the moral decline of a formerly strong nation. Marxist false teaching had caused the Volk, already in the broadest circles, to forget the concept of national honor. Then came the madness of the Marxist revolt of November 9, 1918 and with it the final collapse of the German nation. Party quarrels and squabbles fragmented the Volk. Always standing upon a national basis, I made a spiritual search for an unknown power, which embodied the notion of a national and social Germany. Standing amidst the maddening struggle of self-sacrifice in a life of sales, this vision grew stronger and stronger. The faith was certain in me that only a strong personality could vanquish the hate and strife through a national and social greatness.[76]

The Nazi reaction to the profound changes of the Weimar period was obviously extreme. Many who became Nazis interpreted this period as not simply hard times but, in apocalyptic fashion, as a total "collapse" of German civilization. Once again, the apocalyptic construction of reality reflects, in part, a collapse of an inner perception of order. Not consciously aware of this, these individuals projected their inner chaos onto a world that was in extreme disarray, though by no means approaching apocalypse. Viewing the world through apocalyptic lenses, many early Nazis believed that Germany was at best threatened by "enslavement" and, more frequently, "annihilation." One early Nazi supporter said of the times that "Germany seemed doomed" in a "struggle against an overwhelming fate," where "the world was turned upside down" and the "the suffering and despair of the people, subjected to foreign occupation and a number of communistic uprisings, was terrible . . . there was a constant tension in the air . . . there was no unity of purpose anywhere."[77]

Weimar was conceived as a time of apocalypse or salvation. One Old Guard Nazi, Wilhelm Scherer, recalled the German Day celebration of 1923 as the awakening of a faith that could forestall apocalyptic collapse:

> That was a new milestone, the movement had awakened, and one saw the honest enthusiasm of the co-fighter, a stimulus to press further ahead and not to lose from sight the goal despite this time of despondency and general dissolution. Precisely this day nourished and strengthened the faith that we must be victorious or Germany would go to the abyss.[78]

This sense of imminent annihilation was common as, another early Nazi noted, "Germany staggered more and more towards the abyss."[79] That Weimar was generally described by such words as "disorder," "confusion," "abyss," and, most often, "chaos" points to a psychological inability to structure a perception of reality into a coherent and meaningful pattern. Gustav Bonn wrote of the postwar period that "the disorder was too great to comprehend," while Albert Barnscheidt felt that "it was a spiritual and corporeal struggle—the disorder nearly overpowered me— no party, nor person, could help me."[80]

Occurring simultaneously, the converging catalysts of political, economic, social, and cultural change in Weimar Germany were extremely disorienting and caused great insecurity for those who eventually converted to Nazism. Like most apocalyptic movements, Nazism viewed these changes as resulting, in part, from a dissolution of moral standards and the "relativization" of reality that this entails. This view can be seen in the following excerpt from an essay by Gregor Strasser, an important leader of the Berlin Nazis:

> There is a dreadful hopelessness in the souls of humanity, a disintegration of all firm values, an instability which looks in vain toward a focal point which it finds no more in religion and has lost in morals! "Relativ-

ity"—that is the motto of the culture of our times—relativity in all things, relativity in all knowledge, relativity in feeling—and the dull anxiety of a bad conscience that attempts in vain to conceal the inner stability with "psychoanalysis." The core itself is eaten away and had to a great extent already gone missing![81]

On the anniversary of the first year of Nazi rule, Hitler made a speech in which he looked back on the Weimar era as a time of collapse and impending apocalypse, marked by an inversion of moral and ethical standards in which the positive force of preservation (the Aryans) battled the negative force of destruction (Jewish Bolshevism):

Fourteen long years Germany had suffered under a decay unparalleled in history. It brought into action an inversion of all conceptions. What was good was bad and what was bad, good. The hero was scorned and the coward honored, the honest punished and the corrupt rewarded. The decent man had but to expect ridicule. The depraved however found praise. Strength decays with condemnation; weakness, on the other hand, gains with glorification. Value means nothing. It numbers third place behind inferiority and worthlessness. The historical was defiled in infamy as the historical future was carelessly denied.

Those who had faith in the nation and its rights were attacked with shameless audacity, laughed at and reviled. On the position of love for beauty tread a cult of inferiority and ugliness. Everything healthy ceased to be the guiding star for human striving, while the monstrosities, the sick and depraved, joined in the middle of a so-called new culture.

Every sustaining pillar for the existence of the Volk had been undermined and brought to collapse. And already the existence of millions of the middle class and peasantry fell into ruin, aided, as luck would have it, by dumb citizens in enthusiastic political drudgery, preparing for the final collapse.

Can we seriously believe, that a nation in a state of perpetual collapse can be stopped, without the result of the most extreme and final consequences? No! This must lead to communistic chaos!

Because to the same extent that the nation's leaders consciously departed from all knowledge and laws of reason and instead now prescribed to the insanity of Marxism, the society of people had to suffer an incessantly accelerating disintegration. The positive forces of preservation began to loosen and to fall apart, and only the negative forces of destruction merged into a frightful uniformity in their universal assault against the last remnants of existence.[82]

Germany, according to Hitler, had collapsed, with all sense of morality and righteousness turned upside down. Consequently, Germany, indeed the world, had arrived at a turning point, one that promised eternal salvation or eternal damnation. Typical of the conspiratorial tendency found in apocalyptic thinking, these Nazis found meaning and a sense of order by explaining the chaos as resulting not from chance but from the deliberate tactic of an Evil Other. Weimar chaos was not seen as being simply the sorry consequence of the loss of World War I and the fluctuations of modern economics. Nor was it perceived as resulting from the structural tensions and rapid change wrought by modernity, though in many ways it was. The apocalypse complex constructs a sense of order in differing ways, and one way is to bring meaning to chaos, by explaining it either as the vengeance of a righteous god or as the evil machinations of a satanic antigod and its earthly minions. The early Nazi inner circle found its evil satanic minions in a complex international conspiracy of Jewish Bolsheviks, Freemasons, and Jesuits.[83] It was the Jews, however, who functioned as the apocalyptic Evil Other supreme. Once again, all archetypal visions of the apocalypse complex find expression in a specific historical context. For Hitler and the Nazis, the fear of apocalypse was interpreted in racial terms. This is not surprising, since in the late nineteenth and early twentieth centuries, it was the notion of separate races struggling for existence that informed the construction of historical evolution. According to the Nazi millennial world view, the Germans, indeed the entire Aryan race, were threatened with racial extinction. It was a racial apocalypse that demanded a racial salvation.

2

The Turning Point
Racial Apocalypse or Racial Salvation

The total chaos of the Weimar period, particularly in the early years, elicited a profound sense of collapse for many Germans, outwardly and inwardly. Perched on the edge of an abyss, the Nazis in particular came to believe that Germany, and indeed Aryan humanity in general, had reached a historic turning point. The old order had collapsed, requiring the appearance of a New Order (a new perception of reality, what the Nazis termed *Weltanschauung,* or world view). In true apocalyptic fashion, Hitler explained to a journalist,

> the day is not far off when we shall be living in great times once more. What we now need is that intelligent writers should make clear to the citizens of Germany the historic turning point at which Germany stands today. We are on the threshold of a unique new epoch in our history. We have reached the turning point when the bourgeoises must decide whether it will choose Bolshevik chaos in Germany and therefore in Europe, or a National-Socialist Germany and a new order on our continent.[1]

Alfred Rosenberg likened this turning point to those that ushered in the Renaissance and the Enlightenment: "today is again a turning point in the history of the world. At the beginning of the sixteenth century one began in Europe; at the end of the eighteenth century another set in; at the beginning of the twentieth century is again decline and rebirth." According to Rosenberg, it was a rebirth into a "new synthesis of life," not simply a new form of government but an inner spiritual transformation: "today we are all inwardly experiencing a collapse, and we have a deep longing for a new form of life."[2]

The testimonials of the Old Guard clearly reflect a sense of living at a time that would bring either apocalypse or salvation. Jakob Hoffmann stated that "I always believed a union of the best forces of Germany must bring about a turning point in order to save Germany from chaos."[3] Wilhelm Scherer remarked that he was happy to have been "able to contribute" to what he termed "a world-historical epoch." Describing this epoch, he explained,

> a presentiment arose in me that only revolution must follow, like one that the glorious history of Germany had not yet experienced. Yes, like one world history had not yet, till now, produced. Germany put into effect a world turning point, brought about by our Führer, his movement, and many of our best who had sacrificed their sacred blood.[4]

Heinrich Maxeiner exclaimed that "I, however, rejoiced that a benevolent fate had placed me in this great destiny and turning point of our Volk— to have allowed me to experience the striving and struggling for it."[5] Similarly, another minor Nazi stated that "we are thankful to our Creator to be able to live in this age," while yet another proclaimed that "the greatest fortune that could befall me was the circumstance that I was born into a time like no other."[6] Finally, Arno Belger, a local propaganda leader from Halle, described this "world turning point" in language reflective of his role within the movement:

> An over-strained, spiritually hollow age drew to its close, as antiquated and decaying liberalistic social orders and forms collapsed into themselves. Europe breathed with difficulty under the stifling nightmare of that Uncertain yet Inescapable which was summoned by the shot at Sarajevo as a purifying bath of steel closed upon the civilized world, and so produced the pre-condition for the evolution of the new man of community.[7]

This turning point marked the death of one age and a rebirth into a new age. Rosenberg's notion that out of the collapse of civilization there is rebirth is a significant and recurrent element of Nazi millennialism. For many Nazis, the death of their world necessitated the birth of a new world. According to Hitler, it was the Nazis' mission to help finish off the dying old world so that the new one could be born. As he explained to Otto Wagener,

That is precisely the most profound secret of the entire revolution we are living through and whose leadership it is our mission to seize: that there has to be overthrow, demolition, destruction by force! The destruction must be meaningful not senseless, as under Bolshevism. And it can only become meaningful if we have understood the goal, the purpose, the necessity.[8]

Hitler told Hermann Rauschning similarly, "They regard me as an uneducated barbarian. Yes, we are barbarians! It is an honorable title. We shall rejuvenate the world! This world is near its end. It is our mission to cause unrest."[9] While Rauschning and many later historians took such statements as proof of Hitler's essential nihilism, he and they missed the central point that Hitler, like his beloved Richard Wagner, saw destruction as potentially regenerative, hastening the birth of the millennial Third Reich.[10]

Key events like the loss of the First World War and the collapse of the Hitler putsch were interpreted as part of the divine cycle of death and rebirth. Jakob Heist interpreted the collapse at the end of the war as bringing about a phoenix-like rebirth: "It was for me and my *Volksgenossen* [racial comrades] in my neighborhood an upheaval from which something new must arise from the old ruins."[11] Paul Bierwirth responded to Hitler's failed putsch with a vision of rebirth. Significantly, it entailed a new perception of reality, reflecting the construction of a new sense of order that is at the heart of the apocalypse complex:

In November 1923 I was shaken up by the shots in Munich and began since those days to see the events around me with different eyes. My entire interest, in all matters from then on, was concerned with the rebirth of a national, great Germany and the reparation of the Shame Treaty of Versailles.[12]

Robert Mayer found that after World War I he had lost "all hope of a German rebirth" but that the occupation by French and British soldiers, along with the mass deprivation, had produced an "awakening" of many Germans from a "certain spiritual paralysis."[13] According to one Nazi, National Socialism was specifically designed to bring about this rebirth. He explained that "National Socialism is a conscious rebirth of an ancient Germanic *Volksgemeinschaft* [racial community] that had been deliberately undermined by the Germanic peoples' enemy powers in the false supposition that one could completely destroy a blood- and body-like formed *Volksgemeinschaft*."[14] Similarly, another Nazi claimed that the Party Days were deliberately created to "awaken" *Volksgenossen* [racial comrades] in time "for the coming Third Reich." After the 1929 Party Day, he explained, "success was achieved. Thus I experienced in boundless happiness the rebirth of our people."[15] The choreographed unity of the Party Days was meant to awaken, to bring to consciousness, the racial oneness necessary for rebirth.[16]

Rebirth symbolizes the psychological transformation that occurs when a new construction of reality replaces one that has collapsed, a function of the postconversion mentality that I discuss in the next chapter. Nazi rhetoric and propaganda reflected this psychological process in its presentation of contemporary times. A *Völkischer Beobachter* headline on February 26, 1930, stated plainly, "While the Volk Decays, a New Volk Arises Out of It." Goebbels explained that "distress is the path to happiness. Disintegration and dissolution do not mean perishing but, rather, ascension and opening. Behind the noise of the day the strong powers of a new creation work in stillness." Gregor Strasser noted that "in disaster the seed of the coming redemption is contained, and in death the seed of the coming life."[17] Rosenberg stated that "a new synthesis of state is arising from the collapse and chaos."[18] Ernst Röhm exclaimed that "the time in which we live, in which a world has collapsed in a roar and a young world struggles for life and light, will be designated by later generations as the birth of a New Age."[19] The Old Guard Nazi Karl Hepp described the Weimar period in a similar manner:

> A world was forever submerged, and there was something new in the Becoming. A spiritual unrest had seized the world and especially the German people, and permitted men to experience the labor pains of a New Age. I also was strongly possessed by the inner unrest of the New Age.[20]

In fact, it was the Nazis themselves who heralded the dawn of the New Age. As one early Nazi explained,

> Today I am proud, as a co-fighter under the gifted leadership of our Adolf Hitler, to have stepped over the threshold of a New Age. I am also

proud to have been able to co-fight in the shaping of German men into National Socialists and to have been able to assist in the achievement of a National Socialist Greater Germany of freedom, power and prosperity, which one day in the future will take over the leadership of all people for the welfare of all humanity. That was my dream for all these long years and it will find its fulfillment.[21]

Another man had faith that his storm leaders were "the right men to usher us into the New Age," while still another Nazi proclaimed confidently, "we have helped to win the Third Reich. We have washed away the shame of 1918, and we have marched in victory through the Brandenburg Arch. Some day we shall go down in history as the first champions and prophets of a new, better age."[22] The spiritual nature of this transformation is seen in another Nazi's proclamation: "with us grows the New Age, with us and our Führer grows the faith and an irresistible supernatural power that we designate Providence."[23] Finally, one member of the party's paramilitary force, Willi Altenbrandt, writing about the 1929 Party Day, reported proudly that "five vans stood ready to bring the Fire-bearers of a New Age for the employment of Adolf Hitler's idea."[24]

Adolf Hitler's role in the "becoming" of the New Age was crucial; he was both the prophet who envisioned the millennial Reich and the messiah who would bring it into fruition.[25] One Nazi stated that "Adolf stands for me above every situation, he will lead my Volk again into a New Age, a time in which one will sing again with complete justification: 'Germany, Germany above everything, above everything in the world.'"[26] Hitler's assumption of power was interpreted as the foundation stone of the New Age. Johannes Zehfuss remarked that, with Hitler's chancellorship, "a New Age had dawned and imposed a new mission."[27] Belief in the coming New Age, and faith in Hitler helped many Nazis withstand the strain of the depression. One Nazi noted that, despite the severe difficulties of 1930, there "always lived in us the hope of an imminent New Age and a re-elevation of Germany from the Party quagmire through our Führer, and that righteousness would again find wider acceptance."[28] This "New Age" did not signify simply the appearance of a new political party. For the Nazis, in true millenarian fashion, it meant a fundamental and total transformation of society and humanity, physically and spiritually. As one writer noted, "A New Age has dawned . . . upheavals of enormous proportions, upon all spheres of German life, are leading to a complete transformation of German existence."[29]

Inherently related to the notion of rebirth is the belief in renewal. Psychologically, it reflects the same desire for a new consciousness or world view that reorders one's perception of reality, replacing the perception of chaos. For many would-be Nazis, the postwar experience signified the need for renewal. For some, this meant, at least initially, joining paramilitary groups that were dedicated to promoting renewal through national defense. The future Nazi August Eckart stated that "in the year 1923 I came through friends to the Black *Reichswehr*, where I took an active part in the sense of Germany's renewal."[30] For others, however, something more than paramilitary activity was needed. Friedrich Neuber stated that "after the soldier's experience, and through the betrayal of November 1918, there ripened in my consciousness the notion that a renewal of the German Volk was only possible through the path of German [meaning National] socialism."[31] Similarly, another Nazi explained,

> In the year 1928 I perceived that these paramilitary unions could achieve nothing so long as the German Volk was fissured into parties, interests and classes and that the liberation of the German people was possible only through a freedom movement which brought together all conscious German men from all social stratums and occupations.[32]

The prime factor necessitating renewal in the minds of many Nazis was the division generated by party factionalism. What was termed *German* or *National* Socialism meant a return to unity—a partyless and classless society. This was to be the millennial Reich.

Interpreting the divisiveness of Weimar as a sign of the apocalypse, many individuals searched for a movement that promised to unify Germany and thereby save it. One man believed that he had found this movement in Nazism:

> Finally a practical proposition for the renewal of the Volk—Destroy the parties! Away with the classes! True *Volksgenossen!* These are aims which I could totally support. Yet that same evening it was clear to me where I belonged: to the new movement. From them alone could I hope for the salvation of the German Fatherland.[33]

Another Nazi had a similar view: "The movement was steadfast in its goal—Germany's renewal. Should, however, Germany's renewal succeed, it was necessary that the party quarrels, the inner division of the German people, must come to an end."[34] Still another explained, "here was our great renewal movement of Adolf Hitler of Munich, his struggle and his life delineated the thesis of the holy National Socialist world view."[35] Writing about the martyrdom of Peter Gemeinder, a local Nazi leader who figures prominently in many Old Guard narratives, Georg Schorbach remembered reverently, "Speechless we stood by his stretcher, the stretcher of the man who, out of the deepest divine faith, sacrificed his life for the renewal of his Fatherland, for a new Germany."[36]

Although party and class division were real problems in Weimar society, the situation was inflated and mythologized in an apocalyptic sense. The desire to return to a paradise of primeval Aryan unity was, psychologically speaking, little different from the desire of many Christians to return to Eden. Hitler's assumption of the chancellorship for some marked the beginning of renewal in the millennial Reich. One Nazi stated that "I know that the fact of the seizure of power means not the end, but the beginning of the renewal, and that it depends on the loyalty and the struggle- and sacrifice-readiness of all genuine National Socialists."[37]

Germany, indeed the world, had reached a turning point that meant apocalypse and annihilation or salvation and renewal. A Germany unified through National Socialism would provide that salvation. But the question remains: what or whom had brought the world to this turning point? Was it simply the result of a lost world war? Was it modernity collapsing from within? Or was some hidden demonic force behind it all? To answer how the Nazis answered these questions, we need to look at the origins of the movement in Munich, just as the First World War came to an end.

The Origins of Nazism in the Eschatological War against the Jews

The National Socialist German Worker's Party had its origins in a semi-secret group called the Thule Society.[38] On the surface, the Thule Society was an ariosophical education society. Ariosophy (meaning wisdom of the Aryans) was a form of occultism based on the thought of two Viennese pseudo-scholars, Guido von List and Lanz von Liebenfels.[39] Both men rejected modernity and found solace in a mythic past where Aryan supermen, perfect in body and soul, ruled over inferior humans of mixed blood. Combining theosophy, Social Darwinism, and eugenics, both men came to believe that the world had reached a turning point of either racial apocalypse or racial salvation.[40] If Aryan humanity continued in the direction of miscegenation, then apocalypse was sure to come. However, if the Aryans purified themselves through strict eugenic measures, they would become like the god-men of old and save the world.

To begin the process of salvation, ariosophical groups, some public and some secretive, began to appear in Austria and Germany. One such group was the *Germanenorden* (Teutonic Order), a quasi-masonic lodge.[41] This group was affiliated with the notorious anti-Semite Theodor Fritsch's *Reichshammerbund,* which was itself actively trying to save the world by exposing the alleged nefarious work of the Jews.[42] The function of the *Germanenorden* was twofold; to promote proper racial hygiene (applicants for membership had to reveal color of hair, eyes, and skin, the lighter the better) and to produce and circulate anti-Semitic materials to raise racial consciousness of what was variously termed the Jewish problem or question.

During the First World War, a splinter group, the *"Germanenorden Walvater* of the Holy Grail" was founded in Munich. This group was soon led by Rudolf von Sebottendorff, an eccentric occultist and anti-Semite who funded many of the group's activities. When the war ended and the threat of a Soviet-style communist takeover of Bavaria loomed, Sebottendorff and his lodge members founded the Thule Society to counter the communist threat. On November 9, 1918, a Soviet-style revolution led by the Jewish journalist Kurt Eisner broke out in Munich. The Thulists, like other right-wing volkish groups, were shocked by the sudden turn of events. Sebottendorff's apocalyptic sermon to the Thulists that night was a thoroughly millennial diatribe on rebirth and resurrection through self-sacrifice in an eschatological struggle against the Jews:

> Yesterday we experienced the collapse of everything which was familiar, dear and valuable to us. In the place of our princes of Germanic blood rules our deadly enemy: Judah. What will come of this chaos, we do not know yet. But we can guess. A time will come of struggle, the most bitter need, a time of danger. . . . As long as I hold the iron hammer [a reference to his Master's hammer], I am determined to pledge the Thule to this struggle. . . . From today on our symbol is the red eagle, which warns us that we must die in order to live.[43]

The belief that the turning point of apocalypse or salvation had arrived in 1918–19 seems to have radicalized the ariosophists. No longer was a small group of racial elites sitting around studying rune symbols and listening to Wagnerian grail music enough to usher in the Aryan New Age. A turning point had arrived, and the Evil Other appeared to be winning. The Thule Society was to become the radical arm of the *Germanenorden*, fighting fire with fire.

The ariosophists came to believe that a small group of Jews, three hundred elders or wise men, were using Bolshevism to attract workers in order to divide the Aryans by class and thus divide the race. The Thule Society dedicated itself to winning back German workers and their Aryan brothers and to actively fighting the Jewish Bolsheviks. To do this, Sebottendorff purchased a small, working-class sports paper, the *Munich Observer*, which would later become the *Volkish Observer*, the Nazi official paper. The Thulists also started their own paramilitary group, the Bund Oberland, to battle the Jewish Bolsheviks in the streets of Munich.

In order to attract workers away from the communists, the Thulist Karl Harrer, in October 1918, formed a worker's circle called the *Politische Arbeiter-Zirkel*. Members included Harrer, Anton Drexler, and Michael Lotter. Eventually, from this group was founded the *Deutsche Arbeiter Partei* (DAP), the German Worker's Party. It was this party that one year later became the National Socialist German Worker's Party (NSDAP). Hitler would quickly push all other leaders aside, although his inner circle was replete with Thulists and Thule associates, including Gottfried Feder, Alfred Rosenberg, Rudolf Hess, and Dietrich Eckart.

But, it must be asked, what made the battle against the so-called Jewish Bolsheviks suddenly so central? The earlier reference to three hundred Jewish elders is pertinent, for the belief that the chaos was being caused by Jews was seemingly revealed in a strange document that appeared a mere two months after revolution broke out in Munich and that seemed to explain the origins of the apocalyptic chaos.

The Protocols of the Elders of Zion *as an Apocalyptic Text*

In 1918, Germany was reeling from the seemingly inexplicably lost war and threatened by what appeared to many to be an imminent Bolshevik-style revolution. Hunger was epidemic, the economy was beginning its steady decline, and society in general was politically and socially fragmented. All of this was enacted against a modernist cultural backdrop that simultaneously celebrated and mocked the collapse of a once proud nation. At this time, rumors began to spread that a vast conspiracy of Freemasons and Jews was behind the war, its eventual loss, and the subsequent revolutionary upheavals in Russia, Hungary, and Germany. The sudden and intense nature of Germany's collapse, and its seeming inexplicable causality, led some individuals to search for a simple explanation for the chaos. It was an Evil Other—the Jews.

In January 1919, a book by the editor of *Auf Vorposten* (On Outpost Duty), Ludwig Müller von Hausen, writing under the pseudonym Gottfried zur Beek, appeared. It told a fantastic tale: a group of three hundred Jewish elders had gathered in Basel, in 1897, as part of a congress meeting of the Jewish Zionist Movement. While the public meetings were about the establishment of a Jewish homeland in Palestine, secrets meetings had taken place at which were discussed a true hidden agenda—Jewish domination of the world. The detailed plans for their agenda, titled *Die Geheimnisse der Weisen von Zion* (The Secrets of the Elders of Zion), the book quickly became a best-seller.[44] It would reach thirty-nine editions by 1939 and continues to be a source of anti-Semitic propaganda to this day.[45] For the Nazis especially (they acquired the rights to the work in 1929), it proved to be a crucial source that shaped and intensified their millennial view of world history.

The *Protocols* is, of course, a hoax. But it was, and for some anti-Semites still is, a believed hoax. The forgery, a concoction of the Czarist secret police, the Okhrana, combined an obscure nineteenth-century anti-Napoleon III satire, Maurice Joly's *Dialogue aux Enfers entre Machiavel et Montesquieu* (1864), with *The Rabbi's Speech,* a portion of a novel by Hermann Gödische titled *Biarritz* (1868).[46] *The Rabbi's Speech* is millennial, with references to the imminent coming of the Jewish messianic age that will see the House of David assume leadership of the world in fulfillment of the covenant with Jehovah. The covenant is realized by the Jews through manipulation of the evils of modernity, including capitalism, which is portrayed as centralizing wealth and power in the hands of Jews, and both democracy and socialism, which enable the Jews to manipulate the masses against the aristocratic elites: "By this means we will be able to make the masses rise when we wish. We will drive them to upheavals, to revolutions; and each of these catastrophes marks a big step forward for our particular interests and brings us rapidly nearer to our sole aim—world domination, as was promised to our father Abraham."[47] Jewish messianism and millennialism are thereby turned into a satanic mirror of the desired Christian millennium, a paralleling of millennial desires and fears found later in Nazism.

The Okhrana hoped that by blaming modernity on the Jews, they could lure the Tsar away from the dangerous innovations of the Social Democrats and the even more radical leftists, who were widely considered to be led by Jews. The tactic failed. The *Protocols* might well have disappeared at this point if not for the appearance of Sergei Nilius, a man who upped the millennial ante, so to speak. Nilius was a mystic convinced he was chosen by heaven to save Russia. The third edition of his book *The Great in the Small: Anti-Christ Considered as an Imminent Political Possibility* contained the *Protocols* as an appendix. Nilius was convinced that the Jew was the anti-Christ, and the *Protocols* appeared to support this belief.

For Nilius, the satanic power behind the dark conspiracy of modernity was the Jews. In 1917, with the Russian Revolution unfolding before his eyes, Nilius published another edition of *The Great and the Small* with the chiliastic title (borrowed from Matthew 24:33) *He Is Near, at the Door . . . Here Comes Anti-Christ and the Reign of the Devil on Earth.* According to Nilius, the apocalyptic turning point had arrived; either Russia and the true spirituality of the Orthodox Church would be saved, or the anti-Christ would rule and the world would end. Nilius combined fear and rejection of modernity with apocalyptic fear of the coming of the anti-Christ, both of which he associated with Jews.[48] It was this version of the *Protocols* that traveled to the West with a number of emigrés fleeing Bolshevik terror. One who claimed to have carried it with him was the future Nazi ideologue Alfred Rosenberg.

Arriving in Munich, Rosenberg soon came into contact with the anti-Semitic writer Dietrich Eckart, a man who also believed that the Jews were involved in a conspiracy to take over the world. In 1919, in his paper *Auf Gut Deutsch* (In Plain German), Eckart had written, "The hour of decision has come: between existence and non-existence, between Germantum and Jewry, between all or nothing."[49] The *Protocols* only seemed to prove this to be true, thus legitimating both the conspiracy theory and the anti-Semitism. Rosenberg subsequently became Eckart's Russian expert, writing articles for *Auf Gut Deutsch* on the 1917 revolution and its supposed connection to the Jews. In 1923, he wrote a gloss on the *Protocols* titled *Die Protokolle der Weisen von Zion und die jüdische Weltpolitik* (The Protocols of the Elders of Zion and Jewish World Policy), which approximated an exegesis on Revelation, showing how contemporary world events were but confirmation of the insidious *Protocols*. At the end of his gloss on the *Protocols,* Rosenberg presented a view that invoked the atmosphere of what Norman Cohn aptly called "apocalyptic prophecy." Echoing Hitler's notion of the Jew as an anti-chosen race, which I discuss shortly, Rosenberg remarked that "the Jew stands in our history as our metaphysical opposite." He explained further in a passage replete with apocalyptic and millennial symbolism:

> That was *never* clearly grasped by us. . . . *Today* at last it seems as if the eternally foreign and hostile, now that it has climbed to such monstrous power, is felt and hated as such. For the first time in history instinct and knowledge attain clear consciousness. The Jew stands at the very top of the peak of power which he has so eagerly climbed, and awaits his fall into the abyss. The last fall. After that, there will be no place for the Jew in Europe or America. Today, in the midst of the collapse of a whole world, a new era begins, a fundamental rejection in all fields of many ideas inherited from the past. One of the advance signs of the coming struggle for the new organization of the world is this understanding of the very nature of the demon which has caused our present downfall. Then the way will be open of a New Age.[50]

That Rosenberg believed the imminent attainment of power would ironically signal "the last fall" of the Jews reflects a belief that Eckart and Hitler would share—that the Jews' will to exterminate would ultimately result in their own extermination.

For many in the volkish movement, the *Protocols* was all the proof they needed that the Jews really were the force of evil in the world. Their long-held fear of a racial apocalypse now found its eschaton. The turning point had arrived. With the loss of the war and with Jewish-Bolshevik revolution spreading, the time was now. Looking back at the war, Eckart would write, in 1919, "This war was a religious war, one can now see this clearly; a war between light and darkness, truth and lies, Christ and anti-Christ."[51] The signs of the time could not be more explicit. Hitler, at least, seems to have accepted the *Protocols* in this light.[52] On August 1, 1923, with Germany lost in economic chaos and a new epidemic of hunger striking millions, Hitler gave a speech titled "Rising Prices, Republic and Fascist State." His explanation of the chaos did not speak of modern economics, or of the government's floating of worthless monies. The explanation was to be found in the evil machinations of the Jews and their minions, the Bolsheviks and the Freemasons, as revealed in the *Protocols*. Was not the two-pronged attack of "international bank capital" and Soviet-style revolution revealed in this work? Hitler warned his audience: "We stand before a new revolution." Behind it lies the "Soviet star," which "is the star of David, the true sign of the synagogue. The symbol of that race over the world . . . the dominion of Jewry. The gold star signifies the Jews' glistening gold. The hammer, which symbolizes the Soviet crest, represents the Freemasonic element. The sickle the inhuman terror! The hopeless Helots of the German Volk should create the Greater Jewish Paradise!" Jewish banking, combined with Bolshevik revolution and a little help from Freemasons within Germany, was attempting to fulfill the promise of Jehovah to his race. Hitler continued, "according to the Zionist Protocols, the masses are to be made docile through hunger" and therefore ready "for the second revolution under the Star of David."[53]

The *Protocols* became a key element in Hitler's conspiratorial thinking, for it was used to explain the apocalyptic chaos. The international Jewish bankers, he argued, had created the hyperinflation that had forced Germans into epidemic hunger, making them pliant in the face of a Jewish-Bolshevik type revolution and thereby taking another step toward the creation of the Jewish millennial paradise of world dominion. Hitler's conspiratorial mentality, and its peculiar logic, is also seen in his reaction to the disclosure that the *Protocols* were a fake. He charged that, since the press was controlled by the Jews (part of the plan revealed in the *Protocols*), the accusations of forgery by the press only proved that the *Protocols* were true. Writing in *Mein Kampf*, Hitler stated:

> to what extent the whole existence of this people is based on a continuous lie is shown incomparably by the *Protocols of the Elders of Zion*, so infinitely hated by the Jews. They are based on a forgery, the *Frankfurter Zeitung* moans and screams once every week: the best proof they are authentic. What many Jews may do unconsciously is here consciously exposed. And that is what matters. It is completely indifferent from what Jewish brain these disclosures originate; the important thing is that with positively terrifying certainty they reveal the nature and activity of the

Jewish people and expose their inner contexts as well as their ultimate final aims.[54]

We see here Hitler's belief that Jews instinctively strive toward world domination, even if unconscious of this striving. The *Protocols* reveal the eschatological "ultimate final aims," world domination and thus world annihilation—apocalypse. Hitler, like Rosenberg, used the *Protocols* like a prophetic text, rereading history as prophecy fulfilled or, in this case, as the working out of the Jewish covenant with Jehovah, increasingly associated not with God but with Satan. All this talk of an instinctive Jewish will to take over the world, and its resultant apocalypse, needs to be further elucidated.

Dietrich Eckart, Hitler, and the Will to Exterminate

Insight into the conspiratorial world of Nazi millennialism can be glimpsed from a relatively obscure early propaganda piece titled *Bolshevism from Moses to Lenin: Dialogue between Hitler and Me.*[55] This brief work is a stylized conversation between Hitler and his intellectual mentor, Dietrich Eckart, published in 1924, a few months after Eckart's death, while Hitler was in Landsberg prison composing *Mein Kampf,* which he dedicated to Eckart.[56]

Eckart's *Bolshevism from Moses to Lenin* attempts to reveal the hidden history of the Jews and their alleged desire, not simply for world domination but for world annihilation. The German reader of the time was clearly meant to see the loss of the First World War and the subsequent postwar chaos as the product of this same "hidden force." The work uses a pseudo-scholarly approach, with citations to various standard anti-Semitic statements by a host of literary and historical figures.[57] More important, however, and this is typical of Nazi propaganda then and later, *Bolshevism from Moses to Lenin* also utilizes Jewish sources, primarily the Old Testament and the Talmud (questionably analyzed and translated) to seemingly unmask the Jews.[58] For example, the Book of Esther is explained as a Purim festival "murder" of 75,000 Persians. It is an event that the authors claim "no doubt had the same Bolshevik background." The Egyptian expulsion of the Jews described in Exodus is used to justify the Nazis' desire to expel Germany's Jewish population.[59] Ignoring the bounds of time (a deliberate technique to show the allegedly eternal nature of the Jewish drive to world domination and annihilation), Eckart likened the alleged Jewish manipulation of the Egyptian "rabble" (*Pöbelvolk,* taken over from Luther's German translation of the Old Testament) or "Bolshevik horde" to the calls for "Liberty, Equality, and Fraternity" that ignited the French Revolution. Eckart implies that the Jews used these catchwords of democracy to incite the mob once again to murder the racial elites; the same implication is later attached to the Russian and German Revolutions. Bolshevism therefore is defined not as a contemporary Marxist political theory but rather as a ancient Jewish technique for manipulating the mixed-race subhumans against the racial elites.

Joshua 6 is cited as further proof of the Jewish tendency to "exterminate" Gentiles "root and branch," a phrasing, perhaps not ironically, the Nazis liked to use for their solution to the Jewish Question. Hitler referred to the destruction of Jericho as an "uninterrupted mass murder of bestial cruelty and shameless rapacity and cold-blooded cunning," a "Hell incarnate."[60]

While the Old Testament, "Satan's Bible" or the "Book of Hate," as Hitler refers to it, is presented as a history of the Jewish will to exterminate, the New Testament is likewise transformed. Here we find an Aryan Jesus, in John 8:44, yelling at "the Jews": "Your father is the devil." Much is made of Jesus' whipping the "Children of the Devil."[61] The work of Jesus the anti-Semite, however, is soon deflected by the apostle Paul (Saul), whom Hitler refers to as a "mass murderer turned saint." *Bolshevism from Moses to Lenin* then leaps to the Middle Ages, claiming that Charlemagne's massacre of his Aryan brothers the Saxons was done at the behest of the Jews. This accusation followed earlier references to World War I and to the Jews' purportedly bringing the British and the Americans into the war. In this way, World War I, like World War II later, is conceived as Aryan fratricide orchestrated by the Jews to further their plans for world domination and annihilation.[62] Hitler then provides a possible solution to this eternal Jewish problem by citing Giordano Bruno. The Jews were, according to Bruno, "such a pestilential, leprous and publicly dangerous race that they deserved to be rooted out and exterminated before their birth."[63] This notion—that the only way to stave off Aryan extermination was preemptive extermination of the Jews—would become a fundamental part of the Nazi millennial world view.

The continuing references to Jewish extermination of non-Jews is deliberate and, from an apocalyptic standpoint, crucial. For *Bolshevism from Moses to Lenin* is proposing that the final battle is approaching. The pamphlet ends with Hitler discussing the "final goal" to which the Jew is instinctively "pushed":

> Above and beyond world domination—annihilation of the world. He believes he must bring the entire world down on its knees before him in order to prepare a paradise on earth. . . . While he makes a pretense to elevate humanity, he torments it into despair, madness and ruin. If he is not commanded to stop he will annihilate all humanity. His nature compels him to that goal, even though he dimly realizes that he must therefore destroy himself. . . . To be obliged to try to annihilate us with all his might, but at the same time to suspect that that must lead irrevocably to his own destruction. Therein lies, if you will: the tragedy of Lucifer.[64]

Even if we are to take these to be solely the words of Eckart, Hitler expressed the same explanation of Bolshevism and its "Jewish" origins. Indeed, in *Mein Kampf,* which was composed at roughly the same time and which is dedicated to Eckart, Hitler argues repeatedly that the Jews were promised in the Old Testament not eternity in the heavenly New Jerusalem but dominion of the temporal earth. It was to this end that the Jew conspired. Hitler explains that his "historical research" led him to question whether or not

> inscrutable Destiny, perhaps for reasons unknown to us poor mortals, did not with eternal and immutable resolve, desire the final victory of this little nation. Was it possible that the earth had been promised as a reward to this people which lives only for this earth?

Later in the book, Hitler, speaking of these alleged Jewish machinations, states, "for the higher he climbs, the more alluring his old goal that was once promised him rises from the veil of the past, and with feverish avidity his keenest minds see the dream of world domination tangibly approaching." This situation would lead to the fulfillment of the "Jewish prophecy—the Jew would really devour the peoples of the earth, would become their master."[65] The end result of the "Jewish doctrine of Marxism" would be the literal end of the world:

As a foundation of the universe, this doctrine would bring about the end of any order intellectually conceivable to man. And as, in this greatest of all recognizable organisms, the result of an application of such a law could only be chaos, on earth it could only be destruction for the inhabitants of this planet. If, with the help of his Marxist creed, the Jew is victorious over the other peoples of the world, his crown will be the funeral wreath of humanity and this planet will, as it did thousands ["millions" in later editions] of years of ago, move through the ether devoid of men.[66]

Hitler continued this theme in his then-unpublished second book. After discussing the supposed parasitic nature of the Jews and their compulsive striving for world domination, Hitler explained,

> His ultimate aim is the denationalization and the chaotic bastardization of other peoples, the lowering of the racial level of the highest, and the domination of this racial mush through the eradication [*ausrottung*] of these people's intelligentsia and their replacement with the members of his own people.

When the Jews have taken over individual countries and eventually the world through race poisoning and the policy of extermination, Hitler again concludes, exactly as Eckart did in *Bolshevism from Moses to Lenin,* the result will be apocalypse:

> The Jewish international struggle will therefore always end in bloody Bolshevization—that is to say, in truth, the destruction of the intellectual upper classes associated with the various peoples, so that he himself will be able to rise to mastery over the now leaderless humanity. . . . Jewish domination always ends with the decline of all culture and ultimately of the insanity of the Jew himself. Because he is a parasite on the peoples, and his victory means his own end just as much as the death of his victim.[67]

Corroborating this account, Otto Wagener recalled Hitler saying much the same thing in the early 1930s. Using the metaphor of the gardener, Hitler stated,

> Nothing upsets Jewry more than a gardener who is intent on keeping his garden neat and healthy. Nothing is more inimical to Jewry than order!

It needs the smell of decay, the stench of cadavers, weakness, lack of resistance, submission of the personal self, illness, degeneracy! And wherever it takes root, it continues the process of decomposition! It *must!* For only under those conditions can it lead its parasitic existence.

Echoing *Bolshevism from Moses to Lenin,* Hitler claimed that this parasitic chaotic nature had led to the expulsion of Jews from Babylonia, Egypt, Rome, England, and the Rhineland, for "in each of these a gardener was at work who was incorruptible and loved his people." Hitler saw in Weimar an increased parasitism of apocalyptic proportions: "But since Weimar, you can once again see an enormous acceleration in the proliferation, the taking root, the stripping of corpses. Truly, if something does not happen soon, it may be too late!" Since Hitler viewed this will to exterminate as being endemic to Jewish nature, it was to a degree an inevitable part of the human experience: "For it *will* repeat itself, it will always return, as long as people live on this earth. And the last ones, God help us, who will proliferate even when the end of man has come—that will be, in spite of everything, the Jews, until they breathe the last of their miserable parasites' lives on the piled cadavers of their victims." To forestall this Jewish apocalypse was his mission and, by extension, the mission of the Nazi movement: "To postpone this point in time as far into the future as possible is our duty, our God-given mission—yes, it is the substance of Divine Creation altogether." This mission was to counter the promise made by Jehovah that the Jews would "one day rule over all mankind." The Nazis, then, had been chosen by God to act the role of Endtime gardener: "But the Jews are *here*, in the world, whether or not we deplore their vile, sadistic parasitism and their will to destroy and exterminate us. . . . The gardener *must* intervene, and he must do soon—as soon as possible!"[68] But how exactly was the gardener to proceed, and with what tools? It is here that Hitler's "Great Idea" and Nazi salvationism become key.

Hitler's "Great Idea": The Nazi Soteriology of Race

Nazi millennialism was rooted in a peculiar mix of eugenic, volkish, and occult apocalyptic ideas of the time.[69] Hitler, however, rarely made direct mention of the sources of this thought. Rather, he presented himself as the prophet who peers into the darkness and glimpses the light, what he termed his "great idea," which he then reveals to others. The presence of the great idea, and a fanatical belief in it, is essential, according to Hitler, if a transformation of humanity is to take place:

> The lack of a great, creative, renewing idea means at all times a limitation of fighting force. Firm belief in the right to apply even the most brutal weapons is always bound up with the existence of a fanatical faith in the necessity of the victory of a revolutionary new order on this earth. A movement that is not fighting for such highest aims and ideals will, therefore, never seize upon the ultimate weapon.[70]

National Socialism, then, is the movement that Hitler created to propagate his great idea to the masses and to ensure its fulfillment: "For the function of organization is the transmission of a definite idea—which always first arises from the brain of an individual—to a larger body of men and the supervision of its realization."[71] Transmission of this idea was to continue after the assumption of power, for the goal of Nazi canvassing was not simply the assumption of political power but the salvation of Aryan humanity. As a party member, Wilhelm Scherer, explained,

> It was clear to me that with the attainment of power in the state the struggle is not yet completed. Now it means to aid our world view's awakening within the outer community, and to erect a unity also within the soul. For in this struggle all powers (Germany's spiritual servants), must struggle against the Jewish spirit within the German Volk's soul, struggle against foreign elements, teachings and religions, which weigh down upon the souls of German men and desecrate their spirit, so strongly embattled in outer unity. Struggle against the hypocrisy outside the movement and also within its ranks. Today we struggle further, for the genuineness of our revolution, for the awakening of our world view. Only when the Volk has risen to our world view—to victory—when it has ripped out root and branch all foreign, Jewish and foreign-type Christian elements, is our mission completed.[72]

The Nazi mission, therefore, was a spiritual one. For this reason, one minor Nazi ideologue maintained that it was "false" to "characterize" National Socialism as an "unspiritual [*sic*] political conception."[73]

The spiritual nature of Hitler's racism, and its millenarian expression, can be readily seen in the following excerpt from a 1931 interview:

The Frenchman Gobineau and the Englishman Chamberlain were inspired by our concept of a new order—a new order, I tell you, or if you prefer, an ideological glimpse into history in accordance with the basic principle of the blood. We do not judge by merely artistic or military standards or even by purely scientific ones. We judge by the spiritual energy which a people is capable of putting forth, which will enable it in ten years to recapture what it lost in a thousand years of warfare. I intend to set up a thousand year Reich and anyone who supports me in battle is a fellow-fighter for a unique spiritual—I would almost say divine—creation. At the decisive moment the decisive factor is not the ratio of strength but the spiritual force employed. Betrayal of the nation is possible even when no crime has been committed, in other worlds, when a historic mission has not been fulfilled.[74]

In *Mein Kampf*, Hitler wrote about the nationalization of the masses, which entailed a mass conversion to his "great idea." To win the masses, the Jews had to be dealt with: "the soul of the people can only be won if along with carrying on a positive struggle for our own aims, we destroy the opponent of these aims . . . the nationalization of the our masses will succeed only when, aside from all the positive struggle for the soul of our people, their international poisoners are exterminated." Later, Hitler wrote in this regard, "Without the clearest knowledge of the racial problem and hence of the Jewish problem there will never be a resurrection of the German nation. The racial question gives the key not only to world history, but to all human culture."[75] So, in order to win the souls of the masses and achieve Germany's resurrection, the Jew, the poisoner of the blood, had to be destroyed. There could be no salvation without extermination.

The Aryan-Jewish conflict was, quite literally, interpreted as an eschatological war. Hitler defined Marxism as a "poison" deliberately produced by the Jewish "prophet" Karl Marx "in the service of his race" to bring about the "swifter annihilation of the independent existence of free nations on this earth."[76] The final battle would come in a fight to the death with Jewish Bolsheviks. In his first important speech after leaving Landsberg prison, in 1925, Hitler explained that the Nazis' aim was

clear and simple: Fight against the satanic power which has collapsed Germany into this misery; fight Marxism, as well as the spiritual carrier of this world pest and epidemic, the Jews. . . . As we join ranks then in this new movement, we are clear to ourselves, that in this arena there are two possibilities; either the enemy walks over our corpse or we over theirs.[77]

A year later, Hitler reiterated in another speech that "there is going to be a final confrontation, and that will not come in the *Reichstag* but in an overall showdown which will result in the destruction of either Marxism or ourselves." It was the Nazis' mission to prepare Germany for this impending final conflict. He continued, using imagery taken from Revelation 12 and thereby transforming Satan into the Jewish Bolshevik:

> It is our mission to forge a strong weapon—will and energy—so that when the hour strikes, and the Red dragon raises itself to strike, at least some of our people will not surrender to despair. I myself represent the same principles that I stood for a year ago.
>
> We are convinced that there will be a final showdown in this struggle against Marxism. We are fighting one another and there can be only one outcome. One will be destroyed and the other be victorious.
>
> It is the great mission of the National Socialist movement to give our times a new faith and to see to it that millions will stand by this faith, then, when the hour comes for the showdown, the German people will not be completely unarmed when they meet the international murderers.[78]

This notion of the satanic power of the Jews was no mere rhetorical device for Hitler. When Hitler stated in *Mein Kampf* that "the personification of the devil as the symbol of all evil assumes the living appearance of the Jew," he meant literally that the Jew was the force of evil and destruction in the world.[79] Eckart had written, as early as 1919, that "when light clashes with darkness, there is no coming to terms! Indeed there is only struggle for life and death, till the annihilation of one or the other. Consequently the World War has only apparently come to an end."[80] The Nazis believed themselves involved in a cosmic battle between the forces of good and evil, light and darkness. World War I was but one phase of an evolving eschatological war.

This apocalyptic dualism was a central part of Nazi ideology. In his report written for the Nuremberg trials in 1946, *Schutzstaffel* (SS; Hitler's personal bodyguards) Major Dieter Wisliceny, Adolf Eichman's deputy, wrote that Nazi anti-Semitism was based on the "mystical-religious conception that sees the world as governed by good and evil forces." The Jews were the "evil principle," and

> against this world of evil the race-mystics placed the world of good, of light, embodied in blond, blue-eyed people, from whom alone all culture-creating and state-building forces emanate. Now both of these two worlds were alleged to be positioned in a permanent struggle, and the war of 1939, which Hitler had begun, represented only the final altercation between these two powers.[81]

The battle lines were thus drawn. Two opposing forces faced each other; the forces of good and evil, creation and destruction, order and chaos, form and formlessness, God and Satan. Only one force could prevail. It was the mission of Nazism to ensure that Aryan humanity was victorious. The loss of World War I and the chaos that followed made it seem certain that history had reached a turning point of eschatological significance, and the Nazis believed that they, indeed all Aryans, had been chosen by higher powers to defeat the agents of annihilation. It was only a matter of time. One party member, Paul Schneider, described the battle with a dualism typical of apocalyptic thinking:

> In the victory of honesty over vulgarity, in the victory of reason over the irrational, in the victory of one (our world view) over all the unnatural, spasmodic, deformed conglomerate of thirty other parties that wooed the favor of the German Volk, in the victory of the pure over the impure, both in men and in culture, economics, race and all the multifarious signs of life, an entirely great Volk learns what it is to be German.[82]

It was for this reason, then, that Hitler viewed the Aryan race as the true chosen people. Hitler told Rauschning bluntly, "There cannot be two Chosen People. We are God's People." When Rauschning asked whether he meant this symbolically, Hitler sharply retorted,

> Symbolically? No! It's the sheer simple undiluted truth. Two worlds face one another—the men of God and the men of Satan! The Jew is the anti-man, the creature of another god. He must have come from another root of the human race. I set the Aryan and the Jew over against each other;

and if I call one of them a human being I must call the other something else. The two are as widely separated as man and beast. Not that I call the Jew a beast. He is much further from the beasts than we Aryans. He is a creature outside nature and alien to nature.[83]

For Hitler, then, the Aryans belonged to the chosen race of the Creator, while the Jews were the chosen race of the Destroyer, Satan. In Hitler's apocalyptic cosmology, it was the Aryan who was chosen "in the highest image of the Creator" to rule, not only the material world but that which "lies partly above it, partly outside it." The choice humanity faced was between diabolical rule by Jews or divine rule by godlike Aryans. It was for this reason that Hitler proclaimed that he was "acting in accordance with the will of the Almighty Creator: by defending myself against the Jew, I am fighting for the work of the Lord."[84]

Hitler, in a speech early in 1922, *"Die 'Hecker' der Wahrheit!"* (The "Agitator" of Truth), prophesied on the impending apocalypse, and on German's choice between slavery and annihilation at the hands of the Jewish Bolsheviks and victory and salvation for Aryan humanity if they followed National Socialism:

There are only two possibilities in Germany! Do not believe that the Volk will wander everlasting in the midst of compromise! It will devote itself first to the side that has prophesied on the consequences of the coming ruin and has steered clear of it.

Either it will be the side of the left: then God help us, that leads us to the final corruption, Bolshevism; or it is the side of the right, which is resolute . . . it allows no compromise. Believe me, the German Volk lost this World War because it had not grasped that there is allowed on this earth only victor and slave.

And here it is precise; this powerful, great contest can be reduced to but two possibilities: either victory of the Aryans or its annihilation and victory of the Jews.[85]

This "politics of either-or," as the historian Robert Wistrich so aptly labeled it, was rooted in the internal logic of Nazi apocalyptic belief.[86] Hitler and his inner circle believed that world history was essentially the struggle between racial groups and that there were two chosen races, one Aryan, chosen of God, and one Jewish, chosen of Satan. These two races were locked in mortal combat, with a final reckoning imminent. In this scenario, "the Jew" became an abstract and symbolic Evil Other whose extermination was essential for ultimate salvation. Once again, this was not simply rhetoric designed solely for audience affect but a believed vision of a coming eschatological battle that could have only one possible end: extermination of either the Aryans or the Jews. While exactly how this scenario would play out was unknown to Hitler and his inner circle; the belief that it would occur in their lifetimes was absolutely an article of faith. That Hitler believed he could play a role in realizing these exterminatory dreams is apparent in a somewhat obscure account by a man who met Hitler in 1922, the year of the "Agitator of Truth" speech.

In 1922, Josef Hell, staff editor on the Munich weekly *Der Gerade Weg* (The Straight Path) met with Hitler. After a rather dispassionate discussion about the Nazi employment of propaganda techniques, Hell asked Hitler, "What do you plan to undertake, then, once you have full freedom of action against the Jews?" Hell's account of what followed is similar to other reports. Hitler went into nondirected thinking mode, speaking to Hell as if he were a multitude in a typically frantic and near-trance state. The response seemed to have been triggered by the image of the Jew as Evil Other that had to be exterminated if the millennial Reich was to be realized. Hell noted,

> While up until now Hitler had spoken comparatively calmly and moderately, his nature now changed completely. He no longer looked at me, rather beyond me off into space and made his additional remarks with rising vocal expenditure, so that he fell into a type of paroxysm and finally shouted at me as if I were an entire national assembly.

Hitler made it clear, to Hell's horror, that extermination of the Jews was his ultimate aim:

> In the case that one day I actually come to power, then the extermination of the Jews will be my first and most important task. As soon as I have power, I will, for example, have erected in Munich upon the *Marienplatz* gallows next to gallows, and indeed as many as traffic allows. Then the Jews will be hanged, one after another, and they will remain hanging until they stink. They will hang as long as the fundamentals of hygiene permit. As soon as they have been cut loose, the next ones will come to it and so on, until the last Jew in Munich is extirpated. This will proceed

in the other cities in the same way, until Germany is cleansed of the last Jews.[87]

Germany, and the world for that matter, had arrived at an eschatological turning point. It was a time of apocalypse or salvation in a millennial Third Reich. Hitler and his disciples came to believe that they were not only fortunate witnesses to the birth of the New Age but divinely chosen to help bring it into being.

The Mission of the Chosen

The belief in a turning point placed a holy mission upon the shoulders of Hitler and his disciples. This emphasis on a historic mission awaiting the Aryan, and thus German, people is an important and frequently occurring element of Nazi millennialism. In *Mein Kampf*, Hitler repeatedly refers to a "truly high mission" given to Germany by the "Almighty," "Providence," or "the Creator." Hitler explains,

What we must fight for is to safeguard the existence and reproduction of our race and our people, the sustenance of our children and the purity of our blood, the freedom and independence of the fatherland, so that our people may mature for the fulfillment of the mission allotted it by the creator of the universe. Every thought and every idea, every doctrine and all knowledge, must serve this purpose.[88]

For Hitler, fulfillment of this mission was essential if apocalypse was to be avoided:

In a hour when a national body is visibly collapsing and to all appearances is exposed to the gravest oppression, thanks to the activity of a few scoundrels, obedience and fulfillment of duty toward them amount to doctrinaire formalism, in fact pure insanity, if the refusal of obedience and "fulfillment of duty" would make possible the salvation of a people from its ruin.[89]

In Hitler's apocalyptic cosmology, this mission required Aryans to purify themselves in order to reach a stage of biospiritual perfection, thereby achieving a state of godlike capabilities, ruling the earth as god-men as in ancient times:

> Human culture and civilization on this continent are inseparably bound up with the presence of the Aryan. If he dies out or declines, the dark veils of an age without culture will again descend on this globe.
>
> The undermining of the existence of human culture by the destruction of its bearer seems in the eyes of a volkish philosophy the most execrable crime. Anyone who dares to lay hands on the highest image of the Lord commits sacrilege against the benevolent creator of this miracle and contributes to the expulsion from paradise.
>
> And so the volkish philosophy of life corresponds to the innermost will of Nature, since it restores that free play of forces which must lead to a continuous mutual higher breeding, until at last the best of humanity, having achieved possession of this earth, will have a free path for activity in domains which will lie partly above it and partly outside it.
>
> We all sense that in the distant future humanity must be faced by problems which only a highest race, become master people and supported by the means and possibilities of an entire globe, will be equipped to overcome.[90]

If Hitler alone had perceived this sense of mission, that could explain his personal motivation. Many of Hitler's followers, however, accepted this self-perception and thereby legitimated it. Heinrich Grebe explained that "unwavering in our faith in Germany's future and Adolf Hitler's mission, we remained even during the forbidden period loyal followers of Adolf Hitler's party."[91] More significant, however, this sense of mission was shared by many of his followers. Hitler's personal mission became a shared mission of all Germans, and, by extension, all Aryans. For these Germans, to struggle for Hitler's idea was to play a crucial role in their personal soteriological mission. While Hitler believed this mission would entail a final battle with the force of evil, the Jews, for most Nazis the sense of mission itself—of having been chosen to perform some great world important task, whatever that task might be—was powerful enough. Psychologically, it provided a renewed sense of self-worth and meaning in their lives. One man remarked that "it is, however, an up-lifting feeling to have taken part in the holy struggle for Germany's greatness under the Führer and its savior Adolf Hitler."[92] Another explained that "for me the essential point is that I may say: 'You have, through your struggle, helped the Führer to take the leadership of the German Volk in his hands at the right time, and thereby guard it from destruction.'"[93] Finally, Heinrich Götz remarked simply, "so arose in me the resolve to contribute my part in the salvation of the German Fatherland."[94]

Hitler, in his speeches, delegated this mission to his loyal followers. Willi Martin recalled a Hitler speech befitting a prophet and messiah of the Endtime:

> That the Führer had suffered spiritually, we saw in his immensely serious features. However, his words were for us a source of power. These words gave us new courage and resolution for the coming struggle-years. And he admonished us of our mission, and said to us with prophetic words that we, if he could count on us, would obtain an impetus of immense dimensions that would form our battalion into a regiment, this regiment into a division, and this division into a army corp—then the entire Volk would be captured. Thereafter our enthusiasm knew no bounds. And this enthusiasm was for us also the loyalty to this man, who alone had, in the last hour, mastered Germany's fate and had taught us about the future.[95]

Members of the *Sturmabteilung* (SA; the party's paramilitary force) and the *Schutzstaffel* (SS; Hitler's personal bodyguards) especially took pride in their mission. They viewed themselves as holy warriors, crusade knights, fighting with their messiah for the coming millennium. One SA member, Martin Reihl, stated proudly, "truly the SA, and especially our old 6th company, brought with their great sacrifice of blood Germany's liberation and resurrection."[96] A Bavarian State Ministry investigation of the Nazis in 1922 reported that "their aim and their mission is as a shield for the liberating work of our German Volk from Jewish Terror."[97] Theodor Schwindel recalled that, immediately after the failed putsch, many Munich citizens, suffering from hunger caused by the inflation, aided the fleeing SA members. He remarked that "they saw in us their savior and liberator from greatest misery."[98] Still another Nazi, discussing the SS, claimed that "we were not mercenaries, but political soldiers, fighters for a new world view that should and must lead the entire Volk one day into a beautiful future. Only one stood before us: the Führer." The mission of the SA or SS official was to proselytize and to fight for Hitler's idea and thereby to awaken the Volk to the right path to salvation, as well as to serve as its holy protector. Explaining further, the Nazi just quoted said of the mission of the SA, "this is the wonderful thing about the idea, that in each and every German of good blood slumbers a function, perhaps only a sensation (inherited or maturely developed), and it is the mission of the old fighter to awaken this function, and to maintain watch over the movement."[99]

The Nazis hoped to stop the decomposing effects of chaos, renew the spiritual health of the Volk, and usher in the millennial Reich. This was their mission as the chosen elite, delegated to them by their savior. As one man explained,

> Irresistibly time thrust forward. Meanwhile gigantic tasks are discharged by the Führer. We had and will have in the future, more than ever, the mission to gain the confidence of our Volk with the good idea of National Socialism, and this goodness will lead to the ends of the earth. Also, this work demands the whole man. Yet still today the decomposition phenomenon of chaos of the past years and decades demands of us the employment of all powers. This struggle means the complete health of the German soul. It should be cleansed from its foundation up and be purified therewith to be entirely capable of absorbing it [the idea] for our epoch. We National Socialists know that this struggle is perhaps the most difficult, yet greatest ever, and we in these circles are the highest that the Volk knows, and we will lead [the Volk] in loyal discipleship to our Führer Adolf Hitler, and with God's help, to a joyous end.[100]

The awakening to the new world view, the new conception of reality, meant for the Nazis bringing to consciousness the importance of racial unity and thereby ending the chaos of racial decomposition. As one minor Nazi admonished his fellow *Volksgenossen,*

> Be mindful of your holy mission as a Volk upon German native soil. German worker, brains and brawn belong together at all times. Never may you forget this and you must endure all joy and harm and ward off all misery. No longer allow classes and pride of place to get the upper hand—continually resist the *Schweinhund* [pig-dog] in your soul. Germany must become and remain National Socialist and the Volk must maintain itself as a pure race. Vow to yourself this pledge and Germany will exist eternally. Long live our Führer Adolf Hitler, long live Germany and our beloved German Volk.[101]

This collective mission of the Nazis also gave them a sense of community, a solidarity that overcame the alienation wrought by the chaos of Weimar. As one man explained, "we had the feeling of being a new embattled community, the consciousness of a great mission in the service of the German Volk."[102] The achievement of this sense of mission was psychologically liberating. One man found that "the stifling spiritual burden is taken from me, liberated and inwardly joyful and blissful, I have faith again in the future of our Volk and in its mission."[103] Johannes Christ responded to his first Goebbels speech with a feeling of liberation, concluding that "finally we could speak out about the party and its mission. How beautiful it appeared to us that we were convinced by our Führer's idea and had faith in the holy cause."[104]

This sense of mission in turn generated a sense of pride. Johannes Christ noted that "when I was asked about it, I said freely that I was a follower of the Hitler party, because I had seen therein a great and holy mission. Already at that time I said that one day the time would come when each and every German will march with us."[105] Similarly, another SA member stated that "I was a Nationalist Socialist, and today I am proud to wear the brown uniform and as my Führer's brown soldier to have saved the Volk and the Fatherland, and therefore also myself, from destruction."[106] Another man explained that "for us to imagine that we had been allowed to aid in the salvation of the German Fatherland before its destruction by Bolshevism makes the struggle-time the most beautiful period of our lives."[107] Paul Schneider lauded the SA for its "camaraderie, a strong unshakable faith in the mission of our Volk, will to sacrifice, and eternal readiness."[108] Similarly, another man explained that

> the unshakable faith in the epoch-making and great mission of National Socialism and its Führer seized us like a holy fire and dragged us with elemental force to its spell, so that one placed oneself irresistibly from a spontaneous unselfishness unconditionally in the service of the movement. So it brought our all-embracing struggle, that each and everyone of us had to fulfill his mission and thereby maintain inwardly the power to not one day become lost.[109]

This mission, of course, was not taken lightly. For, as is typical with the apocalyptic mentality, it was interpreted as a mission imparted by a higher power to a chosen few.

Inseparably tied to the sense of mission is the sense of being chosen by higher powers to fulfill that mission. In keeping with the archetypal pattern of apocalyptic movements, the Nazis viewed themselves as specially chosen to fulfill this divine salvational mission. Hitler stated bluntly, "The selection of the Führer class is my struggle for power. Whoever proclaims his allegiance to me is, by this very proclamation and by the manner in which it is made, one of the chosen."[110] Indeed, Hitler believed that one did not make oneself a leader but, rather, that true leaders were "born" or "chosen."[111] Hitler certainly believed that he had been chosen, stating that "every man who has ever taken a hand in history must be prepared for responsibility, and since I am certain of my ability to fulfill my role I have no fear of assuming it."[112] One individual described one of Hitler's reveries: "'I am Führer of a Reich that will last for a thousand years to come,' he said suddenly, as if coming out of a distant mental space. . . . 'No power on earth can shake the German Reich now, Divine Providence has willed it that I carry through the fulfillment of a Germanic task.'"[113] His followers agreed with this self-perception; as Otto Besenbruch said of a Hitler speech, "here speaks to us a chosen one."[114]

It was not by mere chance the Nazis found themselves in such times. Hitler explains, "We have been chosen by Fate as witnesses of a catastrophe which will be the mightiest confirmation of the soundness of the volkish theory."[115] Gregor Strasser believed that the Nazis were endowed with the eternal spirit necessary to achieve the millennium:

there is, however, only one "correct" spirit, only one spirit with a constructive view; that is the spirit which through man, in God's image, animates eternal nature! It is our strong faith and our profound knowledge that this spirit is in us, in the idea of National Socialism, and that it and no other will build the Millenial Reich![116]

Gregor's brother Otto likewise interpreted the Nazi role as that of being chosen:

the German Revolution recoils from no battle, finds no sacrifice too great, no war too bloody, for Germany must live! Thus we youths feel the heartbeat of the German Revolution pounding, thus we front soldiers see the face of the future before us and experience, humble-proud, the role of the chosen ones, to fight, to win the battle of the twentieth century satisfied to see the meaning of the war, the Third Reich![117]

As many German soldiers had felt chosen to experience World War I, so many Nazis believed themselves to have been chosen to do their part for Germany's salvation. One man noted that "I am thankful, however, to fate for having led me on its eventful run upon the road of fighting men. Ever deeper the perception penetrated into my heart that future generations will envy our combat veteran's generation for the great experience in the German [period of] radical change."[118] The chosen mission, then, was to proselytize Hitler's idea (the new construction of reality) to the masses in order to save their souls, and the world, from annihilation. Many of those who felt themselves chosen for this divine mission came to this conclusion after a profound conversion experience that changed their lives forever.

3

Seeing the Light
The Nazi Conversion Experience

In 1923, Alfred Rosenberg wrote a little book titled the *The Volkish Conception of the State: Collapse and Rebirth*. Discussing the emergence of the "new way," or, in Nazi terminology, the new view of the world, he wrote,

> There comes a moment for anyone who is truly searching when, out of thinking and fighting, suddenly an experience arises. From this moment on, the present, past and the outlook of the future appear to him in an entirely different light than before. He has perhaps still not been able to create a firm foundation for his life, but has taken a new direction.[1]

The "experience" that Rosenberg describes is one that many Old Guard Nazis report in their autobiographical reports of the *Kampfzeit*, the time of struggle.[2] Many Nazis close to the inner circle also claimed to have experienced such conversion experiences. For a few, Hitler was the primary catalyst. Goebbels converted from the Berlin Nazis' truer form of socialism to Hitler's salvational creed after meeting the Führer. In a letter, he described Hitler as "the fulfillment of a mysterious longing," a savior who, "like a meteor before our eyes," suddenly appeared and "worked a miracle of enlightenment and belief in a world of scepticism and despair."[3] Albert Speer recalled of his first Hitler speech that "three hours later I left the same beer garden a changed person. I saw the same posters with the dirty advertising columns, but looked at them with different eyes. A blown-up picture of Adolf Hitler in a martial pose that I had regarded with a touch of amusement on my way there suddenly lost all its ridiculousness."[4] This was a common experience.

Kurt Lüdecke, an early convert and later apostate, wrote that at his first Hitler speech, "I experienced something like a secular conversion.

The sincerity of his conviction redoubled my loyalty. In the face of every difficultly this man would lead us forward, because in his soul he believed that circumstance had laid upon his shoulders the burden of Germany's salvation." Hitler's utter conviction in his salvational mission was transferred to his listener. When Lüdecke later told Hitler of his experience, the Führer replied, "Yes, National Socialism is a form of conversion, a new faith, but we don't need to raise that issue—it will come of itself."[5] Hitler explained to another associate, Otto Wagener, what he meant by this in terms similar to those used by Rosenberg. Speaking of the "great turning point" that the world was going through, from an individualist world view to a socialistic or communal one, Hitler explained that "a thousand-year-old attitude toward life is being thrust aside by completely new concepts." This transformation could not take place through legislation or through the actions of any government ministry. Hitler explained, "Such a transformation requires an *inner* conversion! A mental, a spiritual, an ethical, even a religious one!" He further explained that the new Nazi government, despite his previous statement, could assist the spread of the conversion beyond the party to the Germans as a whole: "What is crucial is the internal conversion of the people, of the *Volksgenossen,* of the Volk! And that is a political task!" He continued, noting that the transformation was "such a far-reaching and complete conversion that the adult is no longer capable of it. Only youth can be converted, newly aligned and adjusted to the socialist sense of obligation toward the community." According to Wagener's account, Hitler's communalism was not so much that of the Marxist socialist but the millennial communalism of the apostolic or gnostic Christians. Wagener quotes Hitler as saying that "For almost two thousand years the Gospel of Christ has been preached, for two thousand years the sense of community has been taught." But, according to Hitler, that communalism had not been listened to but had been ignored: "We're to believe that we can restore the value of the word of God, the teaching of Christ, the truth of a holy religion, where generations upon generations, nations upon nations, the entire life span of a human cultural epoch, all were unable even to recognize the deep abyss in which they wandered or sojourned!" It was the youth that Hitler believed would ultimately build the millennial Third Reich:

> But when you see the masses streaming to join the SA, when you observe the enthusiasm of youth, when the cheerful hands of a innocent child reach for you, then you will sense the inner conversion; then you will re-

alize the new faith is awakening out of the lethargy of a corrupt epoch and taking to the march—the faith in divine justice, in heavenly truth; the faith in an unworldly, paradisiacal future, where the lust for power, force, and enmity gives way to equality and fraternity, the spirit of sacrifice, love and loyalty, and the will to stand before the throne of the Almighty with the open heart of one ready to believe in God. And they will have sufficient greatness to stammer out the prayer for their brothers and fathers, "Forgive them, Lord, for they knew not what they did." It is on this basis alone that the new world can be built! To lay this groundwork is our task. Our own hopes can aim no further. We must leave some things to be done by those who come *after* us. Your work will be a signpost for the future, a witness to our great intention, but in *our* time we will not be crowned with realization.[6]

If such grand conceptions of conversion and transformation were simply the empty rhetoric or wishful thinking of Nazi elites, then their significance would perhaps be minimal. However, the testimonials of minor Nazis demonstrate convincingly the genuineness and importance of Nazi conversion experiences. The total chaos of the Weimar period, the rapid and radical change in all areas of politics, economics, society, and culture, left many who would become Nazis feeling disoriented and hopeless. The order that they believed, rightly or wrongly, had characterized the Wilhelmian era had, during the Weimar period, collapsed into a chaos of apocalyptic proportions. This loss of order left these individuals in a state of psychological crisis. At this point, they became seekers, lost souls searching for salvation in a new conception of order. Hitler's racial salvationism gave these seekers their longed-for perception of order. Hitler placed the Weimar chaos within an eschatological scenario where the forces of light and order (the Aryans) were locked in an eternal cosmic battle against the forces of darkness and chaos (the Jews). Many Old Guard Nazis described their conversion to Hitler's "great idea" as a sudden experience of light and clarity—of disorder being instantly transformed into order. The converted Nazis felt themselves reborn; faith had been reawakened, and, with it, they experienced a surge of "power." Energized, the reborn Nazis sought to extend their conversion experiences to others, proselytizing Hitler's "great idea" in order to bring forth the New Age—the Nazi millennium. Understanding the nature of this conversion experience, then, is essential for comprehending the astonishing rise of Hitler and Nazism.

From Hopelessness to Salvation

Those who began their search for a new way, a new construction of order, most often began it feeling divided, confused, and hopeless. This period of crisis, the "dark night of the soul," as St. John on the Cross described it, is a common and perhaps necessary aspect of the preconversion mentality.[7] The crisis state is often experienced as a feeling of disorientation. This sensation was especially acute for German front-soldiers who returned home to find a world that seemed, and to a great extent was, quite different from the one they had left before the conflict. Adalbert Gimbel recalled that "as a veteran I came back from the World War and found before me a state where nothing corresponded with that which, as a volunteer, I had left behind." Similarly, Otto Leinweber found that "when I came home after the war, everything was different than one had imagined it." Another veteran explained that "my brain could not grasp that everything should be different than it had been," while Gustav Bonn found that "the disorder was too great to comprehend, so that one interested oneself in what should happen to this knocked down and prone Fatherland." Karl Adinger stated, "with all these experiences it was incomprehensible to me why in our Fatherland such conditions dominated." Finally, one veteran and future Nazi explained that "as a front-fighter the collapse of the Fatherland in November 1918 was to me completely incomprehensible."[8] This sense of confusion and incomprehensibility reflects the inability to reconstruct a perception of ordered reality that has collapsed.

The perception of having seen order dissolve into disorder left many Germans feeling disconnected from the world around them, alienated and lost. A number of future Nazis referred to their condition after the war as "rootless."[9] Others felt hopeless, concluding that the disorder was simply too great to overcome. The story of one man demonstrates this experience. After the war, he found that "a great hopelessness was in me." When the right-wing nationalist Wolfgang Kapp attempted, in 1920, to oust the left-wing government in Berlin, he saw a glimmer of hope. But when Kapp's putsch collapsed, he noted that "again came this dull hopelessness."[10] Perceptions of incomprehensibility, rootlessness, and hopelessness were psychic conditions that mirrored the chaos of Weimar Germany. One man who had "lost faith" in Weimar leadership and had been hit hard by the "inflation frenzy" remarked that "inwardly I had lost my Fatherland and proceeded unsteadily through the bitter times of contemporary events."[11] A young soldier and future Nazi, Emil Schlitz, returned from the war and saw a Germany that made his perception of reality fall like the Tower of Babel: "I had believed adamantly in Germany's invincibility and now I only saw the country in its deepest humiliation—an entire world fell to the ground."[12] Reality, a sense of comprehensible order, therefore collapsed into a psychic disorder of apocalyptic proportions. As Karl Hepp remarked, "the inner confusion, and, with it, the doubt in the dawn of the new, better age, was ever stronger."[13]

According to one early Nazi, this state of psychic conflict was necessary for an individual to find the right path: "He who searches for the right path must be inwardly in conflict." He is correct from a psychological perspective, for it is the resolution of conflict through the construction of a new perception of order that elicits the conversion experience, releasing enormous amounts of energy and giving the "reborn" new meaning and direction in life.[14] A detailed look at this man's conversion delineates elements typical of the Nazi conversion process. It begins with a feeling of inner or psychological conflict and unrest. Referring to his own problems in the early 1920s, he noted that "the struggle set in—a fervent, hard spiritual struggle." This spiritual conflict set him on his path to salvation. He searched from party to party, world view to world view, yet found no solace. He explained that "at this time I went through another inner struggle. Again and again I persuaded myself that it [one path or another] was, and must be, right. But always there was a voice there, very soft and scarcely audible, warning and again warning against it." He remarked that "inwardly dull, a scattered soul—I wandered about lost." After a seemingly fruitless intellectual quest, he found his path to Hitler. In Hitler's words he thought he might have finally found the right path. But, as is typical with many converts, there was a period of hesitation: "Inwardly, however, I was completely confused. Yet when I reconciled what I heard with contemporary events, I had to come to the conviction that the truth had been told." A speech by Goebbels further pushed him along this path. The gradual process of conversion then culminated in what was experienced as a sudden revelation:

It was for me as if he had spoken to me personally. The heart went out from me, the chest heaved, I felt as if something within was being put back together, bit by bit. . . . I plunged myself into some literature that was at hand, read Hitler's speeches, read the program of the NSDAP [National Socialist German Worker's Party] and was gradually politi-

cally born again. . . . A totally pure joy came into my consciousness. . . .
I was a National Socialist. No voice this time inwardly spoke against it,
no mind worried about the thought of being a National Socialist. A joyful knowledge, a bright enthusiasm, a pure faith—Adolf Hitler and Germany.[15]

As Lewis Rambo has noted, a period of hesitation and inner conflict before the surrender of the old self to a new self is common during the conversion process.[16] The new life, and the new world view or construction
of reality that comes with it, is tempting, but yielding control to some
higher power or charismatic messiah/guru is difficult. It is the resolution
of this conflict through the surrender of control to an idea, movement, or
individual, or some combination of all three, that elicits the conversion
experience and the sense of liberation that comes with it. For this man, a
period of confusion was resolved through the millennial rhetoric of Hitler
and Goebbels, and the collapsed old order was replaced with a coherent
and meaningful new order. He had found his path to salvation.

The Path to Salvation

The perception of chaos propels many on a search for a new sense of
order, what has been termed the quest.[17] Many Old Guard Nazis can be
described as seekers, individuals who searched various paths hoping to
find structure and order, meaning and purpose. The sociologists John
Lofland and Norman Skonovd delineated six types of conversion, each
reflective of the mode of conversion, as well as the personality of the
seeker.[18] The first is intellectual conversion, which results from immersion
in a "new way" via books, articles, lectures, or television. The second is
mystical conversion, which occurs after a sudden flash of insight, usually
achieved through ecstatic visions, the hearing of otherwordly voices, or
some other transcendent experience. The third is experimental conversion; especially evident in the twentieth century, this conversion results
from the exploration of a variety of religious options or paths. The fourth
is affectional conversion, motivated by a desire for an intimate experience
of being loved and being part of a close community. The fifth conversion
occurs through what might generally be termed revivalism, an experience
usually induced by conformity to group behavior; individuals are emotionally stirred by being merged with a large crowd, often aided by inspi-

rational music and motivational preaching. The sixth is coercive conversion. This is the rarest form, the result of what has been variously termed brainwashing, thought-reform, or programming. The Old Guard conversions reflect all of these types except the last.

Johannes Zehfuss, dejected by the situation in Weimar, said that "immediately I sought contact with like-minded people, whom I then found." Georg Klinger noted that "we were still only young men, who searched for a new ideal." Heinrich Maxeiner explained that "already in the war my search began for a world view of clarity. . . . I searched for powers which were willing, with me, to struggle for the liberation of our Volk." Describing himself, Wilhelm Reuter remarked that "politically I could neither warm up to the left nor the right, and for the parties of the middle even less so. I was and would be a seeker." Walter Gerwien, frustrated by the party system and the social fragmentation it seemed to reflect, commented, "I did not leave myself for long in the parliamentary quagmire—of all the parties and unions—which had caused the general decline of Germany and only played at the role of savior. Rather I searched for the path to Adolf Hitler." Similarly, Emil Hofmann found his new self in the perceived social unity of the Nazi "people's community." Like many converts, he felt compelled to become an ascetic and to spread the word: "Here I found what I searched for, namely German *Volksgenossen* and no classes. . . . It began a new life for me. While others went after pleasures, I carried the new idea from mouth to mouth and canvassed every single soul for the great *Weltanschauung*."[19]

The search begins for a new way, a new path to salvation. The path is a direction, and the means, to that salvation.[20] One rather descriptive Old Guard Nazi began his testimony with an extended image of apocalypse and salvation through a visionary savior. I quote it at length because of its rich chiliastic and messianic imagery:

When today I observe in retrospect the path that my German Volk, and therefore also myself as a member of that Volk, have traveled the long years from 1914–1933, there stands in my mind before my eyes an image, as if brought forth by a Master hand.

In the distance a vast fire, long raging—a complete catastrophe. Coming out from there a landscape—desolate, rocky, full of thorns, overcast with dark clouds. Paths traverse this land to and fro. Many end in the quagmire, many in the abyss. Only one path leads straight through, if also over many crags and crevices—striving towards a mountain, which rises up from the landscape in the distance. Cloud-covered, this wretched landscape—yet sunbeams on the summit of the mountain.

Upon the one path a man travels, with head erect, in front of the Volk, indicating the destination—the sunlit mountain peak. Again and again he summons a vacillating people, despite disappointments and persecution, through the wasteland and the false paths, to the right path. Only a few at first hear him. Many will not hear him. Many cannot understand him. Others further mock him. Foreign peoples, the Jews and their deceivers hate him and tempt the desperate—but honest searching Volk hold off through lies and deceit, to follow the Summoner.

Still more and more the seduced and wrongly guided Volk awakens to the perception: "That which summons you, you German Volk, can alone lead you on the path away from the quagmire, from the misery and destitution, safely to the light—to freedom and to honor—your Volk's Führer, your Führer!"

All of this is no longer an image, but a reality, a miracle, God's hand over our Führer and our Volk! I am also a son of this Volk, whom God indeed tested and weighed, but has never found too light. I had the fortune to have intuitively found the path to my Führer early.[21]

Like this individual, many of the Old Guard took special pride in having found their path to Hitler early. It is clear from their stories that the path to salvation and the path to Hitler were, in their eyes, the same thing. One man noted that "only, today I know . . . that I must be thankful to fate to have allowed me to have found the right path so early."[22] Otto Glas, another member of the Old Guard, said that "I am as a German especially proud that I had found the path to my Führer so early and was able to struggle for his idea."[23] Wilhelm Fleck, reflecting on the seizure of power in January 1933, noted that "this was the most profound experience of my struggle-time, and I was proud that I was fortunate not to have been the last to find the path to the Führer, and that I had helped the Führer to prepare the path."[24] The Old Guard found a deep sense of personal accomplishment in the Nazis' rise to power. The attainment of the longed-for Nazi millennium caused yet another man to look back with pride at having found his way to Hitler early: "today I know, after the Third Reich (that I struggled for for eight years) is now captured, how thankful I must be that destiny permitted me to find the right path so early."[25] Not surprisingly, those who failed to see the light early felt compelled to explain themselves. One man believed that fear and lack of vision kept him from finding his way to Hitler earlier: "Had I cast off this frightful sorrow and could have perceived into the future, trustfully and unencumbered, then perhaps at this time I would already have found my path to Adolf Hitler."[26]

Other Nazis saw the social context of Weimar, especially the economic chaos, as the most important catalyst that drew more and more individuals to the light. One man explained proudly that "through Germany's economic recession and the acknowledgment of the Volk that it had been deceived in shameful ways, ever more *Volksgenossen* found the path to our local branch, which was quickly so strong in the city that a portion had to be divided into four branches."[27] Others found their path through the Nazi Party Days. Josef Schimmel, discussing the 1923 German Day celebrations, claimed that "from this day on it was completely clear to me that only with his movement can the German Volk be saved before its destruction. We bore this understanding home with us, that we were on the right path."[28] Still others found their path through faith alone. In keeping with the religious nature of the Nazi conversion experience, the new faith was almost always referred to with a sense of righteousness; it was the "correct" or "right" path to salvation. Paul Schneider reported that "our faith had shown us in so many debates the right path and the right answer."[29] Johannes Christ, a SA member, remembered this typically brutish fight song, one that offered liberation through redemptive violence:

> We are the army of the Swastika
>> Raise high the red flag,
>> German work we will be put on the right path to freedom
>> Blood, blood, blood must flow knee high thick
>> We don't give a damn about the Jewish Republic.[30]

Karoline Leinweber took the journey on the path to salvation with her husband. Her account demonstrates the importance of familial networks for the spread of Nazism.[31] It also reflects the possessive quality of Hitler's "idea," as well as the religious nature of her subsequent conversion:

When in the year 1922 I heard our Führer for the first time, I shifted my entire interest to the movement, if only because my husband was seized by the same idea. So we went jointly upon this uncertain path. However, a ray of light showed us the path. What the Führer willed, which was holy to us, we surrendered blood and everything that we had. Insults, knocks and taunts we let make us even harder. So we went side by side through bitter deprivation, yet ever wider triumphed the truth. What the Führer did and said was right.[32]

Heini Bickendorf, something of an intellectual seeker, interpreted the path to Nazism as one of achieving a new gnosis. He explained that, while "I believe myself to be widely versed on this path, it is only a beginning in the new wisdom."[33] Finally, Eduard Hohbein, discussing the difficulties of the struggle years, claimed that, "in spite of all this, and every dark happening, I will never in my life let myself be led astray from the good path. I feel myself to be accountable only to our Lord God and my Führer."[34] Hohbein was convinced he had found the righteous road to salvation. Nothing could lead him astray—not violence, not hunger, not poverty. But what made the Nazi conversion experience seem so powerful and so right?

The Search for Transcendence

The Nazi conversion experience was most often referred to as an "inner" or "inwardly" occurring phenomenon, a description that points to its psychological basis. For many seekers, the primary motivation behind a conversion experience is a desire for transcendence, a wish to search beyond themselves to find meaning and purpose.[35] This is true of many Nazi converts, as well, especially those who rejected modernity and its perceived emphasis on materialism and egoistic selfishness.[36] They craved an experience that was spiritual and communal. Ludwig Heck I, an intellectual seeker, said that he came to the Nazi party through newspaper articles. In these writings, he "found inner contact with the spirit of National Socialism and it was my aspiration to work for this idea at my locality."[37] Similarly, another man, speaking of the early 1920s, remarked, "at this time I studied several propaganda writings of the NSDAP and felt myself intuitively drawn to the spirit which spoke from these writings."[38] This notion of being inwardly drawn to the Nazi world view is fairly common. That the written word could carry such magical power for so many Germans points to the powerful attraction of millennial rhetoric. It was not simply the intellectual force of the Nazi argument but something ineffable. One man stated that if someone were to ask him why he had placed all his power behind the Nazis, he would respond that "to tell the truth, I would not have been in a position to answer. I only know that I followed an inner voice, an impulse, which I was not in a position to withstand."[39] The belief that one is following a higher power or truth is a common and powerful aspect of the postconversion personality, as doubt and confusion are replaced by certainty and clarity.

The spoken word was especially noted for its ability to inwardly draw individuals to Nazism. For some converts, that attraction seemed almost supernatural. Peter Weber attended a gathering and found that "instantly I came to a decision, and I said to myself, that only this party can save Germany. From this time on I attended every gathering—it drew me to it, so to speak, with magical power, and on March 1, 1928, I became a member."[40] Franz Madre first came into contact with the movement when he was fourteen years old. He explained that "while I could not as yet understand everything completely, still something inside me said that here exists something to which I belong."[41] In other words, the Nazis' use of millennial symbols and metaphors deeply touched this man. It was the "awakening" or bringing to light (consciousness) of the new world view (the new construction of order) that led to the Nazi conversion experience. The remarks of another man elucidate this psychological process:

> Through National Socialist propaganda I became aware of the movement and visited several gatherings. Without at first being clear about its goals, I felt instinctively the spiritual transformation that [occurred] inside me [through] the liberating idea. . . . Later I read the Führer's book, then heard him in person and . . . believed.[42]

Often, these converts believed that they had always been Nazis but simply had not been aware of it. Again, this is in accordance with their conviction that Nazi propaganda was simply awakening or bringing to the surface something that lay dormant within the soul or blood of all true Aryans. From a psychological standpoint, this is in fact a more accurate description of the conversion process then perhaps the Nazis themselves were aware. Hitler's "great idea," filled with symbols of annihilation and salvation, messianism and demonism, helped adherents to simultaneously reconstruct a sense of order and create a new life. This process is evident in the following account by Martha von Reuss. Here she relates her first encounter with a Nazi proselytizer:

I could have listened to this man all night. Inside a voice would often say: "Yes, entirely correct, as I have always believed." In this hour I knew finally, after many searches and headaches, where I belonged. Then it was very easy for me to see that I was really always there [a Nazi] without knowing it. There Adolf Hitler's people were willing as fighters to stand up against Marxism, and were willing to bleed and to die for this holy idea of our beloved Führer. It was clear to me that my goal and wish was attained. It kindled in me a fire for this movement, and I perceived that one does not learn National Socialism, rather one must experience it. And for the second time in my life, exactly like with the war, I regretted that I was not a man.[43]

One man explained that he was drawn to the movement not by any social pressures but by an inner spiritual or psychological one:

I always was a National Socialist. The name of the concept is immaterial. Today I know that I was a National Socialist before there was a name for that idea. Today, when the concept and the name have been established, I know that I am a National Socialist and will remain one. There was never any question of compulsion. No outward pressure was brought to bear on me; nor did reason dictate this necessity. My heart commanded it.[44]

As mentioned earlier, social networks are often essential to the conversion process, especially for those termed affectional seekers, individuals who find salvation in attaining emotional connections within a like-minded community. One man who came into contact with a group of Nazis remarked that "in their circle I found that for which I searched. Here I experienced my inner transformation to National Socialism." Another man left his first Nazi gathering with an "inner liberation . . . a greater liberation than I had known."[45] For some followers, this inner transformation mirrored the metamorphosis that their external world was going through. One man explained that many young Nazis were undergoing a "process of a great transformation, an inner complete reshaping renewal." This transformation was a "radical cure" that has "often been accompanied by painful occurrences [meaning the many traumas of Weimar]."[46] For others, Hitler was the primary catalyst for transformation. One individual exclaimed, "with glowing enthusiasm I became aware of his appearance and of his first speech, and was immediately captured by him. Since this time I knew inwardly that I was nothing other than a National Socialist. Here I found that for which I searched."[47]

This spiritual search was, in the words of many seekers, one for "clarity" and "light." One man, impressed by his son's willingness to die for Nazism, recalled,

> that was the crucial hour for me. For a long time I pondered how it was possible that my only son would be willing to let himself be killed for an idea. It struck me that there must be something about the idea other than what I had heard about it. In all secrecy I brought myself a copy of *Mein Kampf.* Then I went to some National Socialist meetings, and I began to see the light.[48]

The common conversion metaphors of moving from confusion to clarity, from darkness to light, reflect the psychological process of having a perception of order collapse into disorder and then having that sense of order reconstructed. The sense of order generated by Nazi apocalyptic cosmology was experienced as a revelation of simple but profound truths. An excerpt from the life of one seeker highlights this process. Poor and hungry, tempted to steal yet holding fast to his values, this man struggled throughout the Weimar years—until Nazism came into his life:

> I had held, up until then, many illusions and had to experience them gradually turn to dust. . . . Then came the economic misery—one experienced its hunger and saw full stores, saw the splendor of the streets of the capital, saw the luxuriant department stores. And yet I held myself straight. And when I alas often had not a bite to eat for three days I lived by the strongly held conviction to pass them by, not to become wicked, but to live in misery, to go into the earth without sin. And then the light came into my life.[49]

Many Old Guard converts believed that struggle itself led one to clarity and therefore to National Socialism: "Life was always constant struggle, thus the generation of the war and postwar periods experienced this in concentrated form, and in their circles one finds clarity and a capacity for life that leads to National Socialism."[50] Rudolf Bergmann found the clarity he sought at a Nazi gathering. He recalled that "I went and was there enlightened about the will of Adolf Hitler."[51] Hermann Hirth explained that Hitler was the first to "demonstrate clearly and meaningfully

his path for the future."[52] Many believed that it was this logic and preci-
sion of Hitler's words, and the way that the speeches were constructed,
that converted so many listeners. One man noted that it was "through the
sharpness of his words and the wit of their spirit which brought the listener in tune. Adolf Hitler's speeches are arranged such that the listener
is entirely convinced and won eternally to him." Another man remarked
that it was the "logic of his conception" that "induced" him "to join the
party that same evening."[53]

The perceived clarity of Nazi ideas and goals, contrary to the view of
many historians, was of paramount importance to many of the converted.
The belief, then, that Nazi propaganda, whether written or spoken, was
a meaningless mishmash of ideas that had little effect on its audience is
simply untrue. Hitler's "great idea," and the apocalyptic, millennial, and
messianic rhetoric contained therein, gave many Germans the new sense
of order they were searching for. Once again, by placing Weimar chaos
within an eschatological time frame, making it a sign of an historic turning point that mandated a divine mission for the chosen few, Hitler transformed disorder into order, hopelessness into faith. And, as we saw earlier, blaming that apocalyptic chaos on an alleged Jewish conspiracy also
acted to structure the disorder. One convert felt that what one Nazi
speaker said was "so clear and self-evident," and "everything so easy to
comprehend, that one could nearly believe that we must again be welded
together into one Volk." Another noted that "the righteousness and necessity of Hitler's mission was ever clearer to me." Valentin Schwöbel was
attracted to the Nazis for "above all things—clarity of goal." Heinrich
Berwig was drawn to Hitler for "his simple, clear expressions," while
Heini Bickendorf was attracted by his "purest, simplest, crystal-clear
idea."[54] Finally, one man, describing a Nazi speaker, proclaimed, "Powerful like a mountain Grauste preaches the gospel of Adolf Hitler to an
awaiting multitude, every single one held profoundly spellbound, drawn
up to the light."[55]

Hearing a "Piercing Voice":
Nazi Rhetoric and the Sudden Conversion

According to many Old Guard Nazis, hearing Hitler speak the first
time motivates them to join the party. Their descriptions portray this
event as offering a sudden conversion. As Lewis Rambo has noted, the

image of the sudden conversion typified by Saul on the road to Damascus is, contrary to popular perception, more the exception than the rule.[56] Conversion is a process that occurs over time, rather than a single transforming event. However, while conversion is a process, the moment when surrender occurs, when the individual gives himself or herself totally to some deity, leader, or idea, is often experienced and is certainly remembered as a sudden event. This is true for a number of the Old Guard. Wilhelm Scherer described his first Hitler speech this way:

> He begins, his thrilling leadership breaks the ice perhaps half-way through his speech. The first applause resounds. Again the man speaks, one senses it—in him is a holy seriousness. The water runs by him as by the stern. It became immediately evident to me: yes, only this man can save us and no one else.[57]

For many individuals, it appears that the explicit millennial rhetoric contained in Nazi speeches converted them. Otto Schroeder recalled his first Hitler speech, in 1921:

> I can remember still quite well what he advised the gathering: "Thus I state here sincerely, the politics that are made in Berlin will end in chaos, and Germany can only be saved through the National Socialist movement." I signed an enrollment certificate that was passed around and was thus in 1921 a member of the NSDAP.[58]

Many other individuals reported converting to Nazism after attending their first Hitler speech. One man remembered that "the Führer's speech was so overwhelming that I declared my entrance to the movement that same evening."[59] An attendee at a Hitler speech during the heated campaign of 1933 recalled,

> I heard the Führer Adolf Hitler speak for the first time in the year 1930 in Königsberg. Here I acquired the conviction that I followed the leader who, in the history of the German people, would one day lead it to first place in the world in prosperity.[60]

Another man, in even more frankly millennial terms, recalled a similar reaction to his first Hitler speech:

His remarks made upon me a deep impression and I was so enraptured and convinced by the correctness of his idea that, from this instant, I acquired again new faith in the resurrection of the German Volk. Now more than ever it was clear to me that only National Socialism could save us and make us free again.[61]

The sudden discovery of a new faith following a Hitler speech is a common theme in the Nazi autobiographies. One man recalled simply, "Adolf Hitler's speech recovered something that had left me—faith." It was, as is typical with any conversion experience, a life-changing event, one that gave many Germans new meaning and direction. As one woman remarked after her first Hitler speech, "since this day Germany had its Führer and savior. Thus I have since this time canvassed, struggled, worked and also willingly sacrificed for him, to complete my prayer to him." Similarly, one man remarked that "from this instant on stood for me no doubt, that Hitler was Germany's coming Führer and he would possess also the power to bring Germany back from its unworthy position." Yet another individual remarked that "still today rings in my ears the speech at the Weimar city theater. There came to me the certain realization: here speaks to us a chosen one."[62]

It was not, however, solely Hitler's speeches that converted Nazis. Therefore, it was not simply Hitler's personal magnetism or charisma, in the common sense of the term, or his unique oratorical abilities that converted listeners.[63] That many other Nazi speakers achieved sudden conversions points to the fact that words did in fact count. Significantly, according to one early study, it was the meetings and speeches of the Nazis, and consequently the millennial message they contained, that impelled most converts.[64] As mentioned earlier, Nazi speeches and propaganda were intended to awaken something within, and, psychologically, they had exactly that effect. One convert recalled after his first Nazi speech that he had no doubt "that this movement must be accepted if the German Volk is not to lose its faith in itself and in the Fatherland. This faith in itself, therefore, only slumbers in the German Volk and only requires a piercing voice to be wide awake."[65]

The message of that "piercing voice" was one of impending apocalypse, with salvation possible only through Nazism. Nazi rhetoric struck a chord with the millenarian longings of many hopeless and frustrated Germans. Elisabeth Kranz recalled that the speaker at her first meeting entered saying, "Give room, you people, give room. We are the last messenger! Thus we are the last—the last contingent, the last bulwark against communism. Behind us comes nothing more, behind us comes chaos—destruction."[66] Emil Schneider attended his first gathering, whose theme was the decline of the German people, and observed that many who attended "hoped perhaps to find a salvation from the general chaos." The speaker, he continued, "stressed that the prevailing world economic crisis was not to blame for Germany's decline, but rather the German Volk itself and its contemporary government. He demanded in fiery words the combining of all powers amongst the united circles to save Germany before its complete ruin." This attendee concluded that "now I knew to which movement I would pledge my life: it was the only movement that was chosen to pull Germany and its Volk up from the contemporary chaos."[67]

The story of the future SA member Johannes Christ demonstrates the life-changing capability of a conversion experience, one in which the old self dies and a new self is born. He remarked that, while attending a speech by Gregor Strasser, he came to the sudden realization that his "inner confusion" simply marked "the end of one world. I was slowly ruled by a different spirit."[68] According to Hans Grün, it was the Nazi explanation of the cause of Weimar chaos that was the catalyst for him; Nazism structured the chaos he perceived around him by placing the German collapse within an eschatological framework. In other words, the chaos was no longer perceived as random and meaningless but was seen as reflective of the historic turning point where Germans could choose annihilation through Weimar politics or salvation through National Socialism. According to Grün,

> The gathering made an incredible impression upon me. Why? I had never yet experienced such a thing. The speaker resolved in me what had until then been unclear with an account of the recklessness of the men of the government system and its institutions, as well as all its spawn. This, as well as the entire course of the rally was for me a life experience. I could not wait until the next gathering was announced.[69]

As with Hitler's speeches, many attendees interpreted the gatherings, and the messages contained therein, in spiritual terms. One SA member, Paul Hainbach, stated that "in my spiritual misery these goals worked upon me like a gospel. I perceived that the Führer pursued the welfare of each and every party member with warm concern and that he himself would not forsake the spiritual needs of his followers."[70] Similarly, another man recalled that Goebbels's speech "was for me as if I heard the gospel." He further noted that "politically at this time I was a completely neutral body, when it suddenly dawned in me the sense of the idea and I found that for which I had so longed searched!: righteousness and forward development." Some individuals claimed that it was no accident that brought them to their first Nazi meeting but the work of a hidden power. This belief reflects the perception that one has been chosen by higher powers for some special salvational mission. For example, one individual witnessed a talk of Hermann Esser and stated, "I attended this gathering and today I still thank Providence that it sent me to this gathering. And immediately, upon the foundation of my entire outlook, I joined the party that same morning."[71] Finally, Heinrich Wick, who attended his first National Socialist meeting in the early 1920s, recalled, "I developed through this gathering the little notion that this was the movement, in embryonic form, which could perhaps save our Fatherland from certain destruction."[72]

The following account, which recalls a Goebbels speech and the subsequent conversion of formerly procommunist workers, presents insight not only into this speaker's style and rhetorical content but also into the profound spiritual effect it had on many listeners:

Small and insignificant, with a hindered walk, he proceeded to the speaker's stand. I was disappointed with this so-called cannon of our movement—until this man began to speak. At first small and diminutive and insignificant. Then, however, increasing and swelling to a gigantic Preacher of a New Age. In an uninterrupted line of reasoning he hammered into the men with the teaching of National Socialism: community before individuality; the whole man is but a soldier, the whole soldier but a mouth and hands to hold spellbound opponents and followers; the whole man a victor of spirit over wickedness, baseness, international scoundrels and Bolshevism. Thus he led the seduced worker back to the Volk and the Fatherland and from there to the Führer Adolf Hitler. Few minds ventured to rebel against this thought-world, and soon he was laughing with several comrades and former opponents of our cause. He had captured the hearts of the opposition.[73]

Other Nazi speakers produced similar results. Robert Mayer, who had believed that "Germany's future appeared ever disconsolate," found after a speech by Gregor Strasser that

my heart and eyes opened forever. I was shaken—then before long I believed nothing more about it [Germany's bleak future]. There were still
in Germany men who understood the truth and could bring our Volk
out of its decay. From this hour I must go with Adolf Hitler and his
movement.[74]

Dora Sott recalled a young Nazi "priest" who gave a "hammering
speech." Her words betray an experience with the archetypal. She found
that

> an extraordinary power emanated from him to us, which lasted for a
> long time. . . . For me it appears always essential, to carry the idea to the
> Volk from mouth to mouth. It was this work, which no one saw, but
> which, however, must be done unflaggingly if we want the victory to
> come. In friend- and official-circles one could experience a miracle of lu-
> cidity.[75]

The Nazi's emphasis on community and unity as being crucial for salvation appears to have been the key metaphor for eliciting the conversion
experience for many of the Old Guard. This was especially true for war
veterans who longed for the lost camaraderie of the field, part of what
George Mosse called "the myth of the war experience."[76] The front itself
was in many ways a transcendent experience, one in which the individual
self was surrendered to the needs of the collective. Selfishness was replaced by sacrifice. Through Nazism, especially when experienced in a
mass gathering, whether a speech-gathering or a Party Day ritual, the lost
unity of the front experienced a rebirth. One veteran described his conversion this way:

> The speaker spoke: naturally and unpolished flowed the words. Every
> sentence preached unvarnished truths. The heart intuitively demolished
> the barriers of my narrow-minded inhibitions. I felt myself suddenly in a
> community. I had, after a long while, a cessation of an inner experience.
> The company community of the field [war camaraderie], from which I
> once subscribed to with life and soul, celebrated a resurrection. From
> this day on I completely supported the idea-world of National Social-
> ism. . . . From day to day I perceived ever clearer that Adolf Hitler
> clothed it in understandable words for my dull senses to lead me to com-
> munity. The unknown soldier Adolf Hitler formed the unequivocal de-

mands of National Socialism. I was again filled with the spirit of community and could no longer escape it.[77]

The reference to the "unknown soldier" who would resurrect the spirit of community and save Germany is one of the common messianic metaphors used to described Hitler. The motif of the "unknown man" who becomes savior is also a theme found in many messianic movements. Interestingly, the notion of an unknown man rising from the masses to save a people is the central theme of Wagner's opera *Rienzi,* a performance of which provided Hitler with the beginnings of his messianic sense of mission. I return to this in the next chapter. But here we must ask what made the image of the coming millennial "community" so powerful an attractor to Nazism.

The Sense of Unity: Nazism and the Community of Blood

The idea that the restoration of "community" was essential for the salvation of Germany is a common theme found throughout the autobiographies of minor Nazis. As the politics and social fragmentation of the Weimar period imparted an apocalyptic sense of division within many German psyches, the Nazi millennial world view in turn conferred a sense of oneness via its racial concept of a unified Volk, a community of blood.[78] Hitler exclaimed that politicians who turn workers against employers are turning racial brother against racial brother, a "sin against the blood." He countered that "we must release these misled people from foreign allurements! These people who feel abandoned by the Volk even though they themselves are the Volk—we must reunite them with the other racial comrades! A united Volk must come into being! One faith! One will!"[79] As division creates chaos, unity generates order. This type of reasoning can be seen in the following testimonial:

> The struggle of a few SA men, workers, white-collar workers and peasants—almost entirely unemployed for a lengthy period—was almost desperate. Each and everyone of them was a hero. More and more, however, through the indefatigable canvassing of the Führer and his faithful, knowledge of the correctness and purity of the Idea, and, above all, the single most possibility of a turning away from communistic chaos, penetrated the masses. Helpers and fighters from all political camps gradu-

ally came to assist. The will to sacrifice knew no bounds. Long hours, day and night, and the last penny, were joyfully given up. With helplessness the government at that time watched as Adolf Hitler's followers grew. The movement went through the most difficult struggles and calumny on its path to certain victory. I myself did what I could, especially in my district, to enlighten the worker. I said to myself, then, that the worker, in his loyalty and simplicity, is assured for the movement. It is a fundamental error, if one believes, that the intellectual has a better political understanding for things of the world than the worker.[80]

This sense that Nazism was a heterogenous movement was not lost on its members. Indeed, for many it was precisely this perception that gave them the sense of unity that they longed for. Georg Klinger recalled that he first heard of the Nazis from a friend, who "recounted to me that he had known in Bavaria that the worker, the craftsman, the peasant and the professor marched behind the swastika flag." Another convert, after hearing a Nazi speech, found his desired clarity in the conception of German unity. He stated that "I agreed with what he said, and everything that the speaker had spoken was so clear and self-evident and everything so easily comprehensible, that one could nearly believe it, that we all could again be welded together as one Volk." Paul Schneider described his fellow party members, in a phrase that typifies the Nazi tendency for verbosity, as an "eternally welded together sworn fanatical community." Still another party member defined the Nazis as a "strongly tight knit unity which struggled for Adolf Hitler's idea."[81] Speaking of the SA, one man explained that "in these days the SA represented a unity of purpose such as has never been achieved, nor shall be hereafter." According to another, the quest for unity was the hidden power of the National Socialist idea, explaining, "This then is the secret of our idea, and in it lies the power of National Socialism: unity is the goal of our leader, who wants to make the people strong, so it may become powerful again."[82]

The Nazi Party Days, for many converts, were the most powerful symbol of this unity. Witnessing tens of thousands of individuals, all in uniform, melded as one was a powerful and near-transcendent experience. This was especially so in contrast with the social fragmentation that many perceived around them. One individual recalled that "the men at this celebration were of one heart and one soul and one enthusiasm, which appears no more capable of increasing." Hermann Jung noted that "the days from Potsdam to May Day united our classes, parties and job interests and adapted an entire Volk into a German nation." The observations of Franz Madre demonstrate powerfully the symbolic importance of the Party Days, as well as Hitler's key role as the embodiment of unity:

> For the first time I saw before my eyes the power of the movement. For the first time I was permitted to see the Führer, and since then I have borne in my heart the strong certainty that we will capture Germany. We all were intoxicated by the powerful experience—100,000 men and all harnessed by one man; 100,000 men and all had one goal and one will, to capture this Germany so that the Führer can build a new Reich, a Reich which should stand after us for a millennium.[83]

According to one Nazi it was the *Führerprinzip* (Leadership Principle) that "eradicated class hatred, class spirit and pride of place." He explained, in thoroughly millenarian fashion, that

> There is only one German Reich, one German Volk under one Führer Adolf Hitler, who leads us out of darkness to the light, from misery to happiness. All of Germany strongly supports him and all know that this Third Reich that our Führer created will stand for a millennium, and that after us the Hitler Youth will take this great earth in their loyal hands and build strongly upon it. Thus with a sense of the National Socialist world view as an eternal value and as God sent we will be able to hand over to the loyal hands of the coming Hitler Generation. And still I know one day that through Hitler and his world view not only Germany, but the entire world will recover. Truth lights the road ahead and so one day the rest of the world will view us as the most harmonious Volk on earth.[84]

The assumption of power for many Nazis marked the coming of unity. One Nazi said that "finally our fullest wish of the heart was fulfilled, and in a short time the Führer had made from a divided Volk a single German Volk."[85] Elisabeth Kranz agreed, proclaiming that "a miracle is seen, a powerful, great thing! Germany is one, it follows one Führer and one flag! God bless you my Führer, and you, my Fatherland!"[86] In this way, political and social unity through Nazism would lead to spiritual unity, a further indication of the spiritual power of Nazism.

New Power and New Faith

As is typical of those who have undergone conversion experiences, converted Nazis acquired a new sense of faith, one that replaced the preconversion sense of hopelessness. With the sudden realization or intensification of faith, listlessness and depression disappeared and the convert subsequently felt an infusion of power or energy.[87] Faith was an essential aspect of the new world view, and of the new life of the converts. One Nazi described himself during the struggle-time in this way: "unwavering in faith in the mission of the National Socialist world view I fought this struggle . . . in spite of all my injuries and my sickness, I struggled unshakably further in the faith in the victory of the National Socialist world view." Recalling the final years before the assumption of power, when the "terror" was at its peak, another individual explained that "there one saw, and profoundly experienced, the struggle for German humanity, for its soul." Struggle itself, in the minds of some Nazis, generated the needed faith. Karl Dörr explained that "as the Führer was what he was through his war experience, I was through the war made a faithful fighter for the Führer's holy idea."[88] Faith in Hitler and his "great idea" held Old Guard Nazis to the movement like a spell; as one man explained, "We acted as if under a compulsion. Even had we wished to, we could not have been untrue to the movement without having our hearts turn out of our breasts. Unshakeable faith and unselfish devotion to the hallowed cause were our weapons against apparently invincible opponents."[89]

Hitler was often interpreted as the embodiment of this faith. As Heinrich Oesterling explained, "the faith in the Führer Adolf Hitler, who was indeed the last and strongest pillar, permitted us to never abandon the struggle." This tendency can also be seen in the recollections of Roman Pornschlegel. His story demonstrates how Hitler's charisma was to a great extent projected on him by devoted and adoring followers: "up until this time I had not yet heard our Führer speak, although I had personally registered myself to the party in Munich at the *Schellingstrasse* in the year 1926. I stayed on a few more days, to quiet my senses to be able, one day, to secretively see the man of my faith." Wilhelm Schneider explained that he joined the party "with the strong faith that only this idea and their Führer Adolf Hitler alone would lead our Fatherland again towards better times." The perception of faith also acted as an inducement for some individuals. After meeting a group of Nazis, one man joined the movement because their "fanatical faith in Adolf Hitler, their willingness for sacrifice and boundless devotion, inspired awe in me." For Anne Heilmann, this faith provided a sense of invincibility. She explained, "Did we need weapons? The faith in our Führer and the good cause protected us."[90]

The Nazi Party Days, not surprisingly, were especially important for instilling faith and power. Highly ritualized, the Party Days acted as a form of choreographed messianism, revival meetings for the Nazi faithful.[91] It was at the Party Days that numerous conversions occurred. Many who had joined the party for political reasons alone found something more at the Party Days—they found faith, and they found a savior.[92] Karl Baumann, in a statement common to many Old Guard Nazis, recalled that "the most beautiful moment of my life was when I was permitted to see the Führer for the first time. With new power I returned to the country energized to carry on the struggle." Hans Schmidt, recalling the Weimar Party Day of 1925, explained that, "enthused we returned from Weimar and further worked like apostles of faith for the movement." The SA member Johannes Christ interpreted one Party Day as a coming-out for the movement. He explained that "finally we could speak out about the party and its mission. As it now appeared to us that we were convinced by the idea of our Führer and had faith in the holy cause." Christ now felt free to call himself a Nazi and to publically give testimony for the new faith: "when I was asked about it, I said freely that I was a follower of the Hitler party, because I had seen there a great and holy mission. Already at that time I said that one day the time will come when each and every German will march with us."[93]

Emil Sauer described his return home from a Party Day in a manner that delineates the process of psychological transformation:

This travel home through the dark night, as our headlights ate into the darkness, was symbolic for us. After the torches of the march-by are extinguished, we must again camouflage our brown shirts, as we witness again the seemingly hopeless darkness of the daily struggle against the Terror of the State and the Sub-humans. However, before us shines a light—faith in Germany's future, and the faith that with Adolf Hitler it will be fulfilled. And this light leads us through the darkness till we have reached the goal, the Third Reich.[94]

As the party rallies came to symbolize the transformation from disunity to unity, from darkness to light, the converted Nazis found themselves energized for the continuing struggle. Speaking about the German

Day celebration of 1923, Karl Müller explained that "here we could create again new power for the next year. In Nuremberg the Führer strengthened our faith in the future of National Socialism." Similarly, Jakob Tritsch proclaimed that "in Nuremberg we acquired new power for the further struggle . . . the struggle for the souls of the German worker and peasant goes further." According to the Old Guard, the path to salvation was a long and torturous one; yet, once achieved, it had to be extended to others. As one man explained, it was "a long way to find one's way from here to clarity. . . . It will be my job to canvass for the German soul."[95] Once this man had found his path to salvation, it was not surprising that he felt compelled to convince others to join that path, making his personal salvation a collective one.

The Struggle Goes Further: Spreading the Word of Adolf Hitler

The presence of the great idea, and a fanatical belief in it, was essential, according to Hitler, if a transformation of humanity was to take place:

> The lack of a great, creative, renewing idea means at all times a limitation of fighting force. Firm belief in the right to apply even the most brutal weapons is always bound up with the existence of a fanatical faith in the necessity of the victory of a revolutionary new order on this earth. A movement that is not fighting for such highest aims and ideals will, therefore, never seize upon the ultimate weapon.[96]

Nazism was the movement that Hitler created to propagate, indeed, proselytize his great idea to the masses and ensure its fulfillment: "For the function of organization is the transmission of a definite idea—which always first arises from the brain of an individual—to a larger body of men and the supervision of its realization."[97] The conversion of individual Germans to Hitler's "great idea" had to continue to ripple throughout the population. Transmission of this idea was to continue after the assumption of power, for the goal of Nazi canvassing was not simply the continued growth of political power but the salvation of Aryan humanity by cleansing it of impurities. As Wilhelm Scherer explained,

> It was clear to me that with the attainment of power in the state the struggle is not yet completed. Now it means [we must] aid our *Weltan-*

schauung's awakening within the outer community, and to erect a unity also within the soul.

For in this struggle all powers (Germany's spiritual servants) must struggle against the Jewish spirit within the German Volk's soul, struggle against foreign elements, teachings and religions, which weigh down upon the souls of German men and desecrate their spirit, so strongly embattled in outer unity. Struggle against the hypocrisy outside the movement and also within its ranks.

Today we struggle further, for the genuineness of our revolution, for the awakening of our *Weltanschauung*. Only when the Volk has risen to our *Weltanschauung*—to victory— when it has ripped out root and branch all foreign, Jewish and foreign-type Christian elements, is our mission completed.[98]

For Scherer, the Nazi world view created political and social unity, which in turn generated spiritual unity, a process that would go from the movement and then, with the assumption of power, spread to the rest of Germany.

Hitler planned to extend this conversion experience to all Aryans of the world, a universal revelation in the way of his new order. He coined the phrase "the struggle goes further" to capture this sense of an idea that is born in the head of one man, then spreads to a select few, then to more and more, until a world is won. It is a phrase that appears repeatedly in the testimonials of minor Nazis. Hitler hoped, according to Rauschning, to devote the last seven years of his life

to the last and greatest tasks, prophecy, the proclamation of the new faith, with which his work will really be completed. For if the Christian era is now to give place to the thousands of years of the Hitlerian era, it will not be because of an external political order, but because of the revelation of the new doctrine of salvation for which mankind has been waiting.[99]

For the Nazi convert, as is typical after any conversion experience, it was imperative to proselytize Hitler's "great idea to every German soul" to ensure collective salvation.[100] Once converted, each person must continue to spread the word. Proselytizing legitimates the conversion by demonstrating that the new life is valid. In other words, by converting others, we prove to ourselves that we did not make a mistake. Once again, the spread of conversion usually occurs within established social networks, such as friends, family, and workplace relationships. Ludwig Heck I explained after his conversion that "I had found an inner contact with the spirit of National Socialism, and it was my endeavor to work for this idea at my place of work."[101] One man noted how important it was "to aid in the awakening of Adolf Hitler's idea to the German Volk." Emil Hofmann found that, by becoming a Nazi, he had "begun a new life," and immediately he set out to "canvass every German soul." Consequently, he explained, "it [the 'great idea'] was cultivated from village to village, from city to city, and we promulgated the new teaching."[102] Hans Otto was so inspired by one of Hitler's speeches that he too immediately dedicated his life to spreading the faith. It was a faith that reflected a deep personal connection to Hitler. Otto recalled,

> The Führer's words worked like hammer hits. Quiet and overcome I listened to the words of the Führer. Quiet and overcome I listened to the words of this man whom I was from now on pledged to, for better or worse. I returned home with the longing for this man and his world view, and if I must die, then it is to be as a simple faith-bearer and faith-bringer.[103]

According to most Nazi converts, "the best propaganda was, however, the personal canvassing from mouth to mouth."[104] Canvassing gave the Nazis a sense of purpose and meaning. One individual who converted after a meeting exclaimed, "Now I had an aim and a purpose." And another explained that "the joy of fighting for Hitler's principle gave my life a new meaning. The philosophy of the movement endowed my hitherto aimless life with a new meaning and a purpose." Still another proclaimed, "When I joined the party, my life once again came to have significance . . . my very family had to admit I was a changed man."[105] For the unemployed, constant proselytizing gave them the sense of self-worth that they had previously lost along with their jobs. As one man perceptively noted,

> We all who supported Hitler and his early work at that time had nothing to lose. I had been dismissed and my comrades were mostly jobless throughout this time. But with and by our struggle we had a world to win . . . so we could yet be proud to count ourselves among the pioneers of the Third Reich.[106]

This sense of being active was important. It gave the converted a new sense of order in their daily lives, for there was no free time. As Emil Wiesemann noted, "every day brought something new." Hermann Eberhardt recalled that he spent "evening after evening" trying to "win" new members. He further explained that this constant activity visibly demonstrated the dynamism and determined will of the faithful: "everyone now saw that through fanatical will and inexorable struggle our members of the movement could no longer be kept dead silent."[107] The constant canvassing provided order, meaning, and purpose on a psychological level, as well. The story of Adalbert Gimbel's conversion illustrates this process. Looking for a movement that "embodied the spirit of the front," he attended his first Nazi gathering. He recalled that "here dominated a spirit that made a profound impression upon me." Subsequently he read the party's Twenty-Five Points of 1920, and "I had become enthusiastic from this day to volunteer for the idea and place myself at its disposal." He then went to hear speeches every Monday evening, and "through these organizational meetings and lectures took hold an instinctive education to become a fanatical fighter for the cause." He eventually joined the SA, which he defined as "the living propaganda of our idea."[108]

The constant activity of the postconversion Nazi therefore legitimated this new life by giving it focus and direction. Georg Dingeldein recalled, "At home I no longer rested. Evening after evening I hurried to *Volksgenossen* to convince them of the National Socialist world view."[109] One man remarked that "day and night we were active with the pasting of placards, with the distribution of handbills and with person-to-person enlightenment." In a similar fashion, Josef Schneider found that "every day brought new work. Every day, however, also brought a new follower. It was to lead further."[110] Finally, one man explained that "the joy of fighting for Hitler's principle gave my life a new meaning. The philosophy of the movement endowed my hitherto aimless life with a new meaning and a purpose."[111] The importance of a finding a new life in the new world view cannot be underestimated.

The story of Emil Schlitz demonstrates the importance of social networks, as well as the centrality of anti-Semitism as a structuring component of Hitler's "great idea." Schlitz noted that he spent all his free time with his friends, enthusiastically attending anti-Semitic lectures and debates about the "new teaching." He and his comrades were "filled with the new idea." He was so inspired that he concluded, "I must on every occasion speak about politics, I must be a propagandist—everywhere I go." This activity included ad hoc canvassing on the streets and at cafes. He said that he had to "make clear" the thought of the Führer "to all men."[112] Another man, equally committed, said that "I bought newspapers, books, and Hitler images, only to be able to struggle further."[113] The holy mission, and the endless canvassing necessary to fulfill it, came at a cost—a sacrifice that the Nazi converts were more than willing to make. For Nazis, as with others who deemed themselves chosen, the willingness to sacrifice was a necessary burden.

"Guts and Blood": The Sense of Sacrifice

As is common with individuals who give themselves over to the apocalypse complex, the converted Nazi felt a strong sense of sacrifice, a form of surrendering oneself that is an important component of the conversion experience.[114] This sacrifice was necessary for collective salvation. It also acted to strengthen social bonds, as well as to demonstrate commitment to the cause. The time of struggle was viewed by many as a period of constant sacrifice, as one Nazi stated, "scarcely a day goes by without some sacrifice." True to form, the sacrificers relished the hardship: "the struggle-time was, despite it being difficult and hard and despite its immense sacrifice (including in blood), something glorious, and I believe that not one of us would have wanted to miss it." Another noted that "above all in the Volk was a sense of sacrifice for our idea awakened and demanded."[115] Still another man recalled, "Who knows the sacrifices and privations of those years of battle, who knows the inner feeling of those party comrades who sacrificed everything in constant faith to the idea and to its first soldier, Adolf Hitler?"[116] Sacrifice was a legitimating force, legitimating faith in Hitler's "great idea" and, ultimately, in Hitler himself, who embodied that idea. Faith in Hitler and veneration of Nazi martyrs gave the Old Guard the strength to endure the struggle and gave its many hardships meaning, as one explained:

> The word "Hitler" became for me a symbol of our future. Those who had fallen before the *Feldherrnhalle* in Munich became martyrs. I preserved the memory of this great event deep in my heart, even throughout the years when it seemed as though everything must drown in materialism and individualism.[117]

The nature of this sacrifice took different forms, including time, money, "guts and blood," and, most important from the perspective of the Nazis, one's life. As Wilhelm Schnabel explained, "one of the keys, I would say to our youth and those who come after us, is to never forget how much blood was shed for this holy cause—the new birth of the new Germany."[118] Wilhelm Jockel remarked that "tremendous sacrifice of guts and blood must still be given until the movement can conclusively carry off the final victory."[119] Speaking at the funeral of some Nazi martyrs, the Labor Front leader Robert Ley exclaimed, in a telling turn of phrase, that "this blood flows not for nothing, this blood cements us together, it is semen that shoots forth and bears fruit a thousandfold."[120]

The holiest sacrifice, the "highest sacrifice," as one Nazi termed it, was to martyr oneself for the cause and for Hitler.[121] Many Nazis could honestly say that "still nothing could hinder us from working for the glorious movement of our Führer, to struggle and, if need be, to die for it."[122] As Julius Stehl explained, "we were instantly ready to dismiss our lives for Hitler, not only to rise up with him, but if it must be, also to sink down. . . . We have sworn our lives to Hitler and it will belong to him until our end." Rudolf Manz proclaimed bluntly that "we were ready to die for the idea." A favorite phrase of many of the Old Guard was "to the Führer until death."[123] Hitler himself, speaking at the funeral of one young Nazi, stated that "his crime was to love his Fatherland. Only because he had loved his Fatherland, he must die."[124]

Other Old Guard Nazis wanted it known that they had sacrificed their health for the movement.[125] Ernst Hass noted that he had sacrificed much for the new Germany, remarking "that is the best distinction, for which I had fulfilled and had sacrificed my job and health."[126] Still other Nazis recalled the sacrifice of their "free time," a modern convention now duly submitted for the good of the cause. One Nazi remarked simply that there was "no free time." Another Nazi ascetic explained further that "truly we made an appeal through the land—not from pleasure, but rather sacrificing our free time. No! We wanted to awaken the Volk, thereby it would catch a glimpse of what today advances as the most harmonious state in the world."[127]

While many Nazis were unemployed when they worked for the cause, many others were relatively well off. Their sacrifice was, as they took pains to note, financial. Walter Gerwein pointed out that "not only our collected time and energy we turned over to the movement, but also our collected financial means we gladly gave for comrades and for the mission and strengthening of the SS."[128] The means of financial sacrifice varied. Some Nazis explained that struggling against the Jews and "subhumans" hurt them financially (primarily via boycotts).[129] Hans Wagner wanted it noted that giving the party "apparatus" working space "free of charge" for a year "had exhausted me financially."[130] Because many Nazis were poor, those that had the means supported others, paying lecture fees, sponsoring Party Days trips, or buying propaganda materials and redistributing them free of charge. Georg Weiss observed that "no one had money and I was always sacrificing for the poorer SA."[131] And, finally, one Nazi from the upper crust, retired major Strelow, wanted it duly noted that since joining the party his financial sacrifices made it impossible for him to go to the theater, concerts, and the like.[132]

Many Germans who became Nazis, then, did so in the fervent belief that they were chosen for a higher mission, a mission that was guided by a messianic Führer. Their devotion to Hitler was so extreme that they dedicated their lives to him and his "great idea." The relationship between messiah and disciple is crucial, not only for legitimating the messianic pretensions of the former but also for forming the apocalyptic movement itself. For an individual cannot play the role of messiah without an audience, and without the actor there is no performance for the audience to follow. Why Hitler was successful in acting out his apocalyptic drama before millions, whereas other would-be messiahs were not, is the focus of the next two chapters.

4

Hitler as Messiah

The Revelations of Adolf Hitler

Adolf Hitler's early childhood in Austria, as far as we can tell, was not unusually difficult.[1] His father, Alois, however, was distant, stern, and probably prone to violent outbursts. His mother, Klara, compensated, perhaps overly so, by protecting and indulging her son's self-absorption. That she had lost three other children in the years prior to Adolf's birth no doubt accentuated her attachment to her only surviving son. Despite his conflicts with his father, Hitler seems to have had a happy childhood, filled with fantasy and play. In elementary school, which Hitler considered "ridiculously easy," his grades were good, but, with his transition to secondary studies at the *Realschule,* his work began to suffer notably. Hitler later described his adolescence as "an especially painful process."[2] It was a period when his childhood fantasies of future greatness met the harsh reality of academic failure. Hitler's conflict with his father about whether he should pursue a future as an artist or as a civil servant perhaps exacerbated these social tensions. The young Hitler became increasingly sullen and sickly, perhaps psychosomatically so. When his father died in January 1903, Hitler left high school under the pretext of an alleged lung ailment.[3] For the next few years, Hitler led a directionless life, looked after by his mother, aunt, and sister. He returned to a fantasy-filled life replete with visions of future greatness and spent most of his time reading, painting, and attending the theater and opera.

Much of what we know of this period comes from the memories of his teenage companion August Kubizek. This account, although occasionally wanting in chronology and other minor factual matters, is largely reliable.[4] Hitler and Kubizek spent many days and nights wandering the streets of Linz and, later, Vienna, young Adolf lost in fantasies, discussing, for example, his architectural plans for one day reconstructing these cities. He also indulged in a fantasy love involving a young women named Stephanie, whom he never had the courage to meet. On another occasion, he fantasized to the point of utter conviction that he would win the lottery, even planning how to spend the money, only to be shocked when he did not win. At night, the two attended the opera, especially numerous performances of Wagner's works. Hitler fantasized that he and Kubizek, a musician, would compose the next great Aryan opera. Hitler's continuing penchant for infantile fantasy, well into young adulthood and beyond, is important because it is sign that Hitler easily lapsed into nondirected thinking, letting his unconscious intrude into his waking life. That he often mistook his fantasies for reality is especially noteworthy. Kubizek provided Hitler with a captive audience for the oral expression of his interior fantasy life. As Kubizek noted, "he had to speak and needed someone to listen to him."[5]

Hitler's messianic aspirations began as early as these teenage years in Linz. Hitler, like many would-be messiahs, was a dreamer, full of grandiose visions of future greatness but lacking direction and purpose in life. And then an experience occurred that began a profound psychological transformation for the young Hitler. It was certainly not an instant transformation but a slow process that unfolded over some fifteen years. It was deeply significant, however, as it marked the beginning of Hitler's personality change from dreamer to visionary, rabblerouser to prophet, ne'er-do-well to savior. Hitler and Kubizek went to Wagner's operas dozens of times. Hitler was especially attracted to the messianic Grail operas *Lohengrin* and *Parsifal,* of which later he would tell Winifred Wagner, "Out of *Parsifal* I make a religion."[6] But it was the performance of one of Wagner's lesser-known works that worked magic on the young Hitler.

According to August Kubizek, a performance of Wagner's opera *Rienzi,* in 1906, elicited a mystical and revelatory experience for Hitler. Although considered by many to be one of Wagner's slightest efforts, *Rienzi* tells a story that, as much as the music, profoundly moved the young Hitler. Based on Edward Bulwer-Lytton's *Rienzi: The Last of the Roman Tribunes,* the opera tells the story of a man of the people, a visionary, who, as one scholar explains, "with the cunning mixture of pragmatism and mysticism, attempted to deliver the city from anarchy and corruption."[7] In one climactic scene beloved by the young Hitler, Rienzi sings, "and if you choose me as your protector of the people's rights, look at your ancestors and call me your Volk tribune!" The masses shout back, "Rienzi, Heil! Heil, Volk tribune!"[8] During their journey home from the

opera, Kubizek reported, Hitler walked in a "totally transported state."
He recalled,

> Never before and never again have I heard Hitler speak as he did in that
> hour. . . . It was as if another being spoke out of his body, and moved him
> as much as it did me. It wasn't at all the case of a speaker being carried
> away by his own words. On the contrary; I rather felt as though he him-
> self listened with astonishment and emotion to what burst forth from
> him with elementary force. . . . It was a state of complete ecstasy and rap-
> ture. . . . He was talking of a mandate which, one day, he would receive
> from the people, to lead them out of servitude to the heights of freedom.

Kubizek insightfully interpreted this event, noting that "it was a state of
complete ecstasy and rapture, in which he transferred the character of
Rienzi, without even mentioning him as a model or example, with visionary power to the plane of his own ambitions . . . a special mission
which one day would be entrusted to him."[9] In 1939, Hitler invited Kubizek to Bayreuth for the annual Wagner festival. When Kubizek mentioned this episode, he reports that Hitler explained to Winifred Wagner
that "in that hour it began."[10]

While some historians have questioned the validity of Kubizek's account of Hitler's visionary experience, evidence to support the importance of *Rienzi* for Hitler before the Hitler-Kubizek reunion of 1939 exists.[11] In his memoirs, Otto Wagener describes an incident when Hitler
and he were planning to attend a performance of *Rienzi*. When Wagener
asked him, "You probably attach less value to *Rienzi?*" Hitler responded,
"But why? It's a special favorite of mine!"[12] Hitler later obtained the original manuscript for the opera, which was subsequently lost at the end of
the war.[13] More revealing is the fact that Nuremberg party rallies began
with the overture to *Rienzi,* as Hitler arrived triumphant. According to
Albert Speer, Hitler noted that this was not done "by chance." Rather,
Hitler explained,

> It's not just a musical question. At the age of twenty-four this man, an
> innkeeper's son, persuaded the Roman people to drive out the corrupt
> Senate by reminding them of the magnificent past of the Roman Empire.
> Listening to this blessed music as a young man in the theater at Linz, I
> had the vision that I too must someday succeed in uniting the German
> Empire and making it great once more.[14]

The association of the messianic Roman tribune with the coming re-deemer of the Third Reich was deliberate, and, for Hitler, deeply per-sonal.

In 1906, Hitler and Kubizek eventually moved to the cosmopolitan city of Vienna, where Hitler hoped to prepare for entrance into the Vien-nese Academy of Art.[15] To his shock and dismay, he failed the exam.

Hitler spent his initial period in Vienna once more lost in fantasy. As in Linz, Hitler passed time in theaters and at the opera, and he even began to write the libretto to a Wagnerian opera.[16] Hitler would become mono-maniacally obsessed with utopian building plans and artistic visions, working on these projects nonstop for days, only to suddenly drop them. However, after failing the entrance exam to the academy a second time, Hitler left his only friend without so much as a goodbye. Kubizek would not see him again until that night in Bayreuth when they reflected on the *Rienzi* episode. Shortly before his break with Kubizek, his young friend noted that Hitler appeared increasingly "unbalanced."[17]

In his daily walks around the metropolis of Vienna, Hitler saw a city in the process of transformation from genteel nineteenth-century home of the Strauss waltz to a harsh, modernist incarnation of Schoenberg's seri-alism. Economic gaps were large, with displays of ostentatious wealth ex-isting next to abject poverty. Behind the facade of ornate buildings were slums as wretched as in any industrializing city. Rapid population growth and waves of non-German immigrants, including many eastern Jews, made for a thriving multicultural society, yet one that frightened many of the politically dominant Germans.[18] Racial hatred, particularly anti-Semitism, rose along with the swelling tides of immigrants, as politicians like Karl Lueger, Georg von Schönerer, and others sought to stop moder-nity in its tracks.[19] Hitler would learn much from these proselytizers of hate. Here, too, Hitler would become familiar with the ariosophy of Guido von List and Lanz von Liebenfels, beginning the process of meld-ing the political and the spiritual anti-Semitism that would later be the root of his soteriology of race. It was at this time that Hitler's rather or-dinary or typical racism began its slow radicalization. Like his messian-ism, and in fact proceeding on the same timetable, Hitler's racism fully radicalized and became more apocalyptic only after World War I.

For all of Hitler's confidence in his coming greatness, his life at this time was largely aimless. When Hitler's financial situation worsened, the dark and seamy side of modern Vienna began to reveal itself to him. Gone were the strolls in nice neighborhoods, the nights at the theater and the opera. Hitler found himself living in dingy men's hostels, selling copies of postcards he painted for subsistence expenses. By Christmas 1909, Hitler was homeless. He ended up in a shelter for men, offering diatribes to his fellow bunkmates, especially sparked when conversation turned to Jesuits and communists, but not, it seems, to Jews. It was, however, at this time that Hitler became increasingly obsessed with dirt, disease, and impurity, an obsession he subsequently projected onto first the *Ostjuden,* the Eastern Jews, and then all Jews. Hitler had found his Evil Other. Hitler's search for salvation through biological and spiritual purity began here, as he descended from the margins of Viennese high society during his time with Kubizek to the fringe of poverty in the city's men's hostel. Hitler's anti-Semitism, however, would not reach its apocalyptic dimensions until after the war, in Munich, under the tutelage of Dietrich Eckart and Alfred Rosenberg.

Hitler left Vienna, his school of hard knocks, for Munich, Germany, the land of his dreams. It was while in Munich that war broke out and Hitler found new meaning and purpose in life. Like many of the Old Guard Nazis quoted previously, Hitler experienced the outbreak of World War I as form of salvation. He wrote in *Mein Kampf,* probably genuinely in this case, "To me these hours seemed like a release from the painful feelings of my youth. Even today I am not ashamed to say that, overpowered by stormy enthusiasm, I fell down on my knees and thanked Heaven from an overflowing heart for granting me the good fortune of being permitted to live at this time." In true millennial fashion, Hitler interpreted World War I as a holy war and a great turning point, writing that "a fight for freedom had begun, mightier than the earth had ever seen." It was not simply the fate of Serbia or Austria that was in question but whether Germany, in his typical apocalyptic either-or reasoning, "was to be or not to be."[20] For Hitler, it was also a chance at personal redemption:

Thus my heart, like a million others, overflowed with proud joy that at last I would be able to redeem myself from this paralyzing feeling. I had so often sung *Deutschland über Alles* and shouted *"Heil"* at the top of my lungs that it seemed to be almost a belated act of grace to be allowed to stand as a witness in the divine court of the eternal judge and proclaim the sincerity of this conviction. From this hour I was convinced that in case of a war—which seemed to me inevitable—in one way or another I would at once leave my books. Likewise I knew that my place would then be where my inner voice directed me.[21]

Hitler joined the Bavarian List Regiment, a bastion of intellectuals and artists, accomplished or not. Hitler was elated, remarking later, "For me, as for every German, there now began the greatest and most unforgettable time of my earthly existence."[22] Hitler now had a purpose in life; he had direction. He was to participate in a great struggle of world historical importance. Hitler became a runner, taking messages from trench to trench, showing bravery to the point of foolhardiness. He was injured twice and on a number of times narrowly escaped death—a sign of Providence, or so it seemed to him.

Toward the end of the First World War, as he lay in Pasewalk hospital after his final injury, Hitler received a second revelation concerning his personal mission.[23] Hitler had been blinded in a gas attack; he eventually regained his sight, only to lapse back into darkness upon hearing that Germany had lost the war.[24] In 1919, Hitler was telling soldiers of his future greatness. This was well before the so-called Führer myth had developed as a tool of propaganda. He told an aide later that during this period of darkness he had had a supernatural vision that he would one day save Germany.[25] A *Frankfurter Zeitung* editorial of January 1923 reported that, while blinded, Hitler was "delivered by an inner rapture that set him the task of becoming his people's deliverer."[26] Ludwell Denny, writing for *The Nation,* in 1923, reported of Hitler that "during the war he was wounded, or through fright or shock became blind. In the hospital he was subject to ecstatic visions of Victorious Germany, and in one of these seizures his eyesight was restored."[27]

That the story of this event was being circulated as Hitler was just beginning his first ascent to national prominence certainly betrays its propaganda or myth-building usage, but that does not mean that Hitler and his followers did not believe in its occurrence and its legitimacy. Interviewed by the Office of Strategic Services (OSS) during World War II, Hitler's former confidant Ernst Hanfstängl recounted that Hitler had made it known privately that at Pasewalk he had had a "supernatural vision which commanded him to save his unhappy country. As a result of this experience, he resolved to become a politician and devote his energies to carrying out the command he received."[28] Hitler later told another man that "as I lay there, it came over me that I would liberate the German people and make Germany great."[29] Hitler would return to the incident again and again throughout his life. This was as much a means of messianic self-legitimation as it was a tool for convincing others. For instance, during the 1923 putsch, when the vision seemed on the verge of becoming reality, Hitler gave an impassioned speech in which he referred to the Pasewalk episode, using apocalyptic metaphors of annihilation and resurrection:

> I am going to fulfill the vow I made to myself five years ago when I was a blind cripple in the military hospital: to know neither rest nor peace until the November criminals had been overthrown, until on the ruins of the wretched Germany of today there should have arisen once more a Germany of power and greatness, of freedom and splendor.[30]

While in prison for his part in the failed putsch, Hitler wrote his memoir, *Mein Kampf*. In it, Hitler again returned to his vision, saying of his period of blindness, "in the days that followed, my own fate became known to me."[31] Years later, in a speech in 1937, Hitler made a prophesy regarding the fate of the "destroyers of German unity." To those who might question his prophesy, Hitler retorted, "How did I come, as a soldier in the year 1919, to prophesy that I would create a movement which would one day captivate Germany?"[32] Hitler subsequently dated the beginning of his political mission to 1919.

With war over, the meaning and purpose Hitler had found in that apocalyptic struggle were gone. While most soldiers mustered out of the service, Hitler remained in the army until April 31, 1920. The loss of the war is exactly why this vision makes so much sense. The vision was that Hitler would lead Germany back to greatness. With the loss of this supposed holy war, Hitler's identity lost its meaning. He compensated by identifying with a Rienzi-like messiah-figure that arose in his unconscious as he lay blind in Pasewalk. It was for this reason that Hitler claimed he decided to enter politics at this time.[33]

Hitler's two revelatory experiences follow a pattern consistent with those of other individuals who have had messianic pretensions—each occurred during a period of weakened consciousness, a condition conducive to nondirected thinking and the subsequent flow of archetypal material, in this case messianic symbols. The first vision occurred during a time when Hitler was without direction, living a purposeless life, one that consisted of almost constant fantasizing about future greatness. Hitler's penchant for nondirected thinking, as exhibited in his vivid fantasy life, made him susceptible to the intrusion of unconscious imagery into his waking life. The contrast between Hitler's constant fantasies of future greatness and his dismal prospects as an undereducated dropout and orphan is striking, with the latter no doubt feeding the former.

Significantly, the first revelation was sparked by a performance of Wagner's messianic opera *Rienzi*. Most important is the effect Wagner's repetitive music had on Hitler's mental state. According to Kubizek, Wagner's music put Hitler into a trancelike state; Kubizek noted that "a performance could affect him almost like a religious experience, plunging him into deep and mystical fantasies."[34] As Kubizek pointed out, "Listening to Wagner meant to him, not a simple visit to the theatre, but the opportunity of being transported into that extraordinary state which Wagner's music produced in him, that trance, that escape into a mystical dream-world. . . . He was intoxicated and bewitched."[35] Other contemporary observers noted similar effects. Princess Olga, interviewed by the U.S. State Department during the Second World War, noted of Hitler that "during a performance of *Die Meistersinger* he shut his eyes and gave the impression of being in a trance."[36] Ernst Schmidt, Hitler's companion at the end of World War I, recalled that, during a Munich opera performance in 1918, "Hitler was lost in the music to the very last note; blind and deaf to all else around him."[37] In his interview with the OSS, Ernst Hanfstängl recalled that "*Tristan* acts like dope on him."[38] In the *Rienzi* episode, Wagner's repetitive, trance-inducing music, combined with a libretto filled with messianic symbols, pushed Hitler into nondirected thinking mode, a visionary rapture. Rather than project the messiah symbol outward and look for someone to save him, Hitler identified with it, assuming it to be a presentiment of his future greatness. The psychologist George Atwood found that patients who felt themselves called by higher spiritual powers for sacred missions often used imagery that bore a "striking parallelism" with "all those saviors and recurring heroes" in "fairy tales, myths, and the literature of religions."[39] As it did with Hitler, this messianic vision often occurs during a trancelike mental state.[40]

Hitler's second revelation occurred during a time of ill health, both physically and emotionally, a time conducive to messianic visions. As a Nazi party member, Vogel, accurately described this period, it was Hitler's time of "difficult spiritual struggle."[41] The war had provided Hitler's heretofore aimless life with direction and meaning. It was for this reason that he relished it so. The end of the war once again propelled Hitler into a meaningless and directionless life, a personal chaos. His lapse into a psychosomatic blindness upon hearing the news of Germany's defeat symbolically reflected the darkness of his psychic state. It was at this moment of inner chaos and desperation that the archetypal symbols of the apocalypse complex once again appeared before Hitler's eyes, providing him with meaning and direction. As Vogel portrayed it, "in the midst of the chaos of the German collapse he begins, in faithful devotion to his calling, the struggle for the soul of the German people."[42] This type of "difficult spiritual struggle" often precedes a profound personality change or conversion experience, as can be seen in the lives of the messiah/prophets Hung Hsiu-Ch'uan, Handsome Lake, and Te Ua Haumene.[43] Physical and psychological collapse appears to have two important functions in the lives of messiah/prophets. First, it creates a personal sense of chaos that is subsequently inflated into apocalyptic visions, which are projected onto society. Second, the collapse seems to generate a tendency toward nondirected thinking that funnels the millennial symbols of the apocalypse complex into the mind of the messiah/prophet.

Hitler's second messianic visionary experience follows this pattern exactly, occurring as it did during a time of personal and psychic trauma as he lay ill in Pasewalk.[44] Messianic and apocalyptic imagery often appears to individuals during times of great trauma. Hitler's visionary experience was not extraordinary in that regard and need not be dismissed as such. That Hitler had messianic visionary experiences, however, does not mean that he absolutely accepted them as real from the beginning, or believed resolutely in their eventual realization, for individuals with similar messianic visions often experience much doubt and vacillation before they finally accept the mantle of messiah.

Hitler: "Drummer," Prophet, Messiah

In *Mein Kampf,* Hitler discusses how movements come into being. The prophetic role of the great leader is central. He writes, "some idea of genius arises in the brain of a man who feels called upon to transmit his knowledge to the rest of humanity. He preaches his view and gradually wins a certain circle of adherents." As the movement grows, the great idea may be lost if the leader loses direct personal control of his followers. Therefore, Hitler concludes, the authority of the "spiritual founder" must be "unconditional."[45] The true leader should be both prophet and dictator. Here Hitler writes more as a prophetic rather than messianic leader. This does not mean, however, that he had rejected his earlier messianic visions; he tended to encompass both roles in his self-perception, with varying degrees of identification with one or the other as his political circumstances changed. Understanding the shifting nature of this self-perception is crucial for gaining a better grasp not only of how Hitler saw himself but also of how others came to perceive him.

One historian has concluded that Hitler first viewed himself as a prophet, a John the Baptist, preparing the way for the coming Führer-messiah, and only later identified with the messianic role.[46] There is some truth to this. The Nazi apostate Otto Strasser certainly agreed, saying of Hitler's early development that "next he was St. John the Baptist, preparing for the coming of the Messiah, then the Messiah himself, pending his appearance in the role of Caesar."[47] An early speech of 1923 appears to support this, as Hitler concluded by referring to himself as the "drummer" who gathered the masses for the imminent arrival of the messianic Führer:

> What can save Germany is the dictatorship of national will and national resolution. From this emerges the question: is a suitable personality here? Our duty is not to search for such a person. He is either sent by heaven or not. Our duty is to furnish the sword which that person will need when he is here. Our duty to the dictator when he comes is to present a Volk which is ripe for him! German Volk wake up! The day is near![48]

In another early speech, he asked Germans to "pray to our Lord God that he gives us the right Leader," and on another occasion he referred to Erich Ludendorff, in true eschatological fashion, as the "leader of the coming great showdown."[49] Hanfstängl recalled,

> In the early days, however, he did not conceive himself as the chosen leader. Even in 1923 he still referred to himself in his meetings as the "drummer," marching ahead of a great movement of liberation which was to come. Even after this time he frequently used the words of St. Matthew and referred to himself as a voice crying in the wilderness and describing his duty as hewing a path for him who was to come and lead the nation to power and glory.[50]

One true believer, Georg Schott, wrote, in 1924, that a conversation with Hitler turned to the relevance of contemporary events to the "last things," meaning the apocalypse. Schott remembered that Hitler, "with a voice and with eyes that I will never forget, said: 'We are indeed all a little John-like in nature. I await the Christ.'"[51] On another occasion, Hitler purportedly remarked to the Third Reich visionary Arthur Moeller van den Bruck that "I am nothing more than a drummer and rallier [*Trommler und Sammler*]."[52] According to the editor of the *Deutsche Zeitung*, Hitler remarked that he was not the Führer who would "save the Fatherland that was sinking into chaos" but only "the agitator who understood how to rally the masses." Nor, he continued, was he "the architect who clearly pictured in his own eyes the plan and design of the new building and with calm sureness and creativity was able to lay one stone on the other. He needed the greater one behind him, on whose command he could lean."[53]

Ian Kershaw interprets such statements as proof that during the early 1920s Hitler did not see himself as he portrayed himself later in *Mein Kampf*, as "Germany's future leader in waiting, the political messiah whose turn would arise once the nation recognized his unique greatness."[54] But vacillation in accepting one's messianic calling is actually quite typical. Messianic self-legitimization takes time and often necessitates signs of having been chosen, whether attracting disciples, performing miracles, or surviving near-death experiences. How Hitler found legitimation of his early messianic revelatory experiences is intimately tied to his transformation from postwar soldier to the leader of the nascent millenarian political movement, the NSDAP (National Socialist German Worker's Party).

Only a few days after his Pasewalk vision, Hitler returned to a Munich he barely recognized.[55] The November Revolution was less than two weeks old. The local government was administered by a mixture of moderate and radical socialists, as Spartacists roamed the streets battling newly unemployed soldiers, now *Freikorps* members. The communist leader Karl Liebnecht was murdered by the Thule Society wannabe Prince Arco-Valley, while seven actual Thule members were executed by the communists, becoming the first martyrs of what would soon become the Nazi party. This was also a time of epidemic hunger, with many thousands dying of starvation. Worker strikes were frequent and often violent, and a general state of terror was enforced by the much-hated *Räterepublik*, the Soviet-style communist Bavaria.

It was during this apocalyptic chaos that Hitler truly began his political career, taking the first halting steps toward realizing his messianic self-perception. This is not to say that Hitler ever had a clear idea of how or when his calling as Germany's messiah would be revealed or that he was an active agent in its revelation, but simply that his messianism largely lay dormant until the chaos of postwar Munich slowly made its realization possible, though certainly not probable. Hitler was an opportunist above all, but not solely in the sense of someone who takes advantage of circumstances for selfish reasons alone. He truly believed in Providence, in waiting for the right time and place, in listening for his inner voice to tell him that "now is the time." Munich in 1919 was that time and place.

The soldier barracks in Munich were organized into soviets, councils run by the soldiers themselves. In fact, the young corporal Hitler was elected as a representative of a soldier's soviet.[56] After the Bolshevik revolution collapsed, the army decided it needed to re-educate its troops in proper anti-Bolshevik and nationalist sentiments. Courses were set up to prepare speakers to lecture to troops on politics and history, as well as to covertly infiltrate various political groups on the right and the left. The man put in charge of this project was Captain Karl Mayr, Hitler's commanding officer during and after the war. It was Mayr who chose Hitler to educate other soldiers, most likely because of his growing reputation as an anticommunist orator in the soldier's barracks.[57] Mayr sent Hitler to education courses at Munich University from June 5 to 12, 1919. Speakers included Gottfried Feder and Graf von Bothmer, both of whom wrote for Dietrich Eckart's *Auf Gut Deutsch* (soldiers were given copies of this paper as educational material), as well as the historian Karl Alexander von Müller. Hitler's assignment was to learn from these men and then in turn to teach his fellow soldiers.

One night, the postlecture discussion turned into a lively debate. As Müller attempted to leave the lecture hall at the University of Munich, he noticed a group "riveted to a man in their midst who, with a strangely guttural voice incessantly and with mounting passion, spoke to them. I had the peculiar feeling that the excitement generated by his performance at the same time gave him his voice. I saw a pallid, gaunt face under strands of hair hanging down in unmilitary fashion. He had a close-cropped moustache and strikingly large, light blue, fanatically cold, glowing eyes." It was, of course, Adolf Hitler. Müller reported that the next day he asked Karl Mayr, "do you know that you have an oratorical natural [*Naturtenor*] among your instructors?" Mayr replied, "Oh, that is Hitler from the List Regiment."[58] Shortly thereafter, Hitler began giving propaganda lectures to troops stationed in Munich. According to Hitler's account of this episode, which does not mention Müller or Mayr but does discuss the future Nazi Gottfried Feder, his diatribe was sparked by one soldier who, in the minority, according to Hitler, had the temerity to defend the Jews. Hitler recounted in *Mein Kampf* that he had found the place for his special talent: "I started out with the greatest enthusiasm and love. For all at once I was offered an opportunity of speaking before a larger audience; and the thing that I had always presumed from pure feeling without knowing it was now corroborated: I could 'speak.'"[59] Hitler's penchant for extemporaneous diatribes was no longer an annoyance but an asset.

Hitler was extraordinarily successful in his new position. For perhaps the first time, his speaking ability was recognized as both useful and important. Hitler's audience was no longer a solitary Kubizek, or the captive few in the men's hostel in Vienna, or those in the trenches during the war. Hitler's millennial and apocalyptic rhetoric now struck a chord. One stretcher-bearer, Lorenz Frank, reported, on August 23, 1919, that "especially Herr Hitler is, I should truly say, a born popular speaker, who by his fanaticism and his populist demeanor in a gathering compels the listener unconditionally to be attentive and to share his views." An airman, Ewald Bolle, pointed out that "the historical lectures of Mr. Beyschlag found less of an accord or met with less favor . . . than the ebullient lectures (with examples from life) of Mr. Hitler." Hans Knoden, a gunner, was likewise impressed, finding that Hitler's lectures "revealed an outstanding and passionate speaker who gripped the attention of all the listeners for his remarks."[60] Much of Hitler's passionate rhetoric was directed at Jews, his postwar Evil Other, blaming them for the apocalyptic chaos in Munich and in Germany as a whole.[61]

It was at this point that Mayr purportedly sent Hitler to investigate the German Worker's Party (DAP). According to the traditional account, Hitler went to a meeting with Ewald Bolle and Hans Knoden. Dietrich Eckart was scheduled to speak, but instead Gottfried Feder gave his usual "interest slavery" talk, which Hitler had heard earlier at the school lecture. Professor Adalbert Baumann spoke against Feder and for the Bavarian separatists, which elicited a typically excited response from Hitler, who defended Feder. The passion and eloquence of Hitler's rebuttal supposedly attracted Anton Drexler's attention. This leader of the DAP then gave Hitler a copy of his pamphlet "My Political Awakening," which details his conversion to anti-Semitism. Michael Lotter, a founding member of the DAP and secretary of the Political Worker's Circle within that party, reported that Drexler said that Hitler spoke in "marked words which went to everyone's heart" and in such a way that Baumann "took his hat and went." Drexler concluded, regarding Hitler, "Such people we could use." When Hitler subsequently joined the fledgling party, Drexler remarked, "Now we have an Austrian, one who has such a gift for gab."[62]

Hitler now was in a position to begin his ascent to the position of national redeemer, although few as yet would have recognized him as such. While this account is generally accurate, the notion that Mayr just happened to send Hitler to the DAP as one of many such assignments is most likely inaccurate. As we saw before, Hitler had had earlier contacts with DAP and Thule Society associates, such as Feder, Esser, and perhaps even Eckart, through his work as an educational officer. Mayr was likewise well connected with Thulists (Esser was his press secretary) and DAP members, and Mayr's office was in the Hotel Four Seasons, on the same floor as the Thule office. The notion that Mayr sent Hitler and the others to do surveillance on the DAP is suspect, to say the least. It is known that the Thule Society, through the DAP, was looking for a mass orator as described, to woo workers away from the alleged Jewish Bolsheviks who were operating in Munich. Hitler's talents as an orator, his passionate anti-Semitism, and perhaps his familiarity with ariosophy made him a perfect candidate for the Thule-created German Worker's Party. It is quite possible, then, that Mayr, perhaps on Eckart's advice, deliberately sent Hitler to the fledgling movement to serve at least as the "drummer" it sorely needed, and perhaps even to be the savior it fervently desired.

Hitler's oratorical abilities quickly became indispensable for the movement, whose speech gatherings now began to grow exponentially. Hitler used his new power to become sole leader of the soon renamed National Socialist German Worker's Party, arguing in an early speech that the movement could not be run by "any lodge," an oblique reference to the Thule Society and perhaps the *Germanenorden*. In any case, there is evidence that by 1922, Hitler began to be accepted in the role of messianic Führer. In September of that year, Kleo Player dedicated a gift of his poem "Winter Solstice" to "the greatest man of action Adolf Hitler, the fearless Führer of Germany's resurrection." In a speech in November that was reprinted in the *Völkischer Beobachter,* Karl Mayr's former press spokesman and now Nazi Hermann Esser proclaimed Hitler "Germany's Mussolini."[63] In December 1922, two recent party converts, Schmidt and Neuhäusler, sent a work by Eduard Heilfon to Hitler and inscribed a ded-

ication to "the indefatigable, devoted, resolute Führer of the National Socialists."[64] In the same month, the *Völkischer Beobachter* proclaimed
Hitler for the first time a "special Führer." Hitler supporters, leaving a
pro-Nazi parade in Munich that year, were said "to have found something which millions are yearning for, a Führer."[65]

This growing messianism attached to Hitler continued the next year, as
letters poured into Nazi offices lauding Hitler as Germany's "Redeemer."
Nazi converts sold photos of their beloved Hitler, contributing to the
spread of the Führer cult, which was messianic to the core. It is not surprising, then, that, in 1923, Hitler became secure enough in his messianism to betray it publically. More and more, a blurring of the distinction
between the role of drummer and that of leader, or, more precisely,
prophet and messiah, becomes evident.[66] Hitler said in one speech at this
time that he "felt the call to Germany's salvation within him, and this role
would fall to him, if not now, then later."[67] However, Hitler still vacil-
lated, saying, in October 1923, that the leadership question must wait
until "the weapon is created which the Führer must possess." At that
point the time would be ripe to "pray to our Lord God that he give us the
right Führer."[68]

With his growing popularity, Hitler was brought into a circle of famous and influential individuals. Many of them accepted Hitler as the
coming savior of Germany, further legitimating his preexisting messianism. That the family of Hitler's beloved Wagner was for the most part enthusiastic was especially important. After meeting Hitler, Winifred Wagner, the English-born wife of Wagner's son Siegfried, saw Hitler as "destined to be the savior of Germany."[69] Houston Stewart Chamberlain, the
noted anti-Semitic scholar, received a deathbed visit from Hitler. He subsequently wrote a letter to Hitler in which he declared,

> My belief in the Germans has always been strong, although—I confess—
> it had ebbed. With one stroke, you have changed the state of my soul.
> That Germany gives birth to a Hitler in a time of direst need is proof of
> her vitality. . . . I could easily go to sleep and have no need to wake up
> again. May God protect you. Chamberlain.[70]

At this time, the first party rally in Munich, January 27–29, 1923, was
designed to promoted Hitler as Germany's redeemer. The crowed responded approvingly. A newspaper reported that when Hitler entered the
banquet hall of the *Hofbräuhaus* during opening ceremonies, he was

greeted "like a savior."[71] Foreign journalists also reported Hitler's grow-
ing messianism, at least from the standpoint of his disciples. Ludwell
Denny, writing for the *Nation,* covered one of Hitler's feverish rallies, in
February 1923. Ludwell's account, despite the obvious error regarding
Hitler's occupation, is interesting for several reasons. First, it reveals that
Hitler's audience already saw him as savior, before the Nazi myth-mak-
ing machine was a major force, and that the Pasewalk vision was being
used by his audience to legitimate that messianism, a process not uncommon for the messiah-prophet and his or her disciples. Second, Denny's
characterization of Hitler as a mass speaker and as an individual supports
the view many other witnesses had in the 1930s. Denny, using the reportage style of the time, wrote,

> Hitler, going from meeting to meeting, is received with enthusiasm. He is
> an extraordinary person. An artist turned popular prophet and savior, is
> the way members of the audience described him to me as we awaited for
> him to appear. A young man stepped on the platform and acknowledged
> the long applause. His speech was intense and brief; he constantly
> clenched and unclenched his hands. When I was alone with him for a
> few moments, he seemed hardly normal; queer eyes, nervous hands, and
> a strange movement of the head. He would not give an interview—said
> he had no use for Americans. Later I learned something of his story. He
> is not an artist but a locksmith, not a Bavarian but an Austrian. During
> the war he was wounded, or through fright or shock became blind. In
> the hospital he was subject to ecstatic visions of Victorious Germany,
> and in one of these seizures his eyesight was restored.[72]

Hitler's growing notoriety undoubtedly also helped legitimate his messianism. By 1923, he was becoming increasingly well known, not just in
Bavaria but around the world. The November 3, 1923, issue of *The Literary Digest,* in an article on the chaos in Germany, contained a boxed set
of images of the "Three Men of the Hour in Bavaria." They were Gustav
Von Kahr, labeled "The Bavarian Dictator," Crown Prince Rupprecht, labeled "King of Bavaria," and Hitler, labeled "The 'Gray-Shirt' Leader."
Underneath that caption, Hitler is quoted as saying that the Nazis would
be "the sledgehammer of Germany's resurrection." Such notoriety goes a
long way to explaining Hitler's belief that it would soon be time to push
for power (as he would attempt the following week). Paul Gierasch, writing for *The Current History Magazine* of the *New York Times,* astutely

noted Hitler's use of emotion to gather his faithful and, although clearly uncertain of its deeper significance, remarked on the use of apocalyptic fear contrasted with millennial hopes of a better world, renewed through racial cleansing and led by a coming savior figure:

> Their leader, Hitler, had worked up these emotions by using the reactions to economic and spiritual distress that pervade the psychology of the German people today. Radical antipathies and religious motives are fused with dreams of a better day to come. Hitler asks that the German nation be cleansed of all non-Aryan elements and that it find renewal in a church of the people in which the belief in the nordic Wotan shall be merged with that in Christ. To the purified nation shall at the appointed time come forth a new German emperor-king who, as the national messiah, shall free German from the bondage of her foreign taskmaster.[73]

Despite its failure, the putsch of 1924 gave Hitler the national exposure necessary to further legitimate his messianism. In testimony at the putsch trial, Hitler claimed that "the people must understand that German misery has an end, salvation could only come about through a rising."[74] During the trial, Hitler refused to talk to the prosecutor, saying, according to one observer, "It was a matter for him of justifying before history his action and his mission; what the court's position would be was a matter of indifference to him. He denied the court any right to pass judgment on him."[75] From this point on, the messianic Führer cult became more and more prominent. While General Ludendorff was still portrayed as the military leader of coming apocalyptic showdown with the demonic forces of the left, Hitler now was envisioned as the sole political leader.[76] General von Lossow told the court that he thought Hitler wanted only to work "as propagandist and awakener to arouse the people." He said that Hitler had remarked that he did not want the petty position of a ministerial post but wanted to be the destroyer of Marxism. That was his chosen task. Accounting to Lossow, Hitler remarked, "Not from modesty did I want at that time to be the drummer, on the contrary, that is the highest [thing]. The other is a trifle."[77] From the trial on, however, Hitler's dual roles as prophet and messiah tended to merge.

The trial publicity, and the public adoration that followed, more than ever seemed to legitimate Hitler's messianism. For instance, when Hitler's closing statement at his putsch trial became public, many came to see in Hitler Germany's future redeemer, a man whose God-given gift of gab would provide the key to salvation. Joseph Goebbels, who had been searching for his personal savior for some time, wrote Hitler in prison, stating, "What you said there is the catechism of a new political creed coming to birth in the midst of a collapsing, secularized world. . . . To you a god has given the tongue with which to express our sufferings. You formulated our agony in words that promise salvation."[78]

Hitler's increasingly public statements of divine mission have led some historians to conclude that it was only at this time, after the putsch, that Hitler saw himself as the savior of Germany. Yet it is probable, as has been shown, that as early as his Linz days Hitler had messianic inclinations. It is more accurate to view Hitler, like many leaders of apocalyptic movements before and since, as assuming the roles of both messiah and prophet, identifying with one or the other at different times and with varying degrees of confidence. In Hitler's case, it is likely that, while he envisioned himself as assuming a messianic position in German history as early as the *Rienzi* experience, it was only in time that his mounting successes convinced him of the reality of that vision.

The national publicity after the putsch undoubtedly played a role here, as thousands of letters and many distinguished individuals who visited Hitler while in Landsberg prison praised him as Germany's savior. Dietrich Eckart, who ironically had introduced Hitler to Munich high society as "Germany's young Messiah," worried about his protege's increasing "messiah complex" while in Landsberg.[79] Rosenberg had a similar fear, saying of Hitler's belief in his "special providence," "This was noticeable when he came out of Landsberg in 1925 and then increased after he came to power, until at the end of the war this belief had begun to assume really distressing aspects."[80] Putzi Hanfstängl agreed,

After his imprisonment, the "drummer" pattern dropped out very rapidly and he referred more and more to himself as the Führer. This may have been due in part to Hess who coined the term and did his utmost to build a cult around it. But outside of this there was more and more evidence that he was thinking of himself as the Messiah and it was he himself who was destined to lead Germany to glory. He used quotations from the Bible more frequently when referring to himself and separated himself from the others as though he were a special creation.[81]

It should be remembered that *Mein Kampf* was written, or dictated, under this increasing messianic worship, as Hitler was lauded by millions, visited and lionized by dignitaries, and personally bolstered by Rudolf Hess's hero worship. The process of dictating *Mein Kampf* seems to have helped Hitler to see his life even more clearly as divinely ordained. By the time he left prison, Hitler's messianism outweighed his desire to be solely a drummer, although his belief in his prophetic abilities would remain strong until the end. Are Hitler's statements reflecting the shift from "drummer" to messianic Führer therefore clear evidence of a transformation in Hitler's self-perception from Endtime prophet to messiah, from a John the Baptist to a Jesus Christ? Such a radical and sudden change rarely occurs. Most individuals who come to see themselves as messiah figures have a period of hesitation after their initial visions, a transitional phase that not infrequently lasts years. The time Hitler spent in Landsberg prison after the putsch, when he went from Bavarian rabblerouser to national savior, was certainly a pivotal time, and it was perhaps indeed then that the final transformation occurred. However, Hitler's tendency to vacillate between prophet and messiah was still evident even as late as the early 1930s. Speaking to Otto Wagener, Hitler discussed his vision of a community of nations that would be a realization of Christ's philosophy. The creation of such a community would be "the final goal of human politics on this earth." He explained,

> The peace on earth Christ wanted to bring is the very socialism of nations! It is the new great religion, and it will come because it is divine! It awaits the Messiah!
>
> But I *am* not the Messiah. He will come after me. I only have the will to create for the German Volk the foundations of a true Volk community. And that is a political mission, though it encompasses the ideological as well as the economic.
>
> It cannot be otherwise, and everything in me points to the conviction that the German Volk has a divine mission. How many great prophets have foretold this![82]

The undying faith that the so-called Hitler cult had in him also seems to have encouraged Hitler's messianic self-perception. The Hitler Youth leader Baldur von Schirach stated that "this unlimited, almost religious veneration, to which I contributed, as did Goebbels, Göring, Hess, Ley and countless others, strengthened in Hitler the belief that he was in league with Providence."[83] Another man noted that "ever since Dietrich von [*sic*] Eckart discovered him in Munich, Adolf has never lacked people who encouraged his belief in his mission."[84] Perhaps the most significant individual who helped bring Hitler's messianism to the forefront was Rudolf Hess, who came to see in Hitler the "coming man" he longed for, the man who would save him and Germany from misery.

Like Hitler, Hess had been a soldier in World War I. After the war, Hess came into contact with the Thule Society, perhaps as much because of his inclination to matters occult as because of its right-wing tendencies. Also like Hitler, and like many others who would become Nazis, Hess saw a postwar Germany that resembled a descent into apocalypse more than simply a country that had hit on hard times. Hess joined the German Worker's Party in 1920 and avidly read Eckart's *Auf Gut Deutsch*. During this period, Hess looked for what he termed the "coming man" who would save Germany from utter ruin. After attending a Hitler speech, he was instantly converted, purportedly exclaiming, as he left, "The man! The man!"[85] A week later, Hess was introduced to Hitler by Eckart, and he became a devoted disciple.

In 1921, Hess wrote a prize-winning essay titled "What Will Be the Nature of the Man Who Will Lead Germany Once Again to the Summit?"[86] While he did not mention Hitler by name, it is clear that he was describing him as the coming savior. Hess began by describing the postwar German "body" with imagery that is truly apocalyptic:

> Since then [the war] Germany writhes as in a fever. It can barely hold itself erect. Blood drained for years from its aorta as a consequence of the Versailles Treaty; wasteful state administration—empty coffers . . . grotesque inflation. In the Volk gleaming feasts next to glaring misery. . . . The mightiest strain discharged at a moment's notice in plundering, murder and rioting.[87]

Who could save Germany from this misery? Not the Parliament, which specialized in "twaddle and twaddle." No, Hess proposed that what Germany needed was a "savior from the chaos," a "Napoleon as dictator," a Caesar, or a Mussolini. As "chaos . . . calls forth a dictator," so "it will likewise come in Germany." Germany's dictator must instill in the Volk "faith in the purity of the single cause and in its final victory." Presciently, he noted that "intractable will power gives him the power of enchanting speech that allows the masses to hail him. For the salvation of the nation he will not abhor to use the weapons of his opponents: demagogy, slogans, street processions, etc." While the dictator understands the masses, he is not of the masses: "He himself has nothing in common with the masses, his entire personality is ever greater. This power of his personality radiates from a certain something that brings acquaintances under his spell and cultivates ever wider circles." Thus, Hess concluded, "the Volk longs for a genuine Führer free from all party haggles, for a pure Führer with inner veracity."[88]

Hess argued that the coming great leader, like Bismarck before him, must be prepared to spill blood for the holy cause: "Great questions will again be decided through blood and iron. And the question here reads: decline or ascent."[89] Hess, like a prophet, exclaimed, "yet we know not when the 'man' [will take] the saving grasp. However, that he comes millions can feel."[90] The arrival of the messianic dictator, the coming man, is imminent. Hess ended his essay by quoting Dietrich Eckart's "Germany Awake," which Hess interpreted properly as an apocalyptic poem, in which the bell is sounded that awakens the Germans from their sleep in order to unify and prepare them for the final battle that brings ultimate salvation. Hess wrote, "The day will come to be, of which the poet sings":

> Storm, Storm, Storm
>> Sound the bell from tower to tower
>> Rouse the men, the aged, the boys,
>> Rouse the sleepers from their chambers
>> Rouse the girls down the stairs,
>> Rouse the mother away from the cradle,
>> Roar should they and pierce the air,
>> Rage, rage in the thunder, the fury,
>> Rouse the dead from their tomb,
>> German awake![91]

Writing in the *Völkischer Beobachter* on April 21, 1921, at roughly the same time as the essay just discussed was composed, Hess exclaimed, "Are you truly blind to the fact that this man is the Führer-personality who alone is able to carry through the struggle? Do you think that without him the masses would pile into the Circus Krone?"[92] When Hitler was arrested after the failed putsch, Hess had himself detained so that he could be with the man he loved and to whom he was devoted. Writing from Landsberg prison, Hess reiterated that he was more convinced than ever that Hitler was the "coming man." He even did Hitler's astrological chart to prove it: "I know assuredly that he is the 'coming man' in Germany, the 'dictator' whose flag will sooner or later wave over public buildings in Berlin."[93] Hess wrote that he and Hitler debated about the accuracy of astrology but that he was convinced that Hitler was the man he now referred to in his letters as "Tribune," perhaps an indication that Hitler had confided the *Rienzi* incident to him.[94]

Hess had found his much-longed-for "coming man," the Rienzi-like Tribune, God's chosen Redeemer. Hitler's growing notoriety and the ever-increasing devotion of his disciples, from those closest to him, like Hess, to the many thousands of simple Old Guard party members, no doubt allowed Hitler's messianic self-perception to eclipse the "drummer" role. He could now truly believe that he was indeed chosen for a higher mission, protected and, in fact, spoken to by the Almighty.

Providential Care and the Sense of Invincibility

Hitler's profound sense of divine mission, grounded in his early revelations and visions, was greatly enhanced by a seeming providential care that protected him from death. Hitler, consequently, interpreted his numerous close calls in the First World War, while many of those around him died, as nothing short of miraculous.[95] Those who served with him remembered a man who ran gauntlets of mines and burning houses, clothes singed, with little worry for his safety, always volunteering for "suicide" missions.[96] The Linz vision, and Hitler's identification with the messianic image, may have bolstered his sense of invincibility. One war comrade later reported that Hitler "said that we would hear much about him. We should just wait until his time has arrived."[97] Hitler's actions do not seem to have been motivated so much by bravery as by his deep belief in providential care and in his invincibility. Hitler was fond of reporting one wartime incident:

I was eating my dinner in a trench with several comrades. Suddenly a voice seemed to be saying to me, "Get up and go over there." It was so clear and insistent that I obeyed automatically, as if it had been a military order. I rose at once to my feet and walked twenty yards along the trench, carrying my dinner in its tin can with me. Then I sat down to go on eating, my mind being once more at rest. Hardly had I done so when a flash and deafening report came from the part of the trench I had just left. A stray shell had burst over the group in which I had been sitting, and every member of it was killed.[98]

Hitler's escape from death during the aborted putsch in 1923 as Max Erwin von Scheubner-Richter, who marched arm in arm with Hitler, was shot dead was viewed in much the same way. After another near-death in the early 1930s, this time from an auto accident, Hitler proclaimed that no one need have worried, because "in fact, nothing could have happened to us. We have not yet completed our task."[99] Hitler responded to the failure of a number of assassination attempts as he did to his other brushes with death. The failure of the July 20, 1944, attempt seemed particularly providential to Hitler. His response, as told to a wounded aide, is rife with messianic pretensions:

There you are with serious injuries, and yet you are not the one that was to be assassinated. These gentlemen had me, and only me, in mind. But I escaped entirely. This is the fourth time in this war that my opponents have sought after my life in order to eliminate me for good. However, they did not succeed a single time despite most favorable conditions; on the contrary they suffered a renewed reverse each time, and now the Almighty has stayed their hands once again. Don't you agree that I should consider it as a nod of fate that it intends to preserve me for my assigned task? Must I not recognize therein the governance of a higher power which protects me, so that I can lead the German people to victory? Providence has frustrated all attempts against me. That can have only one historical meaning, that it has elected me to lead the German people. Thus I have been right in my course to date, with my regulations and orders, with my entire work toward the destined end and I see no occasion for deviating from this course. Fate has given me the strength to lead the German people in an incomparable ascent to a height which is unique in their history. And the Lord has blessed our arms in the war to date in such manifold ways. However, my whole fight, my successes and my work, would lose all historical meaning if fate had not intended that I should lead the German people *to victory*. Consequently, the 20th of July can only confirm my recognition that Almighty God has called me to lead the German people—not to defeat, but to victory.[100]

Hitler's belief in himself as an instrument of Providence was a significant element of his personality. That his sense of invincibility was inextricably tied to his sense of mission can be seen in the following remark, which also points to the existence of his prewar belief in his sense of mission: "I always knew I should be a great man, even in my poorest days, and I feel convinced that I shall live to finish my task."[101] On Hindenburg's eighty-fifth birthday, Hitler stated that "I am forty-three and I feel in perfect health. And nothing will happen to me, for I am clearly conscious of the great tasks which Providence has assigned me."[102] On another occasion, he recalled,

> There have been two miracles in my life. Twice have I been face to face with disaster—after the Munich putsch, when I was in jail, isolated, dejected, and made to look ridiculous; and on the very eve of becoming Chancellor, when I seemed to founder in sight of port, swamped by intrigues, financial difficulties, and the dead-weight of twelve million people who swung first one way and then another. Both times God saved me.[103]

That Hitler's sense of providential care was an essential element of his sense of self was not lost on his associates. In his memoirs, Albert Speer, Hitler's architect and, after Hess's flight, his closest underling, explains that Hitler was comforted even during his final days in the bunker by belief in "his mission by divine Providence." Indeed, Speer felt that "if there was any fundamental insanity in Hitler, it was this unshakable belief in his lucky star."[104] Walter Schellenberg, a high-ranking SS officer, reported in his memoirs that Hitler's "one dominant and dominating characteristic was that he felt himself appointed by Providence to do great things for the German people. This was his historic 'mission,' in which he believed completely."[105]

In his monologues and rhetoric, Hitler was quite open regarding the role of Providence in his life. Rauschning recalls Hitler's stating, with characteristic bluntness, "Providence has ordained that I should be the greatest liberator of humanity."[106] Hitler was particularly clear on this point during the *Anschluss,* when he returned triumphantly to Austria, the land where his messianic vision had first occurred. He stated that "when Providence once summoned me from this state to the leadership of the Reich, then it must have imparted upon me a mission, and it can only have been a mission, to restore my dear homeland to the German Reich! I have had faith in this mission, have lived and struggled for it, and I believe I have now fulfilled it." Speaking in Vienna less than a month later, Hitler stated, "I believe that it was also God's will to send from here a lad into the Reich, to permit him to become great, to elevate him to leader of the nation, to make it possible for him to lead his homeland back into the Reich."[107] Significantly, Providence not only protected Hitler but, as with any good messiah, also spoke to him, guiding his decisions and actions.

Hitler's "Inner Voice": Listening to the Whispers of Providence

In Hitler's view, his and therefore Germany's historic mission could be fulfilled by simply following the dictates of Providence. The desire to understand the predetermined flow of history is an attempt to eliminate the process of change by rendering its manifestations part of a knowable divine plan. Those who follow destiny's path walk a changeless and eternal road; time and change are nullified, and the perception of chaos generated by rapid and radical change is replaced by one of preordained order. Destiny therefore is like a hidden road map occasionally revealed to a special few, which when followed leads to the culmination of the Creator's divine plan. Hitler concluded that Providence "imparts a higher determination, and we are all nothing other than its implement."[108] It is in this light that Hitler stated, in 1936, "I go with the security of a sleepwalker the way that Providence commands me to go."[109]

The tool needed to understand providential will, according to Hitler, was intuition, which he considered to be a vehicle of revelation. Hitler believed that intuition was a perfectly natural phenomenon with which he was particularly gifted. His oft-mentioned "inner voice," which he considered unimpeachable, was, according to him, none other than the intuitive revelations of divine Providence—destiny exposed. It was the same voice that he believed had saved his life during the First World War, ordering him to leave a bunker moments before it was struck by artillery. Hitler explained to his associate Wagener that the chosen leader was "responsible only to the Volk and to his conscience, and that has been given him by God, that is the divine voice inside him."[110] According to Rauschning, Hitler explained his decision-making process in a similar way, explaining that, "unless I have the inner, incorruptible conviction: this is the solution, I do nothing. Not even if the whole party tries to drive me to action. I will not act; I will wait, no matter what happens. But if the voice speaks, then I know the time has come to act."[111] The voice that Hitler listened to was the voice of the apocalypse complex. Psychologically, this gift demonstrates Hitler's ability to access the richly symbolic world of the unconscious, a skill prophets, shamans, and mediums have exhibited in the past. It was a skill that helps explain why Hitler was so successful while many other would-be messiahs were not. Hitler's gift would be the world's curse.

With his penchant for pseudo-science, Hitler even found a way to link Einstein's theory of relativity to his faith in intuition. He felt that Einstein had proved that the limits of the "human thinking machine" could be overcome, in this case through higher mathematics. Consequently, he explained to Wagener, Einstein had proved that things could exist that, "recognized by man's senses, nevertheless cannot be understood and justified, though they are true and could form the basis for a new way of thinking, perhaps even of a new conception of the world." Consequently, Hitler believed he could trust his intuitive revelations as fact. When Wagener warned that trusting human senses alone could be dangerous, since perceptions can be incomplete and therefore conclusions drawn from them inaccurate, Hitler protested:

> But I do not receive such perceptions through the human senses at all! If it were that sort of perception, it would be amenable to logical proof. And if it were not, it would undoubtedly be false. Rather, in such cases I feel as if I were taking my perceptions from that super-dimensional world Einstein has looked into, not with his eyes or conscious mind, but with his mathematics.

Wagener then asked Hitler whether he always knew "whether such a perception comes from the beyond or though the agency of the human senses within this world?" Hitler responded:

> I do know each time, without question. But I don't always take that fully into account. That is also why sometimes I heedlessly pass over such transcendental inspirations. In general, at such moments I have a sensation like an inner vibration, as if I have seized the impulse, what I said or did as a result of that feeling always turned out to be correct. Whenever I have let it go, almost invariably it turned out later that it would have been right to follow the inner voice.[112]

These "transcendental impulses" and the "inner vibrations" that they engendered in Hitler point to a direct flow of symbolic material from Hitler's unconscious into his conscious world.[113]

Hitler believed that great historical figures such as Charles V, Luther, Robespierre, and Napoleon were successful because they followed their intuition, thereby preventing events that might have been "catastrophic for mankind." By heeding their intuitions, these men acted in accordance with Providence. Hitler explained that "we can and may only view ourselves as the tools of Providence, some of us more, some less. And no one has the right to evade the task that has been set for him." Hitler naturally included himself in this pantheon of world changers, telling Wagener,

> I, too, may be predestined to march before the rest of you with the torch of perception. Behind me, you must carry out the work. *I* must follow my inspiration and my task. But *you,* behind me, can see and recognize things as they are. The torch only occasionally casts its flickering flame on the path before me. But those of you who come behind me march in its light. That is why we belong together, the rest of you and I! I, the one who leads through the dark, and you who, seeing, are meant to complete the task.[114]

Slavishly following one's inner voice and the predestined path it reveals also serves to eliminate change by eliminating choice. One's life, indeed, the destiny of humanity, is preordained, and therefore one need not worry about choosing this or that path—it has been chosen for one. Hitler's belief in his inner voice and the prophetic ability it gave him provided a means of ordering chaos, of giving direction to his aimless life. The acceptance by many of Hitler in his role as prophet fulfilled the same function in their lives. They now had someone and something to follow. But Hitler's self-perception was not simply that of a prophet or that of "drummer," the agitator who riles up the masses for action. Hitler clearly perceived himself as both messiah and prophet—a Christ-like figure chosen by supernatural forces to fulfill a soteriological mission of eschatological proportions. But many individuals roam the streets, shouting, "The world is ending! Follow me to the promised land!" These lost souls generally attract more flies than followers. Hitler, however, attracted a legion of devoted disciples willing to fight and even to die for their savior and his "great idea."

5

The Messiah Legitimated
Linking the Leader and the Led

That Hitler had messianic pretensions is clear. As we have seen, many in his inner circle contributed to Hitler's messianism not only by publicly promoting the so-called Hitler Myth but also by genuinely accepting him in this role. As we have seen in the Old Guard conversion experiences, many minor Nazis also accepted, and thereby legitimated, Hitler in this role as messiah. But why Hitler? In the 1920s, there were certainly other candidates for savior, as messianism was in the air.[1] What made Hitler acceptable? What legitimated him to them as messiah and prophet? While it is probable that many individuals, under great psychic duress, projected the messiah symbol outside themselves, why was Hitler the recipient of this projection? Hitler's proclivity for nondirected thinking, which he interpreted as a prophetic ability to divine destiny's path, enabled him to access the archetypal symbols of the apocalypse complex. And, significantly, Hitler had the oratorical ability to express accurately and emotionally his vision of the apocalypse complex. Hitler struck a chord with many Germans, revealing to them the archetypal forces that were swelling up under the pressure of psychic chaos, helping them reconstruct a new sense of order.

Hitler Speaking: Giving Voice to the Apocalypse Complex

It is generally accepted that Hitler's special talent as an orator, part natural gift and part the result of studied effort, was one of the keys to his success. Hitler's oratorical abilities attracted disciples to the movement and notoriety to himself, thereby legitimating his preexisting messianic self-perceptions. Hitler was fond of giving long diatribes to his childhood friend Kubizek, to the poor acquaintances at the hostel in Vienna, and to his fellow soldiers in the trenches during the First World War. His audience, while at times captive, was not always receptive, and his talent went largely unnoticed. However, shortly after the war, the insignificant lance corporal's gift for "drumming," for stirring up the masses, was recognized. As seen in the preceding chapter, this first occurred in the barracks in postwar Munich, where Hitler's diatribes against the Jewish Bolsheviks, largely ignored when the war was going well, now with the loss began to find an audience. Hitler was elected to the soldier's soviet. His success here led him to success as an education officer, and that led him to the German Worker's Party. Hitler's apocalyptic anti-Semitism now struck a chord.

The descriptions of Old Guard conversion experiences that took place at Hitler speeches demonstrate a remarkable similarity in tone and content. Typical of conversion experiences in general, they were highly emotional and somatic, in other words, experienced bodily. As one former Hitler Youth member, Alfons Heck, remembered of the effect of Hitler's speaking style, "then his voice rose, took on power and became rasping with a strongly appealing intensity. It touched us physically because all of its emotions were reflected on our faces. We simply became an instrument in the hands of an unsurpassed master."[2] The nonrational effect of Hitler's oratory can be seen in the repetition of words such as "mass hypnotism," "magnetism," "mesmerism," "metaphysical," and "mystical," used in contemporary accounts of converts and observers alike to describe the effect of Hitler's oratory. While the use of such paranormal and pseudo-scientific phrases understandably has left historians skeptical of their usage, from a psychological perspective they are highly telling indicators that unconscious processes are at work. One need not, and should not, accept that mass hypnotism was being successfully practiced by Hitler, but one can perceive that some powerful nonrational process did in fact take place. The conversion experiences of the Old Guard are a testament to this fact.

The Nazi apostate Otto Strasser made an acute observation about Hitler's oratorical gift, especially its nonrational basis and the importance of the rhetor/listener interrelationship:

Hitler responds to the vibration of the human heart with the delicacy of a seismograph, or perhaps of a wireless receiving set, enabling him, with a certainty with which no conscious gift could endow him to act as a loudspeaker proclaiming the most secret desires, the least admissible instincts, the sufferings and personal revolts of a whole nation. . . . I have been asked many times what is the secret of Hitler's extraordinary power as a speaker. I can only attribute it to his uncanny intuition, which infallibly diagnoses the ills from which his audience is suffering. If he tries to bolster up his argument with theories or quotations from books he has only imperfectly understood, he scarcely rises above a very poor mediocrity. But let him throw away his crutches and step out boldly, speaking as the spirit moves him, and he is promptly transformed into one of the greatest speakers of the century. . . . Adolf Hitler enters a hall. He sniffs the air. For a minute he gropes, feels his way, senses the atmosphere. Suddenly he bursts forth. . . . His words go like an arrow to their target, he touches each private wound in the raw, liberating the mass unconscious, expressing its innermost aspirations, telling it what it most wants to hear.[3]

Putzi Hanfstängl's account of his first Hitler speech likewise reflects Hitler's gift for working the group psyche:

Within three minutes I felt the man's absolute sincerity and love for Germany. Within ten I had forgotten everything else but the words which that man was quietly dropping into the consciousness of everyone present—words which burned all the more for their softness; words which lashed us as men who had failed in a great responsibility. . . . He completely mesmerized that audience—without paralyzing it.[4]

According to Hanfstängl's account, it was not solely Hitler's oratorical technique but the messianic and millennial content of his speeches that worked its magic. In Hanfstängl's memoirs, written while still a disciple, yet saying much the same thing as the previous quotation, he explained: "Far beyond his electrifying rhetoric, this man seemed to possess the uncanny gift of coupling the gnostic yearning of the era for a strong leader-figure with his own missionary claim and to suggest in this merging that every conceivable hope and expectation was capable of fulfilment—an astonishing spectacle of suggestive influence of the mass psyche."[5] After his conversion, Hanfstängl would use his considerable social connections for Hitler's political advancement.

Kurt Lüdecke, another Nazi convert turned apostate, wrote of a similar first Hitler speech:

Presently my critical faculty was swept away. Leaning from the tribune as if he were trying to impel his inner self into the consciousness of all these thousands he was holding the masses and me with them, under a hypnotic spell. . . . His appeal to German manhood was like a call to arms, the gospel he preached a sacred truth. He seemed another Luther. . . . I experienced an exaltation that could be likened only to religious conversion. . . . I had found myself, my leader, and my cause.[6]

Lüdecke, like Hanfstängl, tried to use his personal connections to raise funds for the Nazis, and his personal funds helped sustain them during the hyperinflation of 1923. By the end of the year, he was nearly broke. That Lüdecke and Hanfstängl both converted to Hitler because of the combination of his messianism and his millennial message, and subsequently used their personal associations and monies to help the party, argues in favor of Nazi millennialism as an important part of the movement's political success in the early 1920s. Nazism represented not just well-delivered, meaningless rhetoric but a combination of oratorical style and millennial substance.

Hitler seems to have had the ability to become possessed by the power of his own rhetoric, or at least the power of the experience of speaking before thousands of enraptured and screaming believers. This can be seen in the account of Major Francis Yeats-Brown, a British apologist for the Nazis:

During the rhetorical passages his voice mounted to the pitch of delirium: he was a man transformed and possessed. We were in the presence of a miracle . . . the tension was almost unbearable until the passionate voice was drowned by the cries of the audience. The delirium was real—Hitler was in a frenzy at these moments—but he was able to release this infectious atmosphere of quasi-hysteria without losing his self-control: whatever his emotion, a steady fervor and a more-than-feminine intuition are harnessed to a cool brain and a strong will.[7]

As Hitler's speeches were emotionally and physically satisfying for his audience, so he too seems to have achieved a satisfaction that bordered on the sexual. The SS leader Walter Schellenberg recalled that "During his speeches he fell, or rather, worked himself into such orgiastic frenzies that he achieved through them complete emotional satisfaction."[8] That the bodily or sexual experience of a Hitler speech was mutually experienced was also noticed by the contemporary historian Karl Alexander von Müller, who wrote that Hitler "needed a long time to screw himself up to the usual excitement. But the orgiastic outbreak never failed to appear, nor the orgiastic response."[9] Kurt Lüdecke described Hitler's speaking ability as being not "conscious" but rather the "perfect co-ordination of impulse and expression."[10] In other words, Hitler, with his penchant for nondirected thinking, felt the impulse of the apocalypse complex and gave voice to symbols that express it. The audience, having given up its ego-consciousness and immersed itself in nonrational thinking, heard its innermost thoughts made audible and were enraptured.

Another contemporary observer described the participatory nature of a Hitler speech experience, the psychological interconnectedness of rhetor and audience:

The susceptibility of the Chancellor's mind to psychic influences is shown in his public oratory. At the outset of a speech his delivery is sometimes slow and halting. Only as the spiritual atmosphere engendered by a great audience takes possession of his mind does he develop that eloquence which acts on the German nation like a spell. For he responds to this metaphysical contact in such a way that each member of the multitude feels bound to him by an individual link of sympathy.[11]

Another British apologist for Hitler portrayed this process from the perspective of the converted: "And seeing Hitler later, I was confirmed in my view that he drew his power from mystic sources; his is a strangely intuitive nature; he has an uncanny gift of knowing how to strike and of timing his strokes."[12] Still another contemporary observer noted this same oneness between the Führer and his disciples. The profound connection between rhetor and audience is clearly evident:

Hitler is able to hypnotize people *en masse*. His manner of speaking is not ranting. His gestures are not violent. He speaks with great emphasis, but he seldom shouts. And yet he casts a spell. Audiences follow more than his words. They follow his gestures. When he is at climax and sways to one side or the other, his listeners sway with him; when he leans forward, they also lean forward and when he concludes they either are awed and silent or on their feet in a frenzy.[13]

Another witness to a Hitler speech, while not himself affected, noted the loss of self-control by audience members, stating that "they ceased to be beings with minds, they have become a single sounding-board for this man's music." Tellingly, this individual described such a mass meeting as a "revivalist phenomenon."[14] Even reporters who were not personally affected noticed the trancelike response of the audience. Egon Larson somewhat cynically but perceptively reported that

> It was all a primitive yet successful performance, and the repetitive rhythm seemed to produced a kind of hypnotic trance in the crowd. When they woke up at the end and made their way to the exit, we found ourselves amidst shining faces and dreamy eyes. These bemused, insecure people had been given a potent injection of faith in a leader and a movement that would put everything right.[15]

An interesting and overlooked aspect of Hitler's oratorical style was his tendency to orate to individuals or small groups as if they were a mass audience. Asked to speak at a wedding reception, in 1923, Hitler refused, saying, "I must have a crowd when I speak. In a small, intimate circle I never know what to say. I should only disappoint you all, and that is a thing I should hate to do. As a speaker either at a family gathering or a funeral, I'm no use at all."[16] Psychologically, this betrays more than poor social skills—it reflects his tendency to slip into nonrational modes of thinking and speaking seemingly at will. Bella Fromm, a journalist for *Vossische Zeitung*, recalled that "in talking to people you got the impression that he was addressing an audience. Thus the most casual remark was delivered as though to a mass meeting." Another man similarly recalled that during one of Hitler's typical harangues, "I had the impression that he thought he was addressing a large audience." The American journalist Dorothy Thompson noted that "he speaks always as though he were addressing a mass meeting. . . . He gives the impression of a man in a trance." The contemporary historian Louis Lochner similarly recalled observing that "he seems to be in a trance. It is the masses he sees and to whom he is speaking."[17] Another reporter, H. R. Knickerbocker, observed,

> It [Hitler's face] is almost like a mask. He frequently looks straight at you. He has terrific power of concentration and sometimes when he talks he appears to forget his surroundings, and to be conversing with

himself, although he may be shouting loud enough to be heard by a great multitude.[18]

When T. R. Ybarra, a reporter for *Collier's,* asked Hitler if he had anything to say to the American public, he noted that the dictator "resembled the Hitler who has so often swayed mass meetings to tumultuous enthusiasm. . . . He seemed to be trying actually to see the Americans to whom he was addressing his words. Into his face came some of that mystical quality which has helped him to drive audiences to hysteria."[19] Frederick Oechsner witnessed an interview of Hitler by an American reporter. He recalled that

> whether Der Führer realized it or not, he was delivering an address: his eyes flashed, his lips twisted in the movements of speech, his head was thrown up in the familiar imperious motion, and with his right forefinger he jabbed the air with sharp thrusts as if to drive home every point. For all I know, he may have forgotten that we were there and have been speaking to one of his audiences of thousands.[20]

Lothrop Stoddard recalled a similar experience: "now Hitler drew himself erect and by the faraway look in his eyes showed plainly that he was not speaking merely to me; he was addressing an imaginary audience that stretched far beyond the walls of the living room."[21] The notion of the imaginary audience is important. Hitler seems to have had the ability to perform what C. G. Jung termed active imagination, a process whereby one consciously generates a fantasy, then lets go and follows its course in a state of nondirected thinking.[22] Hitler seemed to use this technique, perhaps unknowingly, when composing a speech. He explained to Louis Lochner:

> When I compose a speech, I visualize the people. I can see them just as though they were standing before me. I sense how they will react to this or that statement, to this or that formulation. I naturally prefer off-hand speaking, because than you can adapt every phrase and every gesture to your particular audience, but I don't feel hampered by set address.[23]

That two of the observers cited who witnessed this type of oratorical behavior interpreted Hitler's appearance and demeanor as trancelike is significant. In an OSS interview during World War II, a German emigré filmmaker recalled witnessing one of Hitler's nightly monologues. The emigré "was under the impression that in the course of such a rage Hitler works himself into a trance-like state in which he loses contact with his surroundings and during which he enjoys the uninhibited expression of his feelings." He felt that Hitler goes out of his way to "experience trance-like states."[24]

That Hitler's powers of persuasion were strongest in a crowd can be seen in the putsch attempt of 1923. When Hitler attempted in private to convince Lossow, Seisser, and Kahr to form a new government with Ludendorff and himself, he failed miserably. However, he was much more effective with the crowd in the beer hall. Karl Alexander von Müller provides us with an eyewitness account, and an interesting interpretation:

> Ten minutes must have just elapsed when Hitler returned—alone. He had not succeeded in winning over the others as he had promised. What would he say? A dangerous wave of excitement surged upon him as he again ascended the podium. . . . What followed then was an oratorical masterpiece that would have reflected credit on any actor. . . . I cannot remember ever in my life such a reversal of mass sentiment in a few minutes, almost seconds. Certainly there were yet many who were not converted. But the sentiment of the majority had completely turned around. Hitler had with a few sentences turned them inside out like one turns a glove inside out. It had almost something of a hocus-pocus, of a magic about it.[25]

What enabled Hitler to so easily sway so many people so quickly? It was his ability to access the unconscious mind, to slip into nondirected thinking and to give voice to the archetypal imagery swelling up in the minds of the multitude. It is an ability that needs to be explored in greater detail.

Hitler's Proclivity for Nondirected Thinking

If we are to believe his half-brother Alois, Hitler, since childhood, had a penchant for trance states. Alois Hitler told one reporter that Adolf was happy only when he was in his mother's arms; "the rest of the time he was jumpy and frightened, or lost-looking and far away in daydreams that were almost like trances."[26] And, as was noted earlier, Wagner's music apparently induced a similar trancelike altered consciousness. Hitler's messianic visionary experiences before and after World War I seem to have occurred in such altered states of consciousness. Significantly, a number of observers of Hitler's speech making, in small groups or before a mass audience, reported that he appeared at times to be in a trancelike state. Louis Lochner, who witnessed his first Hitler speech in 1930, recalled,

> I looked about me and saw that his young followers were transported and that he himself seemed in a trance. Yet he exerted no magnetic power over me. His eyes seemed to hypnotize those whom he looked at sharply. Yet his glance left me personally untouched.[27]

Another witness to a Hitler speech noted that "here I could appreciate his effect: in the presence of a audience he went into trance."[28] Otto Strasser described Hitler's speaking style similarly:

> A clairvoyant, face-to-face with his public, he goes into a trance. That is his moment of real greatness, the moment when he is most genuinely himself. He believes what he says; carried away by a mystic force, he cannot doubt the genuineness of his mission.[29]

Still another individual, describing a Hitler speech, noted that "he was like a man hypnotized."[30] That the reception of the audience was an important ingredient in Hitler's speaking style and its nondirected nature was noted by a number of observers, again pointing to the importance of a dialogic relationship between rhetor and audience. Otto Strasser, who witnessed Hitler's rhetorical performance at the putsch trial, noted his "sheer intoxication with his own ability with words; as though he became drunk like his audience, with the emotional appeal of his own oratory." Louis Lochner also noted that Hitler appeared "spiritually intoxicated" by crowds.[31] Even as early as 1922, the ecstatic nature of the rhetor/audience relationship was observed, as a *New York Times* correspondent noted that Hitler's evenings of speeches had the feeling of a "patriotic revival meeting."[32]

Klaus Vondung has convincingly argued that the Nazis deliberately used ritualized settings for speeches, party rallies, and other public performances to alter individual's perceptions of reality. In this way, "social reality" could be manipulated via what he termed "magical consciousness."[33] The mass rallies, with their marching columns of uniformed

"Kampfer," were a visual expression of unity in motion, powerful symbols of the millennial transformation of the chaotic rabble transformed into ordered Volk. The experience of this unity, as individuals lost themselves in the collective, was a means to salvation. As a contemporary writer, Hanns Johst, explained it, the party rallies enabled the individual to experience, "in the community of equally minded, equally feeling, equally believing people the dream of salvation as displayed and envisioned truth."[34] As the conversion experiences of the Old Guard attest, the rallies often had exactly this effect. It was at the party rallies that Hitler's "great idea" was made manifest. Alfons Heck, who experienced the mass rallies as a boy, was impressed by the "pomp and mysticism," which had an effect "very close in feeling to religious rituals," a "gigantic revival meeting but without the repentance of one's sins . . . it was a jubilant Teutonic renaissance." He elaborated that "no one who ever attended a Nuremberg *Reichsparteitag* can forget the similarity to religious mass fervor it exuded. Its intensity frightened neutral observers but it inflamed the believers."[35]

Asked by Hitler what effect a party congress has on the first-time participant, Otto Wagener responded,

> There is no question that he is deeply impressed, stunned by the grandeur of the whole and by its utter novelty. He cannot help but be, as I was, affected to the core by the realization that here a beginning has been made, with consequences and potential that are wholly incalculable. And most evident is the realization that everything that happens, that is expressed, that is demonstrated is permeated and saturated with a single idea, a single will, a single spirit.[36]

Wagener's interpretation of his experience reflects the typical millennial sense of witnessing a turning point, a rebirth interpreted as a social transformation of profound consequences, all brought about through unity—the unity of Führer and Volk, Hitler and the rally participant. This sense of unity was extended to the realm of architecture designed for mass spectacles. Albert Speer's proposed domed stadium, designed to hold 450,000, was meant specifically to unify the mind of the audience. Speer noted that "if people with different minds are all pressed together in such a place, they will be unified in one mind. That was the aim of the stadium; it had nothing to do with what the small man might think personally."[37]

The sociologist Jean-Pierre Sironneau observed that at the rallies "a genuine sacred drama was preformed there, which only the resurgence in the twentieth century of religious drives that were supposed to have disappeared can explain."[38] This drama, Sironneau correctly notes, involved the communion of leader and led, what he termed a "dialectic of possession," for "the crowd leader, possessed by they who surround him, possesses them in his turn; because the crowds recognize themselves in him and somehow create him, he subjugates them."[39] Or, I would add, they subjugate each other. For this conjoining of selves, leader and led, was a deliberate part of the unifying process, of which I say more shortly. In this regard, Rauschning recalls Hitler's saying,

> The day of individual happiness has passed. Instead, we shall feel a collective happiness. Can there be any greater happiness than a National Socialist meeting in which speakers and audience feel as one? It is the happiness of sharing. Only the early Christian communities could have felt it with equal intensity. They, too, sacrificed their personal lives for the higher happiness of the community.[40]

Hitler clearly believed that the New Age of the millennial Reich would bring about a happiness on the scale of the equally millennially charged disciples of the messiah Jesus. The emphasis on communalism is shared by many millennial movements. However, with the Nazis it was ritualized on a much greater scale. The secret power of Hitler's national socialism was that it was conceived from the beginning less as a socialism of occupation and income than as a struggle between individual and collective; therefore, it was aimed not at an economic leveling, as was Marxism, but rather at an experience of communal oneness. As a young Rudolf Hess wrote in 1921, "common interest goes before self-interest; first the nation, then the personal ego . . . this union of the national with the social is the fulcrum of our time."[41] The party rallies would become the main ritual setting for symbolically evoking the dream of a millennial age of communal oneness.

It is possible that individuals under great personal duress, while in a mass meeting where ego is generally subordinated, are particularly susceptible to influence by archetypal contents. The religious rites and ceremonies of the Nazis, complete with chants, flags, banners, music, and torchlit processions, undoubtedly had a powerful psychological effect, as well, inducing nondirected thinking in large numbers of individuals. Karl

Alexander von Müller heard his first Nazi speeches on January 27, 1923, a night that was meant to protest the recent French occupation of the Ruhr. Müller noted how Nazi meetings differed from others held at the oft-used *Löwenbräukeller:*

> How many political gatherings had I experienced already in this hall. But neither during the war nor during the revolution had such a scorching breath of hypnotic mass excitement come over me when entering. It was not only the special tension of these weeks or this day. I noted: "special fight songs, special flags, special symbols, a special greeting."[42]

Perceptively, Müller realized that it was not simply the charged atmosphere resulting from the Ruhr episode but the Nazi employment of colorful flags, swastika banners, the "Heil Hitler" greeting with the upraised arm, and the Nazi songs that played a role in generating what he termed mass hypnotism—in other words, an altering of the audience consciousness. Müller described the transformed beer hall: "a forest of dazzling red flags with a black swastika on white background; the strangest mixture of military discipline and revolutionary zeal, of nationalism and socialism—likewise in the audience: predominantly the downward-sliding middle class, in all its layers—will it here be welded together anew?" Regarding Hitler's subsequent speech, Müller pointedly asked himself, "was it the masses that inspired him with this mysterious power? Or did it flow from him to them?" He further noted his impression of the event: "Fantasizing hysterical romanticism, with a brutal core of will." This same night, the reporter Ludwell Denny attended and said, of the crowd's view of Hitler, "he was a popular preacher turned savior."[43]

While the material trappings certainly helped lead the audience into a state of nondirected thinking, it needs to be noted that Nazi speeches were filled with the rhetoric of the apocalypse complex—talk of turning points, rebirth, resurrection and salvation, of a coming battle of good and evil and the dawn of a millennial Third Reich—all now brought to the surface (in the Nazis' conception, "awakened"). The evenings of speeches therefore elicited a profoundly emotional personal experience that, because of its archetypal basis, was charged with millennial overtones. This process can be seen in the experience of one farmer who recalled his first Hitler speech, in 1932, this way:

In July the Führer came to Tilsit. I saw him for the first time. About 40,000 people from near and far had gathered to greet him. I wore the brown shirt from the first time I heard his voice. His words went straight to the heart. From now on my life and efforts were dedicated to the Führer. I wanted to be a true follower. The Führer spoke of the threatened ruin of the nation and of the resurrection under the Third Reich.[44]

This man was moved not only by his immersion in the collective but also by his devotion to the redeemer Führer, whose millennial rhetoric of approaching apocalypse and resurrection in the coming Third Reich satisfied the millennial longings brought on during the heights of the depression. That it is the millennial content of the speech that this individual remembered, intermingled with a call for unity through the elimination of classes and parties and the destruction of evil communism, is important and telling. This sense of unity, of witnessing a chaotic horde transformed by the messiah-leader into an ordered and disciplined Volk, and the profound sense of communalism attached to the experience of losing one's self in the mass, was and is powerfully attractive. That so many Old Guard Nazis reported that their conversion or intensification experience occurred at a Nazi mass gathering is a testament to the psychological power of this process. The following account, from Louis Lochner's perceptive description of a ritual gathering he witnessed, bears this out:

A search light lays upon his lone figure as he slowly walks through the hall, never looking to the right or the left, his right hand raised in salute, his left hand at the buckle of his belt. He never smiles—it is a religious rite, this procession of the modern Messiah incarnate. Behind him are his adjutants and secret service men. But his figure alone is flooded with light. By the time Hitler has reached the rostrum, the masses have been so worked upon that they are ready to do his will. But the masses also effect a transformation in him. He becomes electrified. He appears to go into a trance. He is carried away by his own eloquence. He returns to his chancellory completely washed up physically but revived spiritually.[45]

The effect for Hitler and his audience was one of an altered consciousness where nondirected thinking predominates, where the archetypal imagery of the apocalypse complex came easily to the surface. The apocalyptic rhetoric of the speeches, and the millenarian desires of rhetor and audience, met in a psychodrama where the apocalypse complex was ritualistically performed. Both Hitler and his audience felt transformed and enlightened, as the paradisiacal New Age appeared manifest in the collective unity of Führer and Volk. Hitler, in the guise of messiah and prophet, functioned much like a medium of ages past, a conduit between the world of consciousness and that of the unconscious, between the rational and the nonrational worlds.

Hitler as Medium

Many observers of Hitler, supporters and detractors, noted what they described as his "mediumistic" nature. One woman explained that "he has a mediumistic time sense of the imminent which is special to dictators."[46] Karl von Wiegand, who had been acquainted with Hitler since the early days of the movement, mentioned, or perhaps "promoted" would be a better word, Hitler's "high degree of mediumistic sensitivity, intensified by diet and meditation in the mountains, and his extraordinary psychic intuition." He elaborated that "Adolf Hitler is that rare phenomenon in high politics and among statesmen—a mystic with strong psychic perceptions and mediumistic sensitiveness. There are times, especially in moments of solitude in the mountains, when he has pre-vision, is momentarily clairvoyant." He further explained that Hitler was not a spiritualist medium in the sense of channeling spirits; rather, "he communes with himself. It is then that his inspirations, if such you want to call them, come to him. From the beginning he has been convinced that he was given a definite 'mission' by Providence."[47] Another individual agreed, stating that "undoubtedly, he has sometimes had the gift of clairvoyance and the sensibility of a medium."[48] Again, one need not ascribe genuine psychic or mediumistic abilities to Hitler, no more than one need accept him as an actual prophet or messiah, to perceive in these descriptions important psychological truths. C. G. Jung's insight into Hitler's psychology is important in this regard. During an interview with the journalist H. R. Knickerbocker, Jung gave his analysis of the secret of Hitler's power:

> There were two types of strong men in primitive society. One was the chief, who was physically powerful . . . and another was the medicine man, who was not strong in himself but was strong by reason of the power which the people projected into him. . . . Hitler belongs in the cat-

egory of the truly mystic medicine man. . . . Now the secret of Hitler's power is . . . twofold; first, that his unconscious has exceptional access to his consciousness, and second, that he allows himself to be moved by it. He is like a man who listens intently to a stream of suggestions in a whispered voice from a mysterious source, and then acts upon them. In our case, . . . we have too much rationality, . . . to obey it—but Hitler listens and obeys. The true leader is always led.[49]

Mediumistic ability then, like charisma, is a negotiated phenomenon between medium and believer. When Max Weber first described charismatic leaders (often, interestingly enough, messiah/prophet figures), he noted that their power lies less in innate or mystical forces emanating from them than in that which is projected onto them by their disciples.[50] A reporter gave some idea of this interactional process when he wrote of a Hitler speech,

> The realm of illusion, always half real to him, becomes intensely real to him and to his German hearers (who are attuned almost mediumistically to his nature) the moment he begins to speak. The opening of his mouth is like the raising of the curtain that instantaneously produces the illusion.[51]

Yet, I would add, one person's illusion is another's holy truth. Furthermore, it is the deep psychological connection between the medium and the believing audience, which projects its archetypal contents into that medium, that is most important. Hermann Rauschning gave some indication of this when he noted of Hitler's mediumistic qualities that "these qualities have nothing to do with the medium's own personality. They are conveyed to him from without. The medium is possessed by them."[52] However, it should be noted, the medium's abilities do have *something* to do with his own personality, for not everyone can assume such a role in society. This was certainly the case with Hitler.

Hitler seems to have believed that he had such mediumistic abilities, a facility for slipping into nondirected thinking and letting the archetypal images flow forth. He explained to Wagener:

> Actually I'm now and then aware that it is not I who is speaking, but that something speaks through me. On such occasions, I frequently feel as if there were a mistake in human logic or as if it had limits of which it is not aware. Now and then ideas, concepts, views occur to me that I

read nowhere, heard nowhere and never before thought, nor can I justify them by logic and they do not seem to me capable of being logically
justified.[53]

Hitler is describing himself as akin to a spiritualist medium like Madame
Blavatsky, the nineteenth-century theosophical medium who claimed that
her occult insight came from magical intuition. Again, the point is not
that Hitler was in reality a psychic medium channeling ideas from the
Otherworld but rather that by turning away from logical, rational modes
of thinking, Hitler was able to let unconscious material flow through him,
material that was often millennial, messianic, and apocalyptic. His listeners, however, often interpreted his oratory as the words of a prophet.
Wagener remarked that Hitler would seem engaged in undirected chatter,
then suddenly catch fire:

> then a speech flowed from his lips supported by gestures and by his gaze,
> which at such moments was absolutely clear and totally compelling. His
> words expressed a wealth of ideas and a view of things and their connec-
> tions that at times sounded as if they came from another world. In fact,
> one was forever enthralled by his discourse and followed his logic with an
> inner conviction that almost lacked all will, since it came from a quite dif-
> ferent viewpoint than one was used to, and everything was developed so
> clearly that a doubt could hardly arise, an objection was unthinkable.[54]

Wagener never lost faith in his messiah and prophet and dutifully
recorded his words, considering himself a keeper of the Grail, the gnosis
of salvation as revealed by Hitler. Even after he was no longer close to
Hitler, Wagener continued to believe the words of his prophet:

> Whatever I did from that time on, I would do as the upholder of a
> deeper knowledge, which it seemed my life's mission to formulate. I felt
> myself committed to this knowledge for all time. It remains untouched
> by all that was to come, untouched also by my subsequent separation
> from Hitler. This knowledge had given birth in me to a world view that
> struggled for realization. And I felt, as Hitler had said, like the guardian
> of the grail that holds the secrets of that world view.[55]

Hitler's talent was a combination of speech pattern, physical gesture, and
an ability to seemingly make sense of nonsense, to order mental chaos; all

these factors combined to give the appearance of a medium or prophet. Wagener's analysis sounds eerily like those of supporters of messiah figures as diverse as Charles Manson, David Koresh, and Marshall Applewhite. It would be a mistake to dismiss such descriptions of Hitler as mere hyperbole or propaganda. For they provide insight into what allowed Hitler to transform himself from nobody to agitator to prophet, and, finally, to messiah. Hitler's psychological constitution was an important factor in making this transition possible, as his ability to access archetypal material, combined with his ability to express it verbally, connected messiah and discipline in a way that was experienced as being deeply personal and utterly profound.

Conjoined Selves: Hitler and His Disciples

A number of individuals who had close contact with Hitler remarked on his almost total lack of human qualities or personality of any real depth. One interviewer described him as "distant, legendary, nebulous, an enigma as a human being," while another noted his general "inhuman quality." Another recalled that while Mussolini seemed very "human," Hitler was not.[56] Dr. Arnold Brecht, a former *Reichsrat* member interviewed by the OSS, described Hitler as an "absolute nonentity." Another observer, describing Hitler, concluded that "the whole man gave the impression of a poor copy of a type existing only in the imagination."[57] Hitler's architect, Albert Speer, spoke of the Führer's inner hollowness:

> There was actually something insubstantial about him. But this was perhaps a permanent quality he had. In retrospect I sometimes ask myself whether this intangibility, this insubstantiality, had not characterized him from early youth up to the moment of his suicide. It sometimes seems to me that his seizures of violence could come upon him all the more strongly because there were no human emotions in him to oppose them. He simply could not let anyone approach his inner being because that core was lifeless, empty.[58]

Magda Goebbels similarly remarked that "in some ways Hitler simply isn't human."[59] Hermann Rauschning also remarked on Hitler's lack of human character:

A quiet conversation with him was impossible. Either he was silent or he took complete charge of the discussion. Hitler's eloquence is plainly no natural gift but the result of a conquest of certain inhibitions which, in intimate conversation, still make him awkward. The convulsive artificiality of his character is specially noticeable in such intimate circles; particularly notable is his lack of any sense of humor. Hitler's laugh is hardly more than an expression of scorn and contempt. There is no relaxation about it. His pleasures have no repose.[60]

Rauschning also noted Hitler's lack of warmth, and his hard, remote, and rigid nature. He also showed little discipline, being prone to temper tantrums. Describing one such incident, Rauschning recalled, "He scolded in high, shrill tones, stamped his feet, and banged his fists on tables and walls. He foamed at the mouth, panting and stammering in uncontrolled fury. . . . He was an alarming sight, his hair disheveled, his eyes fixed, and his face distorted and purple. I feared that he would collapse, or have an apoplectic fit." Later, Rauschning remarked, "My own experience of him and what I have learned from others indicate a lack of control amounting to total demoralization. His shrieking and frenzied shouting, his stamping, his tempests of rage—all this was grotesque and unpleasant."[61] General Halder reported a similar experience, one that supports Rauschning's observation, noting that when Hitler "went off the deep end, he was no longer a rational being . . . he foamed at the mouth and threatened me with his fists, any rational discussion was out of the question."[62] This behavior shows a lack of control, which on one hand made for a rather unstable and unpleasant person but on the other hand enabled him to easily slip into nondirected thinking, which tends to operate when consciousness is weak. In this way, what made Hitler seem inconsequential at best, and irrational at worst, was also at the root of his "gifts" as prophet and messiah. Taken as an individual away from the political stage, he could seem a nonentity; in front of his audience, he became whatever they, the disciples, projected onto him.

The journalist Dorothy Thompson had an interview with Hitler before his assumption of power. Her impression of Hitler's personality is pertinent in this regard:

When finally I walked into Adolph Hitler's salon in the *Kaiserhof* Hotel, I was convinced that I was meeting the future dictator of Germany. In something less than fifty seconds I was sure that I was not. It took just about that time to measure the startling insignificance of this man who has set the world agog. He is formless, almost faceless, a man whose countenance is a caricature, a man whose framework seems cartilaginous, without bones. He is inconsequential and voluble, ill-poised, insecure. He is the very proto-type of the Little Man.[63]

C. G. Jung had much the same reaction after seeing Hitler close-up: "When I saw him with my own eyes, he suggested a psychic scarecrow (with a broomstick for an outstretched arm) rather than a human being."[64] Hitler's lack of true personality or individuality thus imparted a chameleonlike nature that made him an empty vessel for the messianic projections of others. As Otto Strasser noted perceptively,

Hitler loses himself completely in a speech, forgets himself utterly. Thus, once he has determined the emotional and mental "vibrations" of his audience, the rest, for him, is easy. It is as though he could assume any character, any mental outlook, at will, living it completely during his oration.[65]

It is perhaps this lack of true individuality that led Hitler to identify with the messiah symbol as it arose from his unconscious. His followers tended to project the messiah symbol onto Hitler, whose ability to express the archetypal elements of the apocalypse complex made him seem to be their desired savior. This conjoining of selves, Hitler's and his loyal disciples, is what links the leader to the led. When the Nazi disciples listened to Hitler speaking, as Otto Strasser noted, "it was not the voice of Hitler speaking out to them; it was their own voice, the voice of Germany."[66] In other words, it was the voice of their collected selves.

A contemporary observer and supporter of Hitler explained that when he was speaking, he had the "power of making his audience feel that he is voicing their thoughts and speaking for them." A physician exhibited this experience when he stated that "the speaker's ideas were so thoroughly after my own heart, that he seemed, in fact, to be expressing my own thoughts and desires. I was swept off my feet, and I made up my mind to join the party without delay." Another man, previously apolitical, responded, "Much was touched upon that had long been in my subconscious mind, and was now called forth into consciousness. I went home deeply moved, thinking that if the aims and purposes outlined by the speaker were capable of achievement, then life would once more be worth living."[67] Similarly, many individuals reported that they were moved by Hitler because words came from the soul—his and theirs. One Old Guard Nazi, Otto Schiedermaier, recalled that "his comments at this time were as spoken from his soul, and acted upon me in such a way that I decided to become a loyal follower of Adolf Hitler. From then on no gathering was given that I did not attend."[68] As Putzi Hanfstängl put it, "He had the priceless gift of expressing exactly their own thoughts."[69] Franz Hemmrich, warden of Landsberg prison, remembered how Hitler's manner of speaking affected conversions. Hemmrich reported that he had to limit even his being around Hitler: "As a rule when I had to 'take' one of these visits, I made a point of having a paper on hand, in which, for appearance's sake, I could appear to immerse myself. Very often, though, I just used it to screen the intense interest I myself was feeling in the conversation. Hitler's way of putting things was not mere talking: he made you feel the point come right home: you yourself *experienced* every word."[70] Rauschning, for all his eventual distaste for Hitler, experienced much the same thing: "I must admit that in Hitler's company I had again and again come under a spell which I was only later able to shake off, a sort of hypnosis. . . . He is simply a sort of great medicine-man."[71] The hypnotic power that these individuals were experiencing was based as much on what they projected on to Hitler as it was on what he revealed to them through his rhetoric.

Accounts of personal encounters with Hitler, at speeches and at march-bys, reflect the fact that these individuals were having encounters with their own selves. As is common in such experiences, many Nazis felt Hitler and his "great idea" had instantaneously "addicted" or "seized" them. One man explained, "Whoever may see Adolf Hitler in the eyes one time is completely addicted and devoted to him and his idea, and there with, his Volk and his Fatherland, and even willing to sacrifice to the last and highest!"[72] Once again, the party rallies were particularly powerful experiences. Johannes Zehfuss, recalling the 1927 Party Day, stated that "there I saw the Führer at close range for the first time and was from this instant on completely addicted to him and his idea."[73] The experience of another convert reflects not only the sense of being possessed by something but also the reality-shattering nature of Hitler's new conception of existence. He stated that "whoever has the occasion to hear and see the Führer one time is seized by him and torn into pieces."[74] Another Nazi's conversion demonstrates the physical nature of the experience, something that reflects the somatic aspect of the archetypal encounter. He recalled that "on this evening I was permitted for the first time to grope for these earnest words and found out about National Socialism. Indeed, I had trembling in my legs, but from out of this rapturous feeling formed in my mouth the words 'faith' and 'loyalty' to Adolf Hitler."[75]

These experiences were so powerful that some individuals felt a loss of individuality as they gave up their selves to Hitler. One man found that after his first Hitler experience, "I belonged no more to myself, but to the movement." He explained further that "the idea seized us. It would not let us go. Therein lies the secret of our following and the victory of our movement."[76] In other words, the archetypal imagery of the apocalypse complex possessed this man and consequently impelled him to serve the movement. Psychologically, this may well have been the "secret" to the success of the movement. Such an experience, not surprisingly, was believed to be something deeply spiritual—an encounter of the soul. As Josef Richter remembered his first meeting with Hitler, "he greeted every single one of us and we saw in him to the foundation of his soul. It was a real experience, and since then I came to no other path and I joined the party that same day."[77]

Some Nazis, as was seen earlier, felt that Hitler had "awakened" something that was already within them. According to the Nazi elites, this was a deliberate process. Dietrich Eckart's phrase "Germany Awake" was meant literally. The truth, the gnosis of race, was slumbering in the souls of all Aryans and needed only to be awakened or brought to consciousness. The Nazis aimed to raise race consciousness, as opposed to the class consciousness of Marxist millennialism. The rhetorical content of speeches, the symbolic rituals of the party rallies, the songs, the art and architecture, all were meant to awaken race consciousness, which the Nazis interpreted in millennial forms. These Nazi converts were experiencing an encounter with an archetypal element to which Hitler had given voice and that had, according to one early Nazi, "awakened" unconscious "sympathies."[78] The account of the following man demonstrates this process, as well as the psychological restructuring that occurs through the symbolism of the apocalypse complex:

what the Führer had spoken there was what was not perceptible to us, yet had slumbered in our souls all along. Now so much discord, which had unfolded in me, broke apart, and with an unparalleled feeling of good fortune, I perceived the truth of the idea preached by Hitler.[79]

Other individuals felt as if Hitler had implanted something in them, almost as if against their will. Paul Then, an Old Guard Nazi, remarked that "his speech was as though he implanted his idea in me. I would have retained him and his idea within me even if I had no longer caught a glimpse of him."[80] This sense of having had something implanted, of having been penetrated from without, was an emotionally overwhelming experience. Georg Schorbach, who had been asked to act as stenographer for a Hitler speech, recalled that "I was also penetrated by the words of the Führer, which for the first time in a hour so gripped and so overwhelmed me that I no could longer keep my eyes off him and thought no more of my stenography."[81] Heinz Hermann Horn's account of his conversion likewise betrays not only the depth of the emotions felt but the oft-mentioned "hypnotizing" effect of the experience:

> I no longer knew what he spoke about. I only knew that I scarcely dared to breath, I was completely seized in a spell by the person of the Führer. And then when he had finished, again this jubilation, an enthusiasm like no one had ever been acquainted with before. This was fanatical veneration, like the will of complete devotion.[82]

Whether the idea was awakened within or implanted from without, the effect was that the individual was possessed by Hitler and his "great idea"—both symbolic expressions of the apocalypse complex.

It was perhaps for this reason that meeting Hitler in person was, for many individuals, an ineffable experience. In meeting Hitler face to face, these converts were meeting their own selves projected onto him. Willi Schondorff, recalling Hitler's review of the SA, noted,

> A brief instant in the eyes of the individual, an instant which tries the heart and the reins of each of us. Then a powerful handshake and on to the next man. I perceived this handshake of the Führer's as the taking of a pledge of loyalty, which we have maintained until the last. This half hour is for me among the most beautiful and most unforgettable of a great series of experiences from the struggle years and will remain unforgettable in memory.[83]

Adalbert Gimbel described a similar experience: "This handshake and the eye-to-eye with the Führer gave us such an inner strength that one can scarcely clothe it in words." Using similar phrasing, another man found that "it is impossible to cloth in words this experience. We experienced such strength through the Führer's words that, now more than ever, we could draw from new, unexpected powers to struggle again for the German Freedom movement." Another recalled that "this instant has been for me an experience so great that I cannot describe it with words." Heinz Schmidt, recalling the Weimar Party Day of 1925, stated that "the days in Weimar have remained unforgettable for us all, especially, however, the instant where we were permitted to behold the Führer Adolf Hitler in the eyes and vowed with the hand to be loyal to him until death."

One party member, Hermann Jung, found such a "one-to-one" encounter with his savior Hitler to be a unifying experience, reflecting something akin to the mystical union felt by the medieval visionary. In this case, however, it is not the mystic's union with God but the Nazis' union with the messianic Führer and his beloved Volk: "that was the most beautiful instant, to be able to stand up against our Führer eye to eye. It was a splendor, and these seconds, with their unspoken speech revealed in the eyes, will be for me be an eternal reminder that we are welded together . . . in success or adversity, and that no one will break us."[84] Indeed, Andreas Dees found the Hitler experience so transforming that his faith in Hitler replaced his belief in traditional religion. He stated that "In religion I am a Catholic. Then I heard the Führer. What occurred inside me, alas, I cannot describe. Then I knew, however, the Man and his movement and nothing else."[85]

Finally, the conjoining of selves, Hitler's and his followers, is reflected in Hitler's identification with his people and their identification with him. In a speech of 1932, Hitler exclaimed, "That is the miracle of our time, that you have found me—that among so many millions you have found me! And that I have found you! That is Germany's fortune."[86] Hitler went so far as to link this identification with the masses with his personal identification with Jesus, paraphrasing Jesus in a speech, saying, "I belong to you and you belong to me." This mixing of self-identifications continued after his assumption of state power. In a 1935 speech, Hitler again identified with both Christ and Volk and again paraphrased the Gospels, saying,

My will—that must be our total creed—is our belief; my belief is to me—exactly as to you—everything in this world! But the highest thing that God has given me in this world is my Volk! In it rests my faith. I serve it with my will, and I give it my life. . . . Just as I am yours, so are you mine. So long as I live, I belong to you and you belong to me![87]

As early as 1924, Georg Schott wrote of Hitler, "He embodies the longing of the nation. That is how Adolf Hitler appears: the living embodiment of the longing of the nation."[88] Rudolf Hess closed his 1934 party speech in the film *Triumph of the Will* with the proclamation, "The party is Hitler, but Hitler is Germany, just as Germany is Hitler." Goebbels promoted a similar idea, saying in a 1935 birthday eulogy to Hitler, "The entire people is devoted to him not only with reverence but with deep, heartfelt love, because it has the feeling that it belongs to him, flesh from his flesh, and spirit from his spirit."[89] In a similar fashion, a Nazi writer explained that "we became one Volk under Adolf Hitler's leadership, Germany's awakener. I belong to you and you to me."[90] Once again, this is more than simple propaganda; the Old Guard narratives demonstrate that this identification between leader and led was powerful and profound. The conjoining of selves, Hitler's and his disciples', provided a shared sense of mission, purpose, destiny. It also provided the sense of unity so central to an experience of the apocalypse complex. The only question for the Nazi movement was whether this sense of unity could be extended to the entire nation.

Hitler's general lack of self control gave him a greater than usual proclivity for nondirected thinking and, therefore, access to archetypal imagery. Hitler's oratorical skills gave him the means to express this archetypal material and in this way to give voice to the collective longings of the German people. The psychological constitution that gave Hitler a proclivity for nondirected thinking and ready access to the symbolic world of the nonrational mind also made him more acceptable as a messiah as he gave form to the archetypal impulse for order and harmony that swelled up from the depths of his admirers' being. Many Germans and non-Germans consequently accepted Hitler's messianic self-perception, his role as both prophet and messiah, interpreting him as a Christ or Godlike figure, sent from heaven to save Germany from utter annihilation.

The relationship between messiah-prophet and loyal disciple is crucial, not only for the legitimation of the messianic pretensions of the former but also for the creation of any apocalyptic movement. For an individual cannot play the role of messiah-prophet without an audience, and without the actor, there is no performance for the audience to follow. Hitler's individual psychology, therefore, was perfectly suited to play the role of messiah and, consequently, to fulfill the psychic needs of a lost generation. Messiah and believers came together, and, with Hitler's assumption of power, on January 30, 1933, the millennial New Age of millennial perfection, the Thousand-Year Reich, was set to begin. But would racial unity be enough to bring salvation, or would the eternal Evil Other, the Jew, need to be dealt with once and for all?

6

Final Empire,
Final War, Final Solution

Lucy Dawidowicz, in *The War against the Jews*, made the following perceptive comment regarding the Nazi conceptualization of the Final Solution: "'Final' reverberates with apocalyptic promise, bespeaking the Last
Judgment, the End of Days, the last destruction before salvation, Armageddon. 'The Final Solution of the Jewish Question' in the National
Socialist conception was not just another anti-Semitic undertaking, but a
metahistorical program devised with an eschatological perspective. It was
part of a salvational ideology that envisaged the attainment of Heaven by
bringing Hell on earth."[1] The same can be said for the Nazi use of the
terms *Endkampf* (Final Battle), *Endsieg* (Final Victory) and the conception of the Third Reich as the *Endreich* (Final Empire), the empire of millennial perfection that would come into being if, and only if, the eschatological struggle between Aryans and Jews reached a definitive conclusion.
Nazi anti-Semitism was conceived, as Saul Friedländer has noted, as an
essentially redemptive enterprise.[2]

As we saw earlier, this linkage of a coming Final War against so-called
Jewish Bolshevism with the subsequent extermination of the Jews was
nothing new for Hitler. From the early 1920s, Hitler and his inner circle
had conceived of the Nazi movement as one day creating a millennial
Reich that was envisaged as a racially pure world empire led by the Nazis
themselves. It was a world that could not be fully realized until a final battle against the demonic force of Jewish Bolshevism had been won, once
and for all. In the apocalyptic atmosphere of postwar Munich, the Thule
Society created the German Worker's Party specifically to attract workers
away from the communist movement (identified as Jewish Bolshevik).
The loss of the war and the seemingly deliberate chaos that followed,
combined with the wide release of *The Protocols of the Elders of Zion*

(which was itself received as an apocalyptic tract), all seemed to indicate that the Jews, the Nazi conception of the Evil Other, were making a final push at world domination. A Jewish-dominated world was conceived as a countermillennium that would ultimately end in the extermination of humanity.

When Hitler and his closest associates (Eckart, Hess, Rosenberg, Feder, Streicher, and Hans Frank, all millennialists associated to some degree with the Thule Society) took over the renamed National Socialist German Worker's Party, they believed that salvation could come about only through the extermination of the Jewish race. Hitler's earliest known political statement, the Gemlich letter of 1919, associated Germany's rebirth and salvation with the "total removal of the Jews from our midst." As early as 1922, this "removal" of the Jews was taken to be but a step to eventual extermination. This is evident in the account of Josef Hell, who recalled Hitler stating that "if I one day actually come to power, then the extermination of the Jews will be my first and most important task."[3] Hitler, in a speech that same year, prophesied that the struggle between Aryans and Jews could end in "either victory of the Aryans or its annihilation and victory of the Jews."[4] As Julius Streicher's most utilized catchphrase puts it, there could be "no salvation without a solution to the Jewish Question." And this salvation could come only with a "final" solution to that question. This early formulation of a coming final battle between Aryans and Jews, interpreted as the forces of light and good versus the forces of darkness and evil, was always conceived as resulting in the extermination of one side or the other. The Final Solution, even if the phrase had yet to be employed, was an eschatological conception from the beginning.

It was this eschatological perspective that led the Nazis to conclude that humanity had reached a historic turning point that could lead only to salvation, envisioned as the millennial Third and Final Reich, or apocalypse, conceived as the extermination of humanity. The Nazis saw themselves as divinely chosen to prevent the latter through a twofold mission. First, after achieving power, they were to purify the Aryan race through employment of racial hygiene measures. This would strengthen the race and better prepare it for the coming final war of extermination against the Jewish Bolsheviks that would simultaneously acquire for Germany the living space necessary for achieving the millennial Reich. Second, they were to remove the Jews from positions of power within Germany and then defeat them in that final war. Within the logic of apocalyptic thinking, this final war of extermination had to occur within Hitler's lifetime, as he was the chosen anti-Semitic savior who would lead the Aryans to victory. If not, the Jewish Bolsheviks would win, and humanity would be doomed to extinction.

Of course, the realization of this part of the millennial myth was not possible in the early 1920s. But events in the 1930s and early 1940s would provide Hitler and the Nazis with exactly the opportunity necessary to induce the apocalyptic war of salvation. By saying this, I do not mean to imply that the road to the Final Solution was not twisted, that the Holocaust was a foregone conclusion. I mean to point out only that when one believes that an apocalyptic scenario is destined to occur and that one is part of a divine plan to help realize that scenario, then, quite often, as the history of millennial movements demonstrates, one finds some way to induce that apocalyptic event. Hitler believed that the turning point had arrived and that the "final showdown," as he put it, between the Aryans and the Jews must occur in his lifetime.[5]

The Coming War of Extermination

The conspiratorial history presented in Dietrich Eckart's 1924 work, *Bolshevism from Moses to Lenin,* with its apocalyptic rhetoric, biblical allusions, and talk of an imminent eschatological war of extermination, continued to appear in Nazi propaganda after the Nazi assumption of power. While the immediate postwar chaos of Weimar, combined with the growing threat of a Bolshevik-style revolution and the sudden appearance of the *Protocols of the Elders of Zion,* seemed to mean that the eschatological turning point had arrived in the early 1920s, the prophesied war of extermination never occurred. The depression and the escalating tension between Nazis and communists during the elections of the early 1930s once again brought the specter of an imminent racial Armageddon to the forefront. For some minor Nazis, the initial successes of the Third Reich made the notion of a Final War less pertinent, but, for Hitler and his inner circle, the crucial time was now, for the Final War had to occur in their lifetimes.

After assuming power, the Nazis continued to present the Aryan-Jewish struggle in apocalyptic terms. Often, Nazi apocalyptic anti-Semitic rhetoric was timed to coincide with significant anti-Jewish legislation or action. A handbill advertising a special issue of Julius Streicher's *Der*

Stürmer, published in conjunction with the 1935 Party Day and the subsequent promulgation of the Nuremberg Laws, which began the process of separating German Jews from Aryan Germans, set the legislation in the context of the eschatological Aryan-Jewish battle. Not surprisingly, the handbill used analogies similar to those found in Eckart's *Bolshevism from Moses to Lenin.* It asked a series of questions: "What is the secret of the world revolution?," "What is the secret of the November Revolution?," "What is the secret of the Soviet Revolution?," "What is the end of this world revolution?," "Who will be dominate in the world?" Then, as in *Bolshevism from Moses to Lenin,* the handbill referred to the supposed nefarious work of Jews in ancient Persia, Egypt, and Rome. It concluded, "The public now for the first time sees the Jews as world revolutionaries and mass murders."[6] The Nuremberg Laws were here presented as a countermeasure to the alleged Jewish push for world domination, which the Nazis believed could end only in human extermination. The first major step toward the final showdown, as Hitler had called it, had been taken.

At the Party Congress of 1936, Goebbels gave a speech titled "Bolshevism in Theory and Practice." Attempting to shed light on the Spanish Civil War, Goebbels characterized Bolshevism as "a pathological, criminal madness . . . invented by Jews with the goal being the annihilation of European people of culture." This goal would be achieved through the "radicalization, anarchinization and Bolshevization of all the peoples of the earth." The Spanish Civil War was interpreted in millennial fashion by the Nazis, conceived as another step in the Jewish grand design for world domination and consequently as another sign that the eschatological turning point had arrived. Goebbels then returned to the theme of Jewish Bolshevism as a satanic force of destruction, saying that "the idea of Bolshevism, that is, the unscrupulous degeneration and decomposition of all morals and culture with the diabolical aim being the annihilation of peoples altogether, could only have been born in the brain of Jews. The Bolshevik practice in its horrible and blood-dripping cruelty is imaginable only by the hands of Jews."[7]

The image of the satanic, world-destroying Jew would reappear in Goebbels's Party Congress speech the following year. Again responding to the Spanish Civil War, Goebbels divided the conflict along two extremes, with one side, Bolshevism, representing "destruction and anarchy" and the other side, authority (meaning fascism), standing for "order and organization." With Bolshevism, Goebbels claimed, the Jews obtained for themselves "in reality the incarnation of everything evil." Consequently, Spain would be another Russia, with peasants "packed together in soul-less collectives." Goebbels argued that the Spanish Civil War was just another domino in the Jewish-Bolshevik march to apocalypse, saying, "as Spain goes, so too the entire world." Spain, therefore, represented the "initiation" of "Bolshevik world domination," as alluded to in *Bolshevism from Moses to Lenin.*

Since Bolshevik Russia had not really led to the apocalypse as prophesied in the early 1920s, the Nazis, like many disappointed apocalyptic prophets, simply restarted the Endtime clock, now viewing Spain as the beginning of the End. Not surprisingly, as Eckart and Hitler had said allegedly happened in ancient Egypt, Persia, and during the French and Russian Revolutions, Goebbels found the eternal enemy behind the Spanish conflict: "Undaunted, we want to point the finger at the Jew as the inspirer, the originator, and the beneficiary of this terrible catastrophe: look, this is the enemy of the world, the destroyer of cultures, the parasite among the peoples, the Son of Chaos, the incarnation of evil, the ferment of decomposition, the plastic demon of the decay of humanity."[8] The Evil Other had surfaced again.

This apocalyptic rhetoric increased as the Nazis moved closer to the Final War for which they were actively preparing. Speaking on November 11, 1938, the day after *Kristallnacht*, the Nazi-organized riots against Jews in revenge for the murder of Ernst von Rath, secretary of the German Embassy in Paris, Himmler spoke to the officers of SS-Standarte "Deutschland." He explained,

> we must be clear to ourselves that in the next ten years we are heading for an unprecedented altercation of a critical type. It is not simply a battle of nations . . . rather it is an ideological battle against the collected Jews, Freemasons, Marxists and Churches of the world. These powers are clear to themselves—whereby I consider the Jews the driving force, as the primal substance of everything negative—then, if Germany and Italy are not to be exterminated, they will be exterminated. That is the simple conclusion. In Germany the Jew cannot remain.[9]

As with Hitler in the early 1920s, removal and extermination were apparently linked eschatological concepts in Himmler's rendering of the coming Final War. Two weeks later, the SS journal *Das Schwarze Korps* reiterated Himmler's statement that Jews could no longer live in Germany. That this presaged more than mere deportation was made abundantly clear: "This stage of development will impose on us the vital necessity to exterminate this Jewish subhumanity, as we exterminate all criminals in our ordered country: by the fire and the sword! The outcome will be the final catastrophe for Jewry in Germany—its total extermination!"[10]

Earlier in the year, Karl Holz, editor of *Der Stürmer,* had written a piece in response to the alleged "Jewish Propaganda war against Germany" of July 1938, a campaign that was in actuality had been initiated by the world's negative reaction to Germany's increasing expansionist tendencies and anti-Semitic activities. Holz, however, concluded that the negative publicity was cunningly calculated to force the remaining Jews out of Germany, thus opening the way for a foreign bombing war of extermination against Germany. Holz wrote,

> that is also the goal and the hope of the Jews in Germany. They devise that they are about to break loose revenge on this land. First they want to leave it. Then, when there no longer are any Jews there, then it [Germany] will be annihilated from the air. Then it will be transformed by bombers into a field of corpses and ruins. It will come, on the contrary, to the opposite. The great vengeance will come upon the Jewish Volk. The vengeance of fate. The vengeance of righteousness. The vengeance of the tortured, non-Jewish peoples. This vengeance will one day break loose and will destroy every Jew on this earth.[11]

In this way, Nazi expansionism and the threat of foreign intervention were transformed into a counterthreat to exterminate the Jews with the righteous vengeance of the Old Testament Yahweh. This inversion of reality typifies the Nazi millennial mentality, and, as will be seen shortly, it became a coping and rationalizing mechanism for German soldiers in World War II, as well.

As world war dawned, Walter Frank, director of the Reich Institute of History, made a two-part radio address, on January 11 and 13, 1939, titled "German Science in Its Struggle against World Jewry." After noting that anti-Semitic parties and groups of the nineteenth century "ran aground" because they never united around a "great general concept," so scientific research on the Jewish question was "frustrated" because it too had "separated itself from the totality of national and world history." What needed to be realized, according to Frank, was that, as "Jewry is one of the great negative principles of world history, it is also only conceivable as a parasite within its opposing positive principle." Thus, Jews were conceived, typically for the Nazis, as a negative force living parasitically within a positive host. Frank then combined this bit of anti-Semitic pseudo-science with a more traditional Christian anti-Semitism that labeled the Jews Christ-killers:

> thus as little as Judas Iscariot, with his thirty silver shekels and the rope with which he ultimately hanged himself, cannot be understood without the Lord whose community he scorned—but whose visage pursued him until the final hour; that dark side of history called Jewry cannot be understood without being arranged within the totality of a historical process in which God and Satan, creation and destruction, lie in an eternal struggle.[12]

According to the leading Nazi historian, the eternal force of evil had been unmasked, and all that was left was a final confrontation. With the new year of 1939, beginning with escalating tensions and talk of war and extermination, it was time for the German messiah himself to speak.

Hitler's Prophecy of Extermination: From Myth to Reality

On January 30, 1939, Hitler gave his yearly speech to the Reichstag commemorating his assumption of power and, with it, the dawn of the millennial Third and Final Reich. He assumed his role as Endtime prophet, proclaiming,

> Quite often in my life I have been known as a prophet and was mostly laughed at. In the time of my struggle for power it was primarily the Jewish people who responded to my prophecies with laughter. I then took over the leadership of the state in Germany and thereby the entire Volk and then, among many other things, would bring a solution to the Jewish problem. I believe that the ringing laughter of Jewry in Germany meanwhile is now stuck in their throats.
>
> I will today again be a prophet: if international finance Jewry within and without Europe should succeed in plunging the peoples yet once again in a world war, then it will result not in the Bolshevization of the

earth and thereby the victory of Jewry, but rather the extermination of the Jewish race in Europe.[13]

The linking of Bolshevism with the Jews and the prophecy of a coming war that would result in the extermination of the Jews is extremely significant. Hitler would return to this prophecy a number of times during the course of the war. Importantly, Hitler, and various Nazi publications misdated the prophecy to September 1, 1939, when the Nazis invaded Poland and began the Second World War. The final struggle against the Jews was therefore inextricably tied to what was termed the *Endkrieg,* the final war itself, for it was conceived as part of the same conflict.[14] The 1939 extermination prophecy is simply a restatement of the apocalyptic formulation of the coming Final War between Aryans and Jews that Hitler and Nazis had prophesied since the early 1920s. Salvation of the Aryan race was always linked to the extermination of Jewish Bolshevism and, consequently, every Jew on earth. Having seemingly secured the west by the summer of 1940, the coming war in the east against the Soviet Union made this scenario possible.

Speaking on January 30, 1941, on the two-year anniversary of his extermination prophecy, and again misdating the speech to September 1, 1939, Hitler stated,

> And I would not want to forget the remark which I had already given at the time, on September 1, 1939, in the German Reichstag. Namely, the remark that if the world would be plunged into an all-out war by Jewry, then collected Jewry will have played out its role in Europe!
>
> They might also still laugh about it today, as they had earlier regarding my prophecies. The coming months and years will demonstrate that I will be seen to have been correct here as well. Already now our race-conscious Volk understands about this people, and I hope that also those who today still stand against us in enmity will one day understand about the greatest inner enemy, and that they will then join with us in a Front.[15]

Hitler's references to an "all-out war" and to the fulfillment of his extermination prophecy in the "coming months and years" indicate that, at least in Hitler's mind, the imminent launching of an all-out or total war against the Soviets, was intimately linked to the coming extermination of the Jews. In part, the eastern war was conceived as something entirely different from the war in the west, which was seen by Hitler as an unfortunate conflict between Aryan brothers. Unlike the war in the west, the war in the east was conceived as both an "ideological war" (*Weltanschauungskrieg*) and a war of extermination (*Vernichtungskrieg*). The two concepts were intricately and inextricably related.[16] Earlier, on February 10, 1939, Hitler had told army commanders that the next war would be "strictly ideological, that is, a deliberately racial war."[17] Hitler was referring not to the war in the west but to the eventual war in the east, later initiated by Operation Barbarossa, conceived as a war against Slavs and Jews.

The connection of ideology, race, and a war of extermination is significant and goes back to the First World War. The historian Michael Geyer makes the important observation that when the German Supreme Command began to see World War I as a "total war," one that involved a struggle between opposing racial and cultural forces, it became an apocalyptic war of survival: "War became truly total once it was seen as an ideological and cultural clash (*Kulturkrieg*) between mobilized nations whose goal was national-racial survival through the subordination of other nations."[18] As the German war effort began to collapse, the Supreme Command more and more began to accept the conspiratorial ideas of the volkish right wing, blaming homosexuals, workers, and especially Jews for that collapse. Consequently, the war began to transform into an apocalyptic struggle. As Geyer states, "Radical nationalists lost interest in even the most ambitious territorial goals as the war became for them a struggle for the liberation of the German race from evil. Germany began to cross over into an apocalyptic war."[19] After the war, the belief that Germany was still in the midst of, and perhaps losing, a racial struggle of apocalyptic proportions (against what were variously described as "Asiatic hordes" and/or "Jewish Bolsheviks") continued. Geyer concludes that the war against the Jewish Bolsheviks that was unleashed in 1941 seemed to be a realization of this vision: "Between 1941 and 1943, the apocalyptic vision of war became strategic reality in the East."[20]

It is important to understand that the notion of a war between *Weltanschauungen*, which means, literally, "world views" but is usually translated somewhat misleadingly as "ideologies," means more than a battle of political ideas (in this case Nazism versus Bolshevism or communism). It was a battle of diametrically opposed world views, conceived as cultural and spiritual forces rooted immutably in two conflicting races, one divinely inspired and constructive, the other demonic and destructive. They were mutually exclusive and, now, with Operation Barbarossa, were locked in that final battle that Hitler had always prophesied.

That the coming eastern campaign was to be the true war of extermination, one clearly interpreted in apocalyptic terms, is seen in Hitler's orders for the conduct of this new stage of the war. On the verge of launching the Russian campaign, Hitler explained to his generals the reasons for and the objectives of the coming "colonial tasks" (from notes made by General Halder on March 30, 1941):

> Two world views battle one another. Annihilating judgment over Bolshevism, the same asocial criminality. Communism immense danger for the future. We must move away from the standpoint of soldierly camaraderie. The communist is not a comrade before and is not a comrade after. It is a question of a war of extermination. If we do not grasp this, we will still beat the enemy, but in thirty years we will face the communist enemy again. We conduct this war not to conserve the enemy. . . .
>
> Struggle against Russia: extermination of the Bolshevistic Commissars and the communist intelligentsia. The new states must be socialistic states, but without its own intelligentsia. That a new intelligentsia reconstitutes itself must be prevented. Here a primitive socialist intelligentsia is enough. The struggle must be waged against the poison of decomposition [Nazi euphemism for the Jews].
>
> That is not a question of the rules of war.[21]

This conception of the eastern campaign as an apocalyptic war of extermination was subsequently put forth in propaganda aimed at the troops. A pamphlet titled "Germany in the Final Battle with the Jewish-Bolshevik Murder-System," given to propaganda officers as part of the 1941 information campaign "Führer Commands, We Follow," included this solemn proclamation by Hitler to his soldiers (the information officers were told to "push this"): "As we at this time enter upon this greatest Front in world history, then it takes place not only on the supposition that it will produce the final settlement of the great war, or to protect the at-present bewildered countries [the newly conquered territories], but rather to save the entire European civilization and culture." The soon-to-be-launched eastern war was presented as an eschatological struggle to save the world. The pamphlet continued, characterizing Bolshevism, "the demonic invention of our time," in this way:

This system of chaos, extermination, and terror was invented by Jews and is led by Jews. It is the action of the Jewish race. World Jewry attempts through subversion and propaganda to bring together the uprooted and lesser race elements to accomplish this war of extermination against everything positive, against nationality and nation, against religion and culture, against order and morality. The aim is the production of chaos through world revolution and the establishment of a world state under Jewish leadership.[22]

Another news sheet for the troops, titled "Salvation from the Gravest Danger," presented the Russian enemy as a demonic host controlled by satanic Jews, a visage part Revelation, part *Der Stürmer,* part *Bolshevism from Moses to Lenin:*

Anyone who has glanced at the face of a Red commissar at once knows what the Bolsheviks are like. Here theoretical discussions are no longer necessary. It would insult the animals if we called these, to a high percent, Jewish slave-drivers beasts. They are the embodiment of the infernal and insane hatred against all noble humanity. In the form of this commissar we experience the revolt of sub-humanity against noble blood. The masses, whom they drive to their deaths with every means, such as ice-cold terror and imbecilic incitement, would have brought the end of all significant life, had this collapse not been thwarted at the last hour.[23]

The apocalyptic war of extermination was not only promulgated to the soldiers through Nazi propaganda. Wehrmacht officers did their part, translating Hitler's earlier conception of the eastern war into their own apocalyptic construction. On May 2, 1941, Panzer Group 4 commander Colonel-General Erich Hoepner not only described the coming eastern war in apocalyptic terms but also used the war's eschatological significance to call for the utmost barbarity—to counter the perceived threat of extermination with a "total extermination of the enemy":

The war against the Soviet Union is an essential component of the German people's struggle for existence. It is the old struggle of the Germans against the Slavs, the defense of European culture against the Muscovite-Asiatic flood, the warding off of Jewish Bolshevism. This struggle must have as its aim the demolition of present Russia and must therefore be conducted with unprecedented severity. Both the planning and the execution of every battle must be dictated by an iron will to bring about a merciless, total extermination of the enemy. Particularly no mercy should be shown toward the carriers of the present Russian-Bolsheviks system [again referring to the Jews].[24]

On October 10, 1941, as the battles raged and with the *Blitzkrieg* having failed, Walter von Reichenau, commander of the Sixth Army, explained to his troops the proper conduct for treating the enemy:

Concerning the conduct of the troops vis-à-vis the Bolshevik system, many as yet unclear conceptions still persist. The essential goal of the campaign against the Jewish-Bolshevik system is the complete smashing of the means of power and the extermination of the Asiatic influence in the European culture circle.

Due to this fact tasks emerge for the troops which transcend the usual military tradition [literally, soldierliness]. The soldier in the Eastern realm is not only a fighter according to the rules of military science, but also is a bearer of an inexorable volkish idea and an avenger for all the bestialities which have been inflicted on the Germans and kindred peoples.

For this reason the soldier must have complete understanding of the necessity for the harsh, yet just atonement of the Jewish sub-humans. This has a further goal—to nip in the bud rebellions in the rear of the Wehrmacht, which experience shows have always been hatched by Jews.[25]

In conclusion, von Reichenau issued the following order:

Beyond future political considerations the soldier has two things to fulfill:
(1) the complete extermination of Bolshevistic false teachings, the Soviet state and its army, (2) the merciless extermination of foreign treachery and atrocity and therewith acheive [*sic*] the security of the lives of the German Wehrmacht in Russia.

Only thus will we satisfy our historical task, to liberate the German Volk from the Asiatic-Jewish danger once and for all.[26]

In von Reichenau's conception, then, the eastern war was an eschatological racial war that could end only with the extermination of Jewish Bolshevism and its alleged progenitors, the Jews, for all eternity.

A little over a month later, on November 20, 1941, with the war now spiraling into an abyss, General Erich von Manstein, commander of the Eleventh Army, using Reichenau's order as a model, made the following declaration:

> Since June 22 the German Volk stands in a life-and-death struggle against the Bolshevik system. This struggle will not be guided by conventional forms against the Soviet army solely according to European rules of war. We also fight behind the front. . . . Jewry constitutes the middleman between the enemy in the rear and the still fighting remnants of the Red Army and the Red leadership. It holds more strongly than in the rest of Europe all the key points of political leadership and administration, commerce and trade, and further constitutes the cells of all unrest and possible rebellion.
>
> The Jewish-Bolshevik system must be exterminated once and for all. Never again should it interfere in our European living space. The German soldier therefore not only has the task to destroy the military means of power of the system; he also marches as a bearer of a volkish idea and an avenger for all atrocities which have been inflicted upon him and the German Volk. . . .
>
> The soldier must be brought to an understanding of the necessity for the harsh atonement to Jewry, the spiritual bearer of Bolshevik Terror. This is also necessary to nip in the bud all rebellions, most of which have been hatched by Jews.[27]

Five days later, on November 25, 1941, Colonel-General Hermann Hoth, commander of the Seventeenth Army, analyzed the world-historical importance of the battle between the German and the Asiatic-Jewish peoples. He concluded with a thoroughly millennial and apocalyptic flourish:

> It has become increasingly clear to us this summer that here in the East spiritually irreconcilable conceptions struggle against one another: German feeling for honor and race, centuries-old soldierly tradition, versus an Asiatic way of thinking and its primitive instincts—whipped up by a small number of mostly Jewish intellectuals: fear of the *knout* [terrorism], leveling down and the jettisoning of one's worthless life.
>
> Stronger than ever we bear in us thoughts of a turning point in which the German Volk is transferred power because of the superiority of its

race and its attainment of the leadership of Europe. We clearly perceive our mission, to save European culture from the advance of Asiatic barbarity. We now know that we have to struggle against an embittered and tenacious enemy. This struggle can only end with the extermination of one or the other; there is no compromise.

Hoth further argued that, in dealing with the Soviet populace, "pity and softness" should be avoided and called instead for the "necessity of harsh measures against racial [Volk] and foreign elements." He concluded that "Russia is not a European land but an Asiatic state. Any step in this joyless, subjugated land teaches us this distinction. Europe and especially Germany must be made free for all time from this burden and from the destroying powers of Bolshevism."[28] Here Hoth encapsulates the now-two-decade-old Nazi millennial myth—that the world had arrived at a historic turning point that imparted a divine mission of world salvation to the Aryan soldier. Only extermination of one side or the other can result. An Aryan victory would ensure the millennial Reich; a victory by the Jewish Bolsheviks would bring certain apocalypse. That the war was in fact going quite poorly at the time this order was given, with mounting causalities among soldiers and civilians alike as ferocious battles raged like something out of Revelation, appeared to be a realization of the millennial myth and, at the same time, a fulfillment of Hitler's extermination prophecy.

Therefore, with the invasion of Russia, Hitler's long-prophesied "final showdown" between Nazism and Jewish Bolshevism had truly begun. As the war in the east was about to be launched, Goebbels noted in his diary that "everything has been accomplished" and that "nothing more" remained but to attack the Jewish Bolsheviks "so that this cancer . . . can be burned out." Significantly, he added, "What we have been fighting against our whole lives is now about to be eradicated."[29] The apocalyptic extermination orders concerning the treatment of Soviet commissars and partisans (including all Jews in the Soviet territories) quoted earlier were quickly carried out with determined ruthlessness. Beginning precisely with the invasion of June 1941, mass killings by the *Einsatzgruppen* (Action Groups) began; these escalated in late July and early August, starting with all male Jews of military age and then expanding to include women and children in August and September 1941, and entire communities in September and October 1941. Nearly one million Jews were dead in the first five months of the *Ostkrieg*, which rapidly became the embodiment of the *Endkrieg*, the Final War.

Could the eschatological imagery imbedded in these orders simply reflect rhetorical licence, designed to motivate the troops and nothing else? Perhaps; however, such pronouncements followed exactly the historical and social perceptions held by the Nazis since the beginning of the movement. They followed Hitler's war prophesy and his extermination directives for that war. They followed Nazi propaganda sheets read to the troops. Hitler's prophesied war of extermination, therefore, seemed to have been fulfilled. More important, the message got through to the troops. Most of the soldiers of the *Einsatzgruppen* as well as the Wehrmacht grew up in the Nazi millennial Reich. Their school books and other cultural media continually prepared them for the coming war against the Jewish Evil Other and their subhuman foot soldiers—all in service of their heaven-sent savior, Adolf Hitler. The apocalyptic propaganda continued throughout the war, coming, as was seen, from both the Nazis and their own officers. We have only to look to the letters of soldiers in the *Einsatzgruppen* and in the Wehrmacht to see that the millennial vision of evil Jewish Bolsheviks and their minions, the Russian subhumans, locked in apocalyptic battle with Germany, the force of order, was accepted by many of those charged with fighting the final war.

Writing to his wife in September 1942, Karl Kretschmer, a member of *Einsatzkommando* (Special Detachment) 4a, conceptualized the war as a battle with Jewry for the existence of the German race:

We are fighting this war today for the very existence of our Volk. Thank God that you in the homeland do not feel too much of it. The bombing raids, however, have shown what the enemy has in store for us if he had the power. Those at the front experience it at every turn. My comrades literally are fighting for the existence of our Volk. They are doing the same that the enemy would do [to us]. I believe that you understand me. Because this in our view is a Jewish war, the Jews are primarily bearing the brunt of it. In Russia, wherever there is a German soldier, the Jews are no more.[30]

Another *Einsatzkommando,* in an interrogation that took place in 1962, attempted to justify his actions by blaming the Nazi prewar demonization of the Jews, noting that the millennial peace could be achieved only through the extermination of the Jews. He explained that "it was hammered into us, during the years of propaganda, again and again, that the Jews were the ruin of every Volk in the midst of which they appear, and that peace would reign in Europe only then, when the Jewish race is ex-terminated. No one could entirely escape this propaganda."[31] Like other German soldiers, he found that the Nazi demonization of the Jewish Bol-sheviks was confirmed by "much of what we experienced in Russia."[32]

Wehrmacht soldiers might be considered to have been less susceptible to the millennial fantasy than the soldiers of the SS, but this was not the case. In July 1941, Frederich Fallnbigl, a private, wrote to his parents, de-scribing the Soviet regime that had "wanted to bring us culture":

> Now I know first hand what war really means. I also know however that we are forced into this struggle against the Soviet Union. For God have mercy on us, for if we had waited, or if these beasts had come to us. For them the most gruesome death is too beautiful. I am fortunate, therefore, that I should be here to put a stop to the handiwork of this genocidal system [*völkervernictenden*].[33]

Captain Hans Kondruss wrote to his local party leader about what he had seen at the city of Lemberg. He said that he had found the scenes of horror worse than anything he had seen in World War I, at Verdun or Reims, or in Flanders. Those horrors, he felt, resulted from the "imper-sonal" nature of the war, leading to "a type of natural catastrophe." This war, however, was different, for here the horrors were created by "beast-men in a blood-frenzy." He explained further, in a manner reminiscent of *Bolshevism from Moses to Lenin*:

> Never in the history of peoples have such horrors been seen, had the an-imal in man been so revealed as here. The realization that humans could be so degenerate is unsettling to be sure. Surely there are among all peo-ples a sub-humanity that find a hiding place in the Great States. They are a symptom of decay, whose numbers depend on the constitution of a people. There will always be bestial creatures, in spite of all the most scrupulous state measures against them. Here, however, an entire Volk has been reared up into sub-humanity. It is without a doubt the most de-monic educational plan of all time, which only Jewish sadism could set up and carry out. It is telling that in the great library in Lemberg, in the Red political headquarters, the only book in another language—ever the Jewish article of war in the struggle against every respectable human-ity—the Talmud! I have taken this book with me as the first example of the activity of this unearthly master.

Why did the Jews create such beasts? Again, Kondruss echoed Nazi apocalyptic mythology from *Bolshevism from Moses to Lenin, Die Spur des Juden im Wandel der Zeiten, Mein Kampf,* and *Der Stürmer,* on down: "The Jewish goal of this beastialization of an entire Volk is to be able to utilize them as serviceable tools in the struggle of Judas for world domination."[34] Like Kondruss, Wilhelm Prüller followed the Nazis in linking the Talmud to Bolshevism as a philosophy of extermination. Writing in September 1943, he noted that "the political doctrine of Bolshevism . . . is but a purely political act of world Jewry. . . . And just as the Talmud teaches nothing except murder and destruction, so Bolshevism knows but one science: murder and destruction, cruel and barbaric murder."[35] Karl Fuchs, a tank gunner, likewise interpreted the eastern war as an eschatological struggle against Jews and their beastly minions the Slavs, writing home that "the battle against these sub-humans, who've been whipped into a frenzy by the Jews, was not only necessary but came in the nick of time. Our Führer has saved Europe from certain chaos."[36]

Other letters reveal cases of soldiers who, while committing horrible crimes themselves, inverted reality, perceiving the victim to be the true beastly murderer. As the war got worse, so did the demonization of the Jew as Evil Other. In July 1942, one soldier wrote home and explained that

> the great task which is imposed on us in the struggle against Bolshevism lies in the annihilation of eternal Jewry. If one sees what the Jews have produced here in Russia, one can more than ever understand why the Führer began the struggle against Jewry. What sorrows would have come over our Fatherland if these beast men had maintained the upper hand?

This soldier then went on to describe his frustration at not being able to fight the enemy in the open, to have to deal with partisans, the "furtive rabble," roaming around at night plundering and murdering. After one such night, he reports, a comrade was found murdered. This was not interpreted as being simply a partisan killing; rather, as this soldier conceptualized it,

> He was cut down from behind. That can only be the Jew who stands behind these crimes. The crack-down that thereupon took place indeed yielded an entirely splendid success. The population themselves hate the

Jews as never before. They now realize they bear all the blame. This struggle must lead to the most extreme limits and we will fight to the end so that this world will find eternal peace.[37]

Besides blaming the mythic "eternal Jew" for the partisan killing, this soldier further mythologized the death as symptomatic of Jews' innate criminality, thereby justifying the mass murders, possibly involving indigenous Ukrainians, alluded to in the conclusion. Moreover, the annihilation of the eternal Jew is once again conceptualized as bringing the eternal peace of the Nazi millennium. For these soldiers, the blame for the mass destruction, starvation, and horrendous death tolls that they saw around them lay not with the Russians, the Germans, or even the reality of modern warfare. Rather, they found the culprit in that same "hidden force" of history seen in *Bolshevism from Moses to Lenin.* The Nazi millennial myth had become reality. In other words, belief in the apocalyptic fantasy had become something of a self-defining principle. The horror of the war on the eastern front, with its extreme barbarity and loss of human life, with half-starved civilians, now eerily resembling the beastlike subhumans of Nazi propaganda, wandering about a war-torn landscape like something out of Hieronymous Bosch, seemed to embody the very apocalyptic war of extermination that Hitler had prophesied for twenty years. The millennial fantasy that provided Hitler, his inner circle, and many Old Guard Nazis with a sense of meaning and direction, not to mention a heightened sense of self-worth, now, through the hell of modern warfare, provided Hitler's soldiers with the meaning and self-perception needed to withstand and comprehend the constant suffering around them. In other words, faith that they were fighting in a holy war of apocalyptic significance both legitimated their own suffering and justified the suffering they imposed on others. The barbarous and often criminal actions of SS and Wehrmacht soldiers were transformed into a sacred struggle for existence and universal salvation.

The Decision to Exterminate the Jews and Question of Intention

The question remains as to when precisely what has been called a "central," "fundamental," or "universal" decision, and subsequent order, was made by Hitler to begin the systematic extermination of all Jews everywhere. For, to envision an apocalyptically mandated extermination is entirely different from actually making it real. Here, too, a recognition of the centrality of millennialism in Hitler's world view can shed some light. The historian Arno Mayer, in his controversial book *Why Did the Heavens Not Darken*, argued that World War II should be seen as analogous to the medieval crusades, as a drive for territory in the east tied to a desire to destroy, not Islam, but communism (here Mayer underplayed the Nazi association of Jews with Bolshevism). The decision to exterminate the Jews of Europe, according to Mayer, did not occur until after it became clear that the war was lost and probably sometime after the Wannsee Conference, in March 1942.[38] Mayer argued that, in the summer of 1941, the Nazis had no intention of killing Jews, only a plan to resettle them. Any killings that took place were essentially pogroms by locals, with few Wehrmacht- or *Einsatzgruppen*-led mass killings.

The evidence proves conclusively that Mayer was wrong.[39] However, the analogy between the war in the east as a crusade against Jewish Bolshevism and the crusades is not without merit; in fact, the idea was not lost on the Nazis themselves, who used the term "crusade," itself filled with millennial connotations, for recruitment and propaganda.[40] Despite these problems, according to Mayer's theory, the motivation behind the decision to exterminate the Jews—that is, failed expectations—could be seen as a case of millennial disappointment. The inability to win living space in the east and thereby vast territorial acquisitions for the millennial Reich was compensated for with a desire to kill all the Jews of Europe. But, once again, Mayer's dating of the decision is not supported by the evidence. However, as we will see, the notion of millennial disappointment tied to the push to escalate the extermination of the Jews may be useful.

So when might a fundamental decision to exterminate all of Europe's Jews have been made, and why? Early works by the historians Gerald Reitlinger, Helmut Krausnick, and Raul Hilberg pointed to spring of 1941, linking the beginning of the eastern war and the mass killings by the *Einsatzgruppen* to a decision (for which no documents are known to exist) to systematically kill all the Jews within Nazi grasp.[41] From the standpoint of the millennial mentality, this makes sense, as the war against the Soviets (led by supposed Jewish Bolsheviks) and the war against the Jews was always interpreted as the same eschatological conflict. Therefore, it follows that, with the commencement of war in the east, a more deliberate and extensive extermination of Jews would begin. As recently as 1994, Richard Breitman argued that Hitler's charge to Heydrich, in

March 1941, to begin plans for a "final solution project" tends to confirm this possibility.[42] Recent scholars have pushed such a decision to later in the year. Christopher Browning has argued for July 1941, when the killings of women and children in Soviet territories began, perhaps the result of a "euphoria of victory," an argument in exact opposition to Mayer's interpretation that the extermination orders resulted from failed expectations.[43]

Ralf Ogorreck and Philipe Burrin suggest that a decision was made in August 1941, when the mass killings expanded to entire Jewish communities, rather than being limited to men of fighting age.[44] And indeed, on July 31, 1941, Göring ordered Heydrich to "make all the necessary preparations—organizational, technical, and material—for a total solution of the Jewish question throughout the German sphere of influence in Europe."[45] Whether or not this meant expelling Jews or exterminating them, however, remains an open question. Christian Gerlach argues that this order was solely about deportation, with "total" or "final" solution not yet connoting extermination. He further argues that "final solution" did not mean "immediate extermination" but "acquired that meaning only later, especially after the war." By this he means that the Nazis envisioned the extermination of the Jews as taking many years to complete.[46]

There is certainly evidence to support this. On July 23, 1941, an *Einsatzgruppen* report noted that "in this area it seems unfeasible to solve the Jewish Problem during the war, as this can only be done by means of resettlement, owing to the immense numbers of Jews."[47] Whether or not it meant immediate or eventual (meaning within ten to twenty years) extermination, to my mind, is somewhat beside the point. Since it was believed that salvation could come only with extermination, exactly when and how the decision was made is not as important as the millennial and apocalyptic nature of the belief itself, without which the "when and how" would be moot. Moreover, a simple statement by *Einsatzgruppen* leaders that extermination was unfeasible for logistic or economic reasons could be interpreted as a response to an order that they believed was, at the time, premature. Ultimately, what the group leaders believed was feasible and what Hitler wanted and had perhaps ordered are two different things.

Peter Longerich places the date for a universal order as the time when the radicalization of *Einsatzgruppen* methods took place, that is, in August 1941. There is evidence, however, that resettlement under the *Generalplan Ost* and preparations for the Final Solution (including not only deportations but work on death camps and gas chambers) occurred at the same time.[48] That plans for resettling Jews were developed simultaneously with plans to murder them confirms the two-decade-old idea that removing Jews from Nazi controlled territory was but a step to realizing the extermination of the Jews.

What we do know is that, as the war in the east stalled and in fact went badly for the Germans, the war against the Jews increased in ferocity. Not surprisingly, Hitler once again linked the escalation of events to his earlier prophecy. On October 25, 1941, speaking in the presence of Himmler and Heydrich, he remarked,

> From the rostrum of the Reichstag I prophesied to Jewry that, in the event of war's proving inevitable, the Jew would disappear from Europe. That race of criminals has on its conscience the two million [German] dead of the First World War, and now hundreds of thousands of more.[49]

The mounting number of German war dead is here tied to the extermination prophecy and then, by inference, to the mass murder of the Jews. In November 1941, work on the death apparatus at Belzec began. Alfred Rosenberg, on November 18, three days after meeting with Himmler, remarked that the Soviet territories were the ideal location for a "biological extermination of the whole of European Jewry."[50] However, it has been argued that he meant a slow process of extermination and not the systematic and accelerated extermination that would develop the following year. Goebbels, writing in *Das Reich,* on November 16, 1941, referred to Hitler's prophecy and the killing of Jews in the east:

> We are experiencing the fulfillment of that prophecy, and it delivers the Jews to a fate which is perhaps severe, but which is more than deserved. Pity, even regret, are totally inappropriate. The Jews are a parasitical race, which is like a festering mold on the cultures of healthy nations. There is only one remedy: a swift incision, and done away with.

He concluded that the Jews were "facing a gradual process of destruction."[51] The extermination prophecy was unfolding, albeit in a slow and uncoordinated way.

Christian Gerlach has more recently argued that a "central" or "fundamental" decision to systematically exterminate all the Jews of Europe (in other words, to realize the prophecy), occurred during the first week of December 1941. It came not because the Nazis saw the war as lost, although a minority did have this opinion as early as November 1941, but because of something else. Gerlach argues that the Soviet counteroffensive of December 5, and especially the Japanese attack on Pearl Harbor on December 7, which ushered the United States into the war, made the war truly a world war. It was only at this time that Hitler's prophecy that "International Finance Jewry" would create another world war was seemingly fulfilled, warranting the prophesied extermination of Europe's Jews.[52]

Gerlach notes that the United States's entry into the war was perhaps a "welcome pretext" for beginning the Final Solution, in part because it removed the notion of using the Jews as hostages. He also argues that a "fortress" mentality was generated with the loss of the Battle of Moscow and with the creation of a two-front war.[53] Only at this point was the prophecy truly realized. I would reinterpret this slightly from the perspective of Nazi millennialism. By taking on the United States, Hitler induced exactly the apocalyptic scenario he had always imagined was destined to happen, in which the existence of the world was at stake, with a victory of either the Jews (more and more conceived not only as the Jewish Bolsheviks in Russia but also the so-called capitalist New York Jews) or the Nazi-led Aryans. It was at this point that Hitler's eschatological vision of Aryans walking over Jewish corpses, or vice versa, came true.

By early December 1941, it was clear that the Germans truly were in a struggle of "existence or nonexistence," as Hitler had prophesied since the early 1920s, and this only heightened the eschatological implications of the war and the desire to fulfill the 1939 extermination prophecy, a central tenet of Nazism for two decades. Notes from a series of meetings between Hitler and members of his inner circle shortly after his declaration of war on the United States lend credence to Gerlach's argument. On December 18, 1941, Himmler, after a meeting with Hitler, jotted down the following notes: "Jewish question | to be exterminated [*auszurotten*] as partisans."[54] It had been policy since the initiation of Operation Barbarossa to exterminate all Jews (beginning initially with all men of military age) in Soviet territories as partisans, potential saboteurs, and "back stabbers." This followed exactly Hitler's war directive and the General's orders, cited earlier. This policy apparently was now to be extended to all Jews everywhere.

Another interesting piece of evidence that Gerlach uses to support his thesis relates back to Hitler's prophecy. It involves Alfred Rosenberg, who made a note on December 16, 1941, concerning a meeting with Hitler two days earlier. Rosenberg and Hitler consulted on a draft of a speech Rosenberg was to give but that they decided to alter after Hitler "remarked that the text had been prepared before the Japanese declaration of war, in circumstances that had now altered." Rosenberg continued,

> With regard to the Jewish question, I said that my remarks about the New York Jews would perhaps have to be changed now, after the decision. My position was that the extermination of the Jews should not be mentioned. The Führer agreed. He said they had brought the war down on us, they had started all the destruction, so it should come as no surprise if they became its first victims.[55]

The extermination prophecy now could be fulfilled, and it should surprise no one. On December 12, 1941, a day after announcing war with the United States, Hitler met with his *Reichsleiter* and *Gauleiter*. According to Goebbels's diary entry regarding this meeting, the prophecy once again appeared:

> Regarding the Jewish question, the Führer is determined to clear the table. He prophesied to the Jews that if they would bring about yet another world war, they would experience their annihilation. That was not empty talk. The world war is here. The annihilation of Jewry must be the necessary consequence. This question is to be regarded without any sentimentality. We are not to have compassion for the Jews but rather *for* our German people. If the German people yet again have to sacrifice 160,000 dead in the eastern campaign, then the authors of this bloody conflict must pay for it with their lives.[56]

Once again the extermination prophecy is linked to the notion of a world war now seen as beginning with the introduction of the United States. *World War* was conceived eschatologically, signifying the *Final War*.

On December 16, Hans Frank, leader of the General Government in Poland and a former Thule Society associate, gave a speech that alluded to both Hitler's 1939 prophecy and his December 12, 1941, speech on the United States's entry into the war:

> As for the Jews, I will say to you quite openly that one way or another they must be done away with. The Führer once uttered the promise: if

the combined forces of Jewry should again succeed in unleashing a world war, then the sacrifice of blood will be made not only by the embattled peoples in the war, but also the Jews in Europe will have found their end. . . . I ask you: agree with me above all on the rule: we will have compassion on principle only for the German people and with no one else in the world. The others have no compassion for us as well. As a long time National Socialist I must say this: if the Jewish tribe in Europe should survive this war, we will have sacrificed our best blood for the preservation of Europe, but this war would be only a partial success. I would therefore concerning the Jews be guided by the expectation that they will disappear. They must be done away with.

How was such a massive project to be realized? Frank continued,

I have begun deliberations aimed at deporting them to the east. In January an important conference will take place in Berlin about this question. I will be sending state secretary Dr. Bühler. This conference is supposed to be held in the Reich Security Main Office with SS-*Obergruppenführer* Heydrich. In any case a great Jewish migration will begin.

But what should happen with the Jews? Do you believe that we will accommodate them in settlement villages in the eastern land? In Berlin we are told: why make this trouble for us? We can do nothing with them in the east land or in the Reich Commissariat. Liquidate them yourselves! Gentlemen, I must say to you, arm yourselves against all considerations of compassion. We must exterminate the Jews wherever we come upon them and where it is at all possible. . . . For us also the Jews are exceptionally deleterious eaters. . . . These 3.5 million Jews we cannot shoot, we cannot poison. However there are some interventions we can undertake that one way or another will lead to a successful extermination [*Vernichtungerfolg*]. And indeed they are connected to the great measures being discussed within the Reich. Where and how this takes place is a matter for the authorities that we must establish and set up here and whose operation I will announce at the opportune time.[57]

It is clear from Frank's statement that resettlement was envisioned simply as a step on the way to extermination and thus the fulfillment of Hitler's prophecy. The Germans were to walk over the corpses of the Jews, as Hitler had always predicted. The apocalypse of the Aryans would be averted as the apocalypse of the Jews began.

The Wannsee Conference: The Prophecy Made Real

In the speech just discussed, Frank refers to a meeting in January at which the details of the extermination of the Jews were to be worked out. This was the Wannsee Conference of January 20, 1942, which was postponed from its original date, December 9, 1941, most likely because of the Japanese attack on Pearl Harbor. Wannsee therefore was not about making the decision to exterminate the Jews. That had already been done. It was about logistics (unifying and coordinating efforts) and the question of ultimate authority (Heydrich through Himmler and then back to Hitler). Wannsee did, however, make it clear to attendees that the killing of the *Ostjuden,* the eastern Jews, which had begun in earnest with Operation Barbarossa, was only the beginning of a much grander and much more horrifying plan. Now it was revealed that all Jews in occupied and allied-controlled territories, including German Jews, who were considered by some attendees as culturally distinct from the "animal hordes" of eastern Europe, as well as part-Jews and Jews married to non-Jews, who had been previously exempt from many anti-Semitic policies—a total reckoned at some eleven million—were to be collected, deported, and exterminated (with some temporarily used for slave labor).[58] With Wannsee, the Final Solution began to be openly discussed, although still under a veil of secrecy.

Two days after this meeting, one participant, SS *Gruppenführer* Gottlob Berger, wrote to Oskar Dirlewanger, commandant of a Jewish labor camp at Dzikow: "Jews are second-class or third-order individuals. Whether or not one is justified in eliminating them is beyond debate. One way or another they must vanish from the face of the earth."[59] Ten days after Wannsee, in yet another anniversary speech, on January 30, 1942, Hitler once again referred to his prophecy (again misdating the original prophecy):

We are clear to ourselves that the war can end only with either the Aryan peoples exterminated, or that Jewry will vanish from Europe. I have already spoken about it on September 1, 1939, in the German Reichstag—and I am careful not to make rash prophecies—that this war will not go as the Jews envisage it, namely that the European Aryan peoples will be exterminated, rather that the result of this war will be the annihilation of Jewry. For the first time that true old Jewish law will be employed: an eye for an eye, a tooth for a tooth. . . . And the hour will come when the most evil world enemy of all time will have played out its role of the last millennium.[60]

As the Final Solution unfolded, the extermination prophecy became a rationalizing mechanism not only for Hitler but for others involved in enacting the Final Solution. A Wannsee participant, SS *Gruppenführer* Otto Hofmann, told a meeting of SS officers, in late September 1942,

> They will no longer recognize any Jewish danger. In twenty years there may not be a single Jew left. In the European part of Russia there are a total of eleven million Jews [*sic*]. So there is still plenty of work to do. I cannot believe that we have exterminated more than one million of them thus far. It will take some time until we have freed Europe from this pestilence.[61]

In motivational speeches to SS leaders in 1942, Himmler paraphrased Hitler's prophecy, saying that "if Jewry should start an international war, perhaps to exterminate the Aryan peoples, so it will not be the Aryan Volk exterminated, rather Jewry."[62] Goebbels, as we saw, made similar references to Hitler's prophecy and to the extermination of the Jews as its fulfillment. Perhaps more surprising, soldiers at the eastern front found some sense of meaning in identifying their murderous actions and the suffering they engendered to Hitler's prophecy. Corporal Heinrich Sachs wrote to a friend, describing the annihilation of the Bolshevik army, a "destiny-intended miracle." In this connection, he also mentioned that the Jewish question was being "solved" with "impressive thoroughness," with the "enthusiastic approval of the indigenous population." He wrote that "as the Führer said in one of his speeches shortly before the outbreak of the war: 'if Jewry should yet once again provoke the nations of Europe in a senseless war, then this will mean the end of this race in Europe!'" Sachs remarked that the "Jew ought have known that the Führer was to be taken seriously with his words, and now had to bear the appropriate consequences." Only extermination of the Jews could bring the millennial peace: "They are inexorably harsh, but necessary, if quiet and peace should finally come among the nations."[63]

With Wannsee, then, the Final Solution, the realization of Hitler's extermination prophecy and his decades-old apocalyptic vision, could now begin in earnest. In his New Year's message of 1943, closing a year that saw more extermination camps erected in Poland, Hitler yet again returned to his prophecy:

> I said that the hope of international Jewry, that it would destroy the German and other European peoples in a new world war, will be the biggest mistake Jewry has made in thousands of years; that it will destroy not the German people but itself—and about that there is today no doubt.[64]

Himmler told SS leaders much the same thing on October 4, 1943, returning to the idea of preemptive extermination found in the apocalyptic logic of *Bolshevism from Moses to Lenin* twenty years earlier:

> We had the moral right, we had the duty to our people, to destroy this people which wanted to destroy us. . . . We have exterminated a bacterium because we do not want in the end to be infected by the bacterium and die of it. I will not see so much as a small area of sepsis appear here or gain a hold. Wherever it may form, we will cauterize it.[65]

The war of extermination continued to go badly for the Nazis for the next two years. Hitler refused to capitulate, for, as he had always prophesied, the Final War could end only with the Aryans or the Jews walking over the other's corpses. Just weeks before the end of his life, Hitler returned one final time to his prophecy. He echoed his statement of January 30, 1941, that Europe one day would understand that war of extermination was a necessary battle if millennial peace was to come to the world:

> I have played straight with the Jews. On the eve of war I gave them a last warning. I warned them that if they again plunged the world into war, they would not be spared this time—the vermin would be finally exterminated in Europe. They replied to this warning by a declaration of war. . . . We have pierced the Jewish abscess. The world of the future will be eternally grateful to us.[66]

Six million Jews died, along with some sixty million soldiers and civilians throughout Europe. It was an induced apocalypse unlike any other in history.

Concluding Thoughts

The difficult search to determine when a central or fundamental "decision" was made may be somewhat misplaced. For one thing, Hitler's decision-making process did not always work in such clearcut ways. For key decisions like this, he waited for his much-vaunted "inner voice," which he believed to be the voice of Providence guiding him, to tell him that "now is the time." He then went into prophet mode, telling those around him what he envisaged, and they subsequently attempted to realize that vision, albeit often in contradictory and competing ways. Moreover, Hitler believed that such a decision was out of his hands, that the decision had already been made by fate, or Providence. Hitler believed that he had been sent by God to realize a divine mission, a mission that entailed creating the millennial Reich, which included winning the final war between Aryans and Jews in his lifetime. When it became clear that *this* war was *that* war, it was more a matter of letting history take its course.

We also need to separate when a fundamental or universal order to exterminate the Jews was given and when the belief in its necessity was conceived. And we need to understand that there was a difference of comprehension regarding what the so-called Jewish Problem or Jewish Question really was. Many outside Hitler's inner circle saw the destruction of the Soviet system and the physical removal of the Jews (resettlement) as a final option, whereas for Hitler, and perhaps for those closest to him, these were always simply steps to the final solution, which, from an eschatological perspective, necessitated the extermination of either the Aryans or the Jews. This Hitler had always envisioned.

Given this, it is perhaps not surprising that as war approached in 1939, Hitler once again brought up the specter of Jewish extermination, linked to a final battle against Jewish Bolshevism. Of course, noting that Hitler and his inner circle envisioned a coming eschatological conflict with Jewish Bolshevism does not mean that they had a concrete plan of when or how this would come to fruition, any more than many millennial movements that have some prophetic vision of a coming apocalypse know exactly when and how events will unfold; they know only that they will and must occur. While some movements have a definite date and a literal reading of a prophecy to guide them, many do not. They believe only that the apocalyptic events will happen in their lifetime, because they are convinced that they have been chosen to fulfill a divine mission to save the world. Importantly, when the prophesied event does not occur, millennial movements quite often attempt to induce the apocalypse in some way, with mass murder being one alternative. Nazi millennialism in relation to the Final Solution should be seen in this light. The Nazis believed that the final showdown was to occur in their lifetime—that the Aryans would win and walk over the corpses of the collected Jews, or vice versa.

With an understanding of the internal logic of apocalyptic thinking, I would break down the unfolding of the Final Solution this way:

- Hitler, and probably those closest to him, believed in a coming final war between the forces of light (Aryans) and those of darkness (Jews), a war that was to be a war of extermination and that was to occur in their lifetime. Either the Jews or the world would be exterminated. Exactly how this was to take place was left, to some extent, to the force of Providence.
- World War II was conceived, even before it started, as Hitler's prophecy in 1939 indicates, as an apocalyptic Final War. However, it was not until the eastern war began that the final battle truly began, and mass killings of Jews in the east therefore occurred at the same time. It was believed that fate was on the Nazis' side and that the *Blitzkrieg* would be successful; the extermination of the Jews could then occur at a leisurely pace, with the mechanics worked out in time. However, with the failure to achieve a quick military victory, and with the failure in some ways of their prophesied apocalyptic victory, the Nazis began to escalate the mass killings and made early preparations for an even more systematic genocidal operation, starting in late summer 1941 and escalating again in the fall. Following Christian Gerlach, when the war became truly global, in December 1941, Hitler announced publicly the plans to exterminate all Jews, and the machinery of Nazism moved into action to realize this apocalyptic vision. Wannsee, in January 1942, began this process in its most systematic and coordinated way.

In other words, as the *Blitzkrieg* victory expected in the early summer of 1941 failed to occur, as Russian tanks proved superior to German tanks and antitank weaponry, as Russian soldiers proved better fighters than imagined, and as a two-front war unfolded, the expectation that the Nazis could take their time in the millennial Third Reich to achieve the extermination of the Jews was dashed, and they responded by hastening the end, rushing headlong into exactly the apocalyptic war of extermination that Hitler had long foretold, with genocide on a grand scale and at a much more rapid pace.

The apocalypse complex and the myths of the millennium, of living at a historic turning point, of having been chosen for a holy mission to give birth to a wondrous New Age, a New Order of communal unity and eternal peace, was enough to convert many Germans, and some non-Germans, to Hitler's "great idea." The early years of this millennial Third and Final Reich seemed to fulfill those dreams. The eschatological and darker side of the myth, that a Final War was imminent between the forces of light (the Aryans) and the forces of darkness (the Jews) was less significant, if at all relevant, to them. But it was there. It was always there. Hitler, and perhaps those closest to him, like many millennialists before them, found a way, twisted though the road may have been, to induce the apocalyptic vision that was both the crux of that turning point and the justification for their salvational mission.

Appendix

The Hitler Gospels and
Old Guard Testimonials:
Reconstructing a Mythical World

The Nazi construction of the millennial myth discussed in this book was gleaned from a variety of sources, many of which, taken individually, could be and have been held suspect by historians over the years. However, understood and used properly, these sources prove essential for an understanding of Nazi millennialism. Indeed, the very subjectivity of these sources provides a perfect vehicle for understanding the use and abuse of myth, for the Nazis, their supporters, and their detractors did both. Discussion of my use of these supposedly tainted sources, some of which have been branded with a historiographic scarlet letter, becomes essential. For instance, Ian Kershaw, in the first volume of his biography *Hitler: Hubris,* views his total avoidance of Hermann Rauschning's account of Hitler's monologues as one his work's strongest assets. Writing in his preface, Kershaw states, "I have on no single occasion cited Hermann Rauschning's *Hitler Speaks,* a work now regarded to have so little authenticity that it is best to disregard it altogether."[1] However, if the content of such a work, properly understood and carefully used, is shown to be supported by other sources, is this avoidance so meritorious? This is especially salient because the sources discussed in this appendix often present us with the most accurate glimpse of the Nazi use of the millennial myth.

I term the first category of tainted sources the Hitler gospels. These are sources that purport to present actual conversations, or, more precisely, reconstructions of such conversations, between various individuals, at one time privy to the inner circle around Hitler and thus, to some degree, acquainted with the esoteric gnosis of Nazi millennialism. These sources should be taken not to be anything like transcripts of actual conversations but as something more akin to the Christian Gospels, with various witnesses recounting in their own words, sometimes a number of years after the fact, similar Hitler monologues. The question, then, is not whether they present the literal words of Hitler but whether they, as a collection, can provide an accurate view of the rhetoric and imagery employed by Hitler and thus faithfully reflect his subjective construction of reality. By utilizing the term "gospels" I do not mean to belittle the Christian Gospels or to equate Hitler with Jesus, but simply make a historically useful source analogy.[2] Historians of Christianity have used the Christian Gospels for hundreds of years as a relatively accurate portrayal of the world view of Jesus of Nazareth, despite the fact that they were composed many years after the fact by different and sometimes multiple authors; each paints a slightly different portrait of Jesus' words as each reflects the time and place of composition as well as the personal world view of the author or authors who composed it. Seen from a historiographic perspective, and not a religious one, the Gospels cannot be taken to be the literal words of Jesus but are a subjective, although not altogether inaccurate, reconstruction of those words (mixed together with folklore and myths popular at the time of the reconstruction). Few historians of early Christianity would ever consider branding the Gospels a forgery or hoax, not to be used under any situation. Rather, they would argue that they should be used in conjunction with apocryphal Gospels (which should not be taken to be false Gospels) and other contemporary non-Christian sources.[3] The Hitler gospels, then, should be used like other reconstructed sayings of prophet-messiahs, pretenders or otherwise, with caution and understanding.

The fact that these kinds of sources have traditionally been ignored (or in some cases misused or misunderstood) is one of the reasons that the millennial aspects of Nazism have been overlooked, or at least undervalued. Generally speaking, these sources are in fact of marginal value for traditional objective history. For example, if one turns to these sources for determining precise chronology of events, one finds most of them wanting. However, the Hitler gospels are essential for grasping the murky but crucially important subjective world of Nazi millennial myth. In this regard, it needs to be kept in mind how Hitler often communicated with those around him. We have dozens of sources that describe interviews with Hitler and accounts by those who spent some time in his presence during one of his hundreds of nightly monologues. During these occasions, Hitler would speak to an individual or a small group as if he were addressing a multitude.[4] He would go into prophet mode, assuming the role of visionary, laying bare to his disciples the secret working of history, past, present, and future. It is in the accounts of these prophet sessions that we get the best glimpse of Hitler's millennial world view.[5] To utterly dismiss such works as suspect, even when they largely present an identical Hitlerian world view, is anything but good scholarship.

The earliest such work is a relatively obscure early propaganda piece by Dietrich Eckart titled *Bolshevism from Moses to Lenin: A Dialogue between Hitler and Me*.[6] This brief work is a stylized conversation between Hitler and Eckart, his mentor, published in 1924, a few months after Eckart's death, while Hitler was in Landsberg Prison composing *Mein Kampf*. Early on, the Nazis themselves considered it an important and genuine work. As a young man, Himmler found it so important that he put it on his short list of essential writings. He described the work as "an earthy, witty conversation between Hitler and Eckart that so genuinely and correctly characterizes both of them. It gives a perspective through all time and opens one's eyes to many points that one had not yet seen. I wish that everyone would read this."[7] The Nazis for the most part, however, suppressed the piece, not because it was an inaccurate portrayal of the Nazi world view but because it was all too revealing. When the work resurfaced in the early 1960s, Ernst Nolte found it useful for understanding Hitler's fundamental view concerning the Jews. He further noted that the language and imagery corresponded quite well to Hitler's later writings and speeches and, perhaps most enlightening, to his so-called wartime table talks.[8]

Margarete Plewnia and Shaul Esh, however, argued against Hitler's direct involvement in the work, which for them rendered it relatively useless as a source.[9] While both authors are certainly correct in stating that Eckart is the sole author, each undervalues or misses entirely the central point as to the nature and function of this source. The fundamental question is whether the work provides useful insight into Hitler's and the Nazis' world view, their millennial construction of reality. And this it most certainly does.[10] In other words, the important question is not whether *Bolshevism from Moses to Lenin* can be taken to present the verbatim words of Hitler but whether it offers an accurate version of his and the Nazi world view in the early 1920s as interpreted and embellished by the man Hitler himself considered his spiritual mentor—the man to whom Hitler dedicated *Mein Kampf* and the individual referred to most by Hitler in that other important Hitler gospel, the wartime table talks, compiled almost twenty years after Eckart's death.[11] Again, one must answer in the affirmative.

Moreover, the central notion of *Bolshevism from Moses to Lenin,* that Jews are destructive by nature and that they were in their final attempt to control the world and thereby annihilate humanity, is repeated by Hitler in *Mein Kampf,* composed at almost the same time and repeated again in Hitler's unpublished second book. Is the symbolic and mythic similarity of all these sources, spanning two decades, simply a bizarre coincidence? Or is it more likely that *Bolshevism from Moses to Lenin,* read along with the other Hitler gospels, does indeed give us a more or less accurate glimpse into the mythic world of Hitler's millennialism? I find the second possibility much more likely. Moreover, simply dismissing a source because it does not present Hitler's words verbatim plays into the historical myth that only Hitler is important for understanding the Nazi world view. This certainly over-values Hitler's importance; most of the seeds of Nazi millennialism had been planted earlier by the likes of Eckart, Rosenberg, and others before Hitler's arrival. Hitler's chief role was to present the archetypal imagery of millennialism in a way that rang true for large numbers of his contemporaries. By successfully playing the role of apocalyptic prophet, Hitler took the first important step in becoming savior. Therefore, like all the sources that constitute the Hitler gospels, *Bolshevism from Moses to Lenin* presents us with a invaluable view of not only Hitler's millennial world view but also that of those in his inner circle.

The next most significant, and certainly most controversial, of the Hitler gospels is Hermann Rauschning's *The Voice of Destruction.*[12] National Socialist senate president of the Free State of Danzig from 1933 to 1934, Rauschning became disenchanted with Hitler and fled Germany, writing a series of books on what he perceived to be Nazism's inherent nihilism. According to Rauschning, *The Voice of Destruction* was based in part on notes taken during his brief time with Hitler, in part on his memory, and in part on other sources.[13] The work has been used repeatedly since its publication, often as if it contains the exact words of Hitler and without much critical assessment. Many scholars, have questioned Rauschning's reliability, but I am in agreement with Theodor Schieder that his book can be used, albeit with care (as should be the norm with any source). Schieder properly notes that Rauschning employed direct discourse as a literary form, much like Eckart so many years before.[14]

Like other Hitler gospels, *The Voice of Destruction* suffers from inaccurate chronology and biased interpretations, in this case by an apostate Nazi who hoped to support his own nihilist myth concerning the nature of Nazism. But it is this subjectivity, the image-world Rauschning paints, that is most important for my investigation. Schieder in the end argued that the work "is not a document in which one can expect to find verbatim, stenographic records of sentences or aphorisms spoken by Hitler, despite the fact that it might appear to meet that standard. It is a document in which objective and subjective components are mixed and in which alterations in the author's opinions about what he recounts become mingled with what he recounts." Despite these caveats, Schieder concludes that "it is, however, a document of unquestionable value, since it contains views derived from immediate experience."[15] Thus, like all such gospels, we have one individual's subjective interpretation of the symbolic world view of Adolf Hitler. Used, therefore, in combination with other such sources, it is certainly a valid source.

Wolfgang Hänel has since cast doubt on Rauschning's authenticity, arguing that he never had such intimate contact with Hitler. Moreover, Hänel argues that Rauschning is a fraud.[16] Eckhard Jesse and Fritz Tobias came to similar conclusions.[17] Hänel's rather narrow argument is unconvincing, as Martin Broszat successfully counterargued, and the same can be said for Jesse's and Tobias's assertions.[18] While it is certainly true that Rauschning did not spend an extraordinary amount of time with Hitler, this was not really necessary. Hitler's conversational style was such that he did most of the talking, sometimes for hours on end. He often repeated himself, and his fundamental ideas remained largely consistent over the years. A few experiences with him would be sufficient to gain insight into his world view. Moreover, Hänel's primary technique for supposedly proving the case for fraud is to point out similarities in phrasing in quotations from other individuals in Rauschning's other books, such as those from Ernst Jünger, and quotations attributed to Hitler in *The Voice of Destruction*. If the two are even remotely similar, Hänel concludes that the latter must *be* concoctions. However, the similarities, which are mostly slight, could exist for any number of reasons. Hitler, for instance, had an extraordinary memory and often made seemingly original statements or used turns of phrasing that in fact originated elsewhere. The similarities need not stem from Rauschning's attempt at forgery. And, again, the contents of Rauschning's book should not be taken in any case as direct quotations of Hitler's but simply as one man's reconstruction of a series of encounters with Hitler. In this light, Eberhard Jäckel, in his assessment of Rauschning, argued that the work should be used not as if it were a primary source in the sense of being a verbatim transcript but as one man's interpretation.[19] I would add that until recently, historical sources have rarely been verbatim transcripts; most are individuals' reconstructions of past conversations, speeches, monologues, and the like. In the end, any source must be judged along with other contemporary sources. Finally, when analyzing the role of myth, symbol, and image, the subjectivity of a source is at times its most important asset. In my study of Nazi millennial myth, how individuals like Eckart, Rauschning, and others interpreted what they perceived to be Hitler's world view is as important as how Hitler himself presented it in his speeches and writings.[20]

Another similar, and in many ways complementary source, is Otto Wagener's *Hitler: Memoirs of a Confidant*. Based on memoirs written in 1946 while Wagener was interned in a British camp for German officers, the published memoir was compiled from thirty-six military notebooks, amounting to some twenty-three hundred pages.[21] Wagener, like Rauschning, claims to have made notes of his conversations or experiences with Hitler, which ended up in his diary. The notes and the diary, however, do not appear to have survived the war, and Wagener certainly did not have them in his possession when he composed his own "conversations with Hitler," a work he considered a reconstruction of his lost diary.[22] So, like Rauschning's, Wagener's subjective reconstruction of his experience with Hitler is not a verbatim transcript, but it is, as the work's editor, Henry Ashby Turner, noted, a valuable source from an individual who had intimate contact with Hitler. For my investigation it is an essential source for analyzing the topics that emerged during some of Hitler's prophecy sessions, as he laid bare his vision of the coming Third Reich. And, just as important, they are an accurate reflection of Wagener's *interpretation* of Hitler and his millennial world view, an interpretation that is unique in some ways (Wagener viewed Hitler as an essentially Christian reformer with messianic and prophetic powers) and dramatically similar to Rauschning in other ways (regarding Hitler's own messianic self-conception, as well as his eschatological conception of the supposed Aryan-Jewish conflict). I agree then with Turner's assessment that Wagener's notes represent "a historical source of exceptional richness and breadth."[23] Not surprisingly, however, given the general misunderstanding of the Hitler gospels, Wagener's work has been little used since its publication.[24]

Wagener's published memoirs cover the period from the summer of 1929, following his conversion to Nazism at a Nuremberg party rally, to his fall from Hitler's grace during the summer of 1933. Consequently, they give us a glimpse into Hitler's idea-world during the period slightly before that covered in Rauschning, ten years after that covered in Eckart's dialogue, and ten years before the table talks. Therefore, used as a set, the Hitler gospels present us with twenty years of Hitler's world view. During this period, Wagener, much more so than Rauschning, in fact, belonged to the inner circle around Hitler.[25] The most important fact, then, is that Wagener's "conversations" come from approximately the same period as Rauschning's and therefore provide an important comparative and complementary source. Both works, therefore, as Turner points out, belong to the same category of historical sources: both written years after the original conversations and both attempt to reconstruct long conversations with Hitler. By using Wagener and Rauschning together, it is possible to get an idea of the symbolic and mythic world view of Hitler in the early 1930s. When used in conjunction with Eckart's dialogue of the early 1920s and the table talks of the early 1940s, what emerges is a remarkably consistent world view. It is one that is thoroughly millennial, messianic, and apocalyptic. The fact that such diverse reconstructions of Hitler's monologues paint such similar images on these key issues is a testament to their value as historical sources. The differences that do appear reflect the times in which they were written and, more important, the authors who composed or compiled them. For instance, while Hitler's millennialism and messianism come through in both Rauschning and Wagener, they are interpreted differently by each, and Hitler's "conversations" are consequently shaped somewhat differently.

It is important to add that Rauschning, an apostate Nazi, composed his work as "a warning to the West," to show that Hitler was a demonic nihilist, while Wagener considered Hitler a messiah and prophet and himself the keeper of the Grail and further hoped his memoirs would reveal the true Hitler (and not the Germany gone astray due to the evil machinations of the likes of Goebbels, Himmler, and Göring). Yet despite subtle differences in tone and motive, the two works are remarkably consistent in presenting Hitler's millennialism and messianism, as well as exposing the apocalyptic anti-Semitism that supported each. If Rauschning made it all up to support not only his nihilist myth but also his own conservative agenda, as his detractors have claimed, then we are left with the stunning coincidence that Wagener, who hoped to portray Hitler as prophet and savior, made up the same Hitler. It seems highly unlikely, then, if not impossible, for Rauschning to be a fraud in the sense that has recently been argued. It is equally unlikely that Eckart's earlier work is solely a product of his own imagination, when we know that Hitler's words as found in the dialogue so clearly match his own words found in *Mein Kampf,* in his speeches of the early 1920s, and in the table talks some twenty years later. When we add to the Hitler gospels the many memoirs of other Nazis of the 1930s and after, some apostate and some still true believers, what emerges is a consistent messianic, millennial, and apocalyptic world view. To simply dismiss all such sources under the guise of sound historiography, while at the same time ignoring the re-markably consistent content, flies in the face of the evidence (and thus is anything but sound historiography). The Hitler gospels therefore provide us with a crucial set of sources for understanding how Hitler constructed his conception of how the cosmos worked, of historical cause and effect. For it is in the subjective world of millennial myth that a deeper under-standing of Hitler, Nazism, and the Holocaust is to be found.

The final source typology that needs consideration is the witness testi-monials of Old Guard Nazis, those who joined prior to the assumption of power in 1933. I term them "witness testimonials," for they are re-markably similar in content and construction to American Puritan con-fessionals of the seventeenth and early eighteenth centuries, German Pietist confessionals such as the much-read and much-imitated conver-sion testimony of Johann Heinrich Jung-Stiling, or the more recent con-version accounts of born-again Christian Fundamentalists. While all such sources are certainly formulaic, this fact does not deny the sincerity of the subjective spiritual experience the authors attempt to reconstruct. These testimonials are a reconstruction of one's past to fit the new, reborn life, but the fact that they are reconstructions does not invalidate the gen-uineness of the original conversion experience.[26] Such conversion testi-monies typically tell the story, or myth, of being lost in chaos and dark-ness, of a journey from darkness to light, from meaningless to meaning and purpose, often but not always the result of a single key conversion experience that occurs after hearing the millennial preaching of a prose-lytizer or charismatic speaker.

The Old Guard testimonies found in the Theodore Abel Collection and in *Die alte Garte sprichts,* discussed in detail later, fit this model perfectly. It would be tempting to conclude that they fit the model too perfectly, implying then that they must therefore be fraudulent constructions, simply another form of Nazi propaganda. This is most unlikely, for a number of reasons. The two collections were gathered for different reasons, written by different individuals at different times; yet, they are markedly similar. To argue that this similarity is rooted in Nazi propaganda, one would have to further argue that the long arm of Nazi indoctrination reached much further than it ever in fact did. Indeed, the testimonials gathered by Theodore Abel in 1934 are in many ways pre-indoctrination, unless one counts the Nazi speech-gatherings as indoctrination episodes (this would be only partially true). Besides, both collections have that unmistakable ring of truth, the tone and feel of memories of real experiences, genuinely felt and sincerely recalled. If the years that passed between experience and recall, from a few years to fifteen or more, leads to a certain sameness of construction, this is not propaganda (any more than it was with the Puritans or the Pietists) but a fundamental part of the postconversion reconstruction of self and part of the joining of a millennial community, a community of shared conversion experiences. The reconstruction of one's past life is a process that validates the personal conversion experience through its repetition in the millennial group.

The two collections used in the present study are the Theodore Abel Collection and *Die alte Garte sprichts* (The Old Guard Speaks). Like the Hitler gospels, these testimonials are remarkably similar sources collected for two different reasons.[27] Theodore Abel was a sociologist at Columbia University who was interested in the social dynamics that propelled the Nazi movement from an insignificant fringe group to a large and powerful state-controlling political force. In 1934, he convinced the Nazis to allow party members from the Old Guard to tell their stories in their own words. To acquire the essays, Abel ran an essay contest offering a $500 prize for the "best personal life history of an adherent of the Hitler movement." The only stipulation was that entrants had to have been members before 1933 (eliminating the masses that joined after the Nazis assumed power) and that they be accurate and detailed, including descriptions of "family life, education, economic conditions, membership in associations, participation in the Hitler movement, and important experiences, thoughts, and feelings about events and ideas in the postwar world."[28] In this way, Abel hoped to acquire the kind of information necessary for sociological analysis, including such things as familial and social networks. The Nazis agreed, as it fit nicely with their goal of telling the world what they considered to be the true history of the Nazi movement.[29] The Nazis helped publicize the contest, eventually eliciting some seven hundred testimonials, from one to eighty pages in length.

Thomas Childers is certainly right when he says that the Abel Collection is the "single most valuable source we have (or will ever have) for evaluating individual grassroots opinion within the National Socialist movement."[30] Childers correctly noted that, while the Abel essays cannot be taken to be a representative sample in a statistically compelling sense, they are invaluable for gathering insight into the social and psychological attractions of the Nazis, precisely the type of source needed to link the millennial and messianic pretensions of the Nazi elite with the rank and file.[31] I agree with this statement and would add *Die alte Garte sprichts* to this short list of Old Guard testimonials. I also concur with Childers, Merkl, Koonz, and Rhodes that the Abel essays have the all important ring of truth, providing us with frank and often unintentionally damning indictments of the writers and the party itself.[32]

The assumption that the Abel Collection, and *Die alte Garte sprichts* for that matter, must have been heavily censored or shaped by the Nazi propaganda machine is unwarranted. For the Nazi political and propaganda reach was not as great in the early 1930s as is commonly believed. Likewise, those who believe that the Abel essays were probably tailored for an American audience would be hard pressed to explain its striking similarity to *Die alte Garte sprichts*, which was collected for the Nazi archives and perhaps an eventual German audience, not an American one. Finally, I agree with Childers as well that one of the chief virtues of *Why Hitler Came into Power*, and the original sources it is based on, is that it allowed the members of the Old Guard to speak for themselves, to explain their varied motivations in their own words, whether they were veterans, factory workers, clerical workers, department store clerks, professors, doctors, or chemists.[33] I have similarly allowed the Nazis of the inner circle and of the rank and file to "speak" for themselves at length. For it is in their own words that we glimpse the sometimes ephemeral world of apocalyptic fears, millennial expectations, and messianic hope.

We are left again with the decision whether to ignore the witnessing testimonies as tainted, since they were composed after the fact, or to recognize that the consistent millennial imagery they exhibit means something. While they were composed in the mid-1930s for different purposes, they are entirely comparable in their apocalyptic sentiments, a fact that I believe strengthens the argument for what I call the apocalypse complex. However, it could be questioned whether the sentiments of the Nazi witnesses, mostly looking back on events ten years earlier, are descriptions of actual experiences or some sort of agreed-upon constructed memory (such as the genre of witnessing literature common to conversion experiences). Certainly something of the latter process has taken place, for as the Nazis compiled their history they clearly placed it in an eschatological time scheme. But this too strengthens my argument. For the construction of memory and history using apocalyptic symbolism points to the construction of a new perception of reality that is at the heart of the apocalypse complex. Therefore, even a symbolically homogenized retelling of the Hitler conversion experience tells us something of the psychology involved, regardless of whether the events happened exactly as Nazis' memories and history portray them. Moreover, there is more to these memories than apocalyptically filtered hindsight. For instance, we know that Hitler and other Nazi ideologues, from the beginning, spoke in apocalyptic terms.

Therefore, there are two possibilities—either the Nazis promoted apocalypticism and their supporters failed to respond at the time and only a decade later gave voice to the apocalyptic in their reconstruction of memory and history or Nazis' supporters heard the initial voice of the apocalypse, responded accordingly at that time with a genuine conversion experience, and then accurately reported this experience in their testimonials ten years later. I find the latter possibility much more convincing. Moreover, evidence for a simultaneous rhetor/listener relationship does exist. Ludwell Denny, in one of the first English-language articles to mention Hitler, noted that Hitler's followers viewed him as "prophet and savior."[34] So, while the mythic construction of memory and history is a factor, so too is the importance of the actual Nazi conversion experiences. If we are to understand the mythic world of Hitler and the Nazis, we need to expand the parameters of our sources to include those subjective sources that have too routinely been dismissed or ignored.

Notes

Notes to the Introduction

1. The convergence of natural disaster and economic despair can be seen in the Eight Trigrams movement in China, in 1813. This Buddhist apocalyptic movement was most successful in the southern portion of the North China plain. A series of droughts and floods in 1811–1812 greatly affected the economy of the area. In the early spring of 1813, the area was again hit by a severe drought that lasted into the summer. Insufficient snows from the previous winter, combined with a lack of rain in the spring, kept the fields dry and hard—they could not even be plowed. Consequently, the price of grain rose, and famine set in. The region was marked by empty houses, abandoned villages, bodies strewn along the road, looters and wolves ransacking villages at night, beggars by the roadside, and children being sold by their parents. When rains did come, only a few weeks before the Eight Trigrams uprising, they caused massive floods as the drought-hardened soil could not absorb the moisture. During this period, a comet appeared, first in 1811 and brightest in the late summer of 1813. In typically millennial terms, it was interpreted as an omen signaling the end of one era (*kulpa*) and the dawn of a new age. Discussed in Susan Naquin, *Millenarian Rebellion in China: The Eight Trigrams Uprising of 1813* (New Haven: Yale University Press, 1976), 111–17.

2. The best comparative study of millenarian reaction to the rapid and radical change wrought by colonization is Michael Adas, *Prophets of Rebellion: Millenarian Protest Movements against the European Colonial Order* (Chapel Hill: University of North Carolina Press, 1979).

3. For instance, the Buu Son Ky Huong movement arose in south Vietnam partly because this region was less developed, socially and organizationally, than the north and center of the country. It lacked such stabilizing influences as village and religious councils, block associations, mutual self-help associations, guilds, and kinship groups. Therefore, the south did not have as strong a network of ordering factors to withstand the extreme social change Vietnam was experiencing at this time. Discussed in Hue-Tam Ho Tai, *Millenarianism and Peasant Politics in Vietnam* (Cambridge: Cambridge University Press, 1983).

4. See Thomas Flanagan, "The Third Reich: Origins of a Millenarian Symbol," *History of European Ideas* 8 (1987): 283–95.

5. Discussed in Naquin, *Millenarian Rebellion in China.*

6. George Shepperson, "The Comparative Study of Millenarian Movements," in Sylvia L. Thrupp, ed., *Millenarian Dreams in Action: Essays in Comparative Studies* (The Hague: Mouton, 1962), 44.

7. As Walter Schmithals noted in *The Apocalyptic Movement, Introduction and Interpretation* (Nashville: Abingdon, 1975), 104, both millennialists and gnostics shared the belief that, as chosen ones, the righteous or spiritual ones, they "do not share the fate of this eon that is passing away, but belong to the other, the higher, or the coming world."

8. George E. Atwood, "On the Origins and Dynamics of Messianic Salvation Fantasies," *International Review of Psycho-Analysis* 5 (1978): 85. On patients with delusions of having been chosen for a messianic mission see John Weir Perry, *The Far Side of Madness* (Englewood Cliffs, N.J.: Prentice Hall, 1974), 20, 96.

9. I have taken the term "nondirected thinking" from C. G. Jung, "Two Kinds of Thinking," *The Collected Works of C. G. Jung* (New York: Pantheon Books, 1953–71), vol. 5, para. 4–46. Others have employed terms such as "infantile thinking" and "magical thinking," but to me these seem both too narrow and pejorative in conception.

10. Names could also be used as agents of legitimation. As Naquin notes, *Millenarian Rebellion in China,* 14–15, the White Lotus sect associated with the surname Li with the coming savior Buddha Maitreya. Interestingly, Li was the traditional surname of Lao-tzu, who for some Chinese Taoist millennialists became a messianic figure who would be reborn to save the world. See Anna Seidel, "Image of the Perfect Ruler in Early Taoist Messianism: Lao-tzu and Li Hung," *History of Religions* 9 (1969–70): 216–47.

11. In the early nineteenth century, the Javanese messiah Prince Dipanagara found legitimacy as a savior figure because of his gifts of prophecy and healing, more so than his high birth and anticolonial rhetoric. His followers subsequently identified him with the *Ratu Adil* (Just King), the longed-for savior-king of Javanese millennialism who, it was for centuries believed, would appear at the end of the final era. Discussed in Adas, *Prophets of Rebellion,* 97.

12. These "Forcers of the End" are discussed in Gershom Scholem, *The Messianic Idea in Judaism and Other Essays in Jewish Spirituality* (New York: Schocken, 1971), 56–57.

13. This book is concerned primarily with the relationship of Hitler to his Old Guard, and how each interpreted the rapid and radical change of the Weimar years apocalyptically and sought salvation through Nazism under a messianic leader. The subject of World War II and the Holocaust as an induced apocalypse is vast, and I hope to make it the focus of an entire second

volume. However, I believe it is important to at least give a cursory look at the subject here as it was a logical, albeit horrible, consequence of Nazi millennialism.

14. I first introduced the idea of the induced apocalypse in a brief essay written in the days following the Heaven's Gate mass suicide. See my "Heaven's Gate and the Induced Apocalypse," *Clio's Psyche* 4 (1997): 1–5. For more discussion of the interrelationship of millennialism and violence see Catherine Wessinger, ed., *Millennialism, Persecution, and Violence* (Syracuse: Syracuse University Press, 2000); Michael Barkun, ed., *Millennialism and Violence: Historical Cases* (Portland: F. Cass, 1996).

15. DeLillo's main character in *White Noise* (New York: W. W. Norton, 1998) is a professor of Hitler Studies. While a typically sarcastic observation on DeLillo's part, it's not too off the mark.

16. Most important, see Hermann Rauschning, *The Revolution of Nihilism: Warning to the West* (New York: Alliance, 1939).

17. The classic studies in English are George L. Mosse, *The Crisis of German Ideology: Intellectual Origins of the Third Reich* (New York: Grosset & Dunlap, 1964); Fritz Stern, *The Politics of Cultural Despair: A Study in the Rise of German Ideology* (Berkeley: University of California Press, 1961); and Roderick Stackelberg, *Idealism Debased: From Völkish Ideology to National Socialism* (Kent: Kent State University Press, 1981). The German word *völkisch* derives from the word *Volk*, meaning people, race, or folk, with a Romantic stress on conceptualizing an ethnic group as an organic entity, bound by a collective spiritual connection that is mystical and ineffable. I have chosen to use the semitranslation "volkish," as the English word "folkish" has a different and less accurate connotation of "countryness."

18. "The Struggle for the Irrational" is the title of James Webb's introduction to his study of modern occultism, *The Occult Establishment* (La Salle, Ill.: Open Court, 1976), which includes a chapter on the possible influence of occultism on Nazism. The introduction to Webb's previous book, *The Occult Underground* (La Salle, Ill.: Open Court, 1974), is titled "The Flight from Reason."

19. For instance, the German historians Götz Aly and Susanne Heim have demonstrated, in works such as *Architects of Annihilation: Auschwitz and the Logic of Destruction* (Princeton: Princeton University Press, 2002), that many of Germany's best and brightest rationalized all aspects of Nazi Germany's economic and social systems, providing eminently logical and efficient means for adjusting the numbers of productive and unproductive groups within the populations under German control. For all its ruthless barbarity, the Holocaust was often perpetrated through highly rational means.

20. More recent scholars writing on this subject have addressed this shortcoming, especially the literary studies of Jost Hermand, *Old Dreams of a New Reich: Volkish Utopias and National Socialism* (Bloomington: Indiana Univer-

sity Press, 1992) and Klaus Vondung, *The Apocalypse in Germany*, trans. Stephen D. Ricks (Columbia: University of Missouri Press, 2000).

21. Robert Pois, *National Socialism and the Religion of Nature* (New York: St. Martin's Press, 1986).

22. Friedrich Heer, *Der Glaube des Adolf Hitler: Anatomie einer politischen Religiosität* (Munich: Bechtle, 1968), uses Hitler's own words to demonstrate the religious character of his world view, while Josef Ackerman, *Heinrich Himmler als Ideologe* (Göttingen: Musterschmidt, 1970), does much the same with Himmler's speeches, writings, and letters. In both cases, the messianic, millennial, and apocalyptic, while not clearly addressed, shines through. J. P. Stern, *Hitler: The Führer and the People* (Berkeley: University of California Press, 1975), finds the messianic dialogue between Hitler and the German people an important aspect of the Nazi leader's political success, although Stern's cynical assessment dilutes his argument. Manfred Ach and Clemens Pentrop, *Hitlers "Religion"* (Munich: Arbeitsgemeinschaft für Religions-und Weltanschauungs-fragen, 1977), likewise analyzes Hitler's speeches and finds them essentially religious in content and even structure. Uriel Tal, in his published lecture *"Political Faith" of Nazism Prior to the Holocaust* (Tel Aviv: Tel Aviv University, 1978), focuses on the importance of the concept of *glaube* (faith) in the Nazi sacralizing of political ideology. Richard Steigmann-Gall, in *The Holy Reich: Nazi Conceptions of Christianity, 1919–1945* (New York: Cambridge University Press, 2003), while largely missing the centrality of Nazi millennialism, does demonstrate that, far from being anti-Christian, most Nazis interpreted the movement's anti-Semitism and anti-Marxism within a largely Christian framework, a so-called positive Christianity that was purged of Jewish, Catholic, and non-German elements.

23. On Nazi use of symbol and ritual, see George L. Mosse, *The Nationalization of the Masses: Political Symbolism and Mass Movements in Germany from the Napoleonic Wars through the Third Reich* (New York: H. Fertig, 1975); Hans-Jochen Gamm, *Der braune Kult: das Dritte Reich und seine Ersatzreligion* (Hamburg: Rütten & Loening, 1962); Klaus Vondung, *Magie und Manipulation: ideologischer Kult und politische Religion des Nationalsozialismus* (Göttingen: Vandenhoeck & Ruprecht, 1971); Sabine Behrenbeck, *Der Kult um die toten Helden: Nationalsozialistische Mythen, Riten und Symbole* (Vierow: SH-Verlag, 1996).

24. Peter Viereck, *Metapolitics: The Roots of the Nazi Mind* (New York: Capricorn Books, 1965). See Eric Voegelin, *Hitler and the Germans* (Columbia: University of Missouri Press, 1999) and *Modernity without Restraint* (Columbia: University of Missouri Press, 2000). For a brief discussion of Voegelin's basic assumptions regarding the concept of political religion see Hans-Christof Kraus, "Eric Voegelin redivivus? Politische Wissenschaft als politische Theologie," in *Der Nationalsozialismus als politische Religion*, ed. Michael Ley and Julius H. Schoeps (Bodenheim b. Mainz: Philo Verlagsgesellschaft, 1997),

74–88. For a different take on the gnosticism approach, see Morris Berman *Coming to Our Senses: Body and Spirit in the Hidden History of the West* (New York: Simon & Schuster, 1989), esp. 253–93. Berman's emphasis is on a gnostic rejection of the body and embrace of an ascent experience. Berman too sees Nazism as essentially gnostic in character.

25. Michael Allen Williams has challenged the validity of the term "gnosticism," since there are so many similarities and differences found among the literature variously designated as gnostic. See Williams, *Rethinking "Gnosticism": An Argument for Dismantling a Dubious Category* (Princeton: Princeton University Press, 1999). There is certainly something to what Williams is saying, but I think that rejecting a philosophical category simply because of diversity of expression misses the point that a core mystical experience can be explained and elaborated in different and often contradictory ways.

26. The literature on the influence of occult thought on Nazism is rife with undocumented, sensationalist works and paranoid histories that tell us more about the conspiratorial fears of the authors than anything concrete on the Nazis themselves. For a good discussion of the myths surrounding Nazi occultism see Nicholas Goodrick-Clarke, "The Modern Mythology of Nazi Occultism," appendix E, 217–25, in Goodrick-Clarke, *The Occult Roots of Nazism* (New York: New York University Press, 1992). For a broader discussion of the claims of alleged Nazi occultism see René Freund, *Braune Magie?: Okkultismus, New Age und Nationalsozialismus* (Vienna: Picus, 1995). Important scholarly works exploring the connection of modern occultism and Nazism do exist. The most complete work is Goodrick-Clarke, *The Occult Roots of Nazism,* which represents an important step in uncovering a possible contributing source of Nazi millennialism; however, a direct connection to National Socialism, despite the implications of the title, is not firmly established. See also Jackson Spielvogel and David Redles, "Hitler's Racial Ideology: Content and Occult Sources," *Simon Wiensenthal Center Annual* 3 (1986): 227–46.

27. Norman Cohn, *The Pursuit of the Millennium* (New York: Secker & Warburg, 1957).

28. The 1970 revised edition of *The Pursuit of the Millennium* rightfully reinstated Cohn's earlier views regarding the archetypal nature of millennialism, as well as its psychological origins.

29. James Rhodes, *The Hitler Movement: A Modern Millenarian Revolution* (Stanford: Hoover Institution Press, 1980). Along these lines see also Jean-Pierre Sironneau, *Sécularisation et religions politiques* (New York: Mouton, 1982), esp. 262–354, which also interprets Nazism as a form of secular millennialism. The distinguished scholar of modern religious movements, Robert Ellwood, building primarily on the work of Rhodes, presents an interesting analysis of Nazi millennialism in "Nazism as a Millennialist Movement," in Wessinger, ed., *Millennialism, Persecution, and Violence,* 241–60.

30. Robert Wistrich, *Hitler's Apocalypse: Jews and the Nazi Legacy* (New York: St. Martin's Press, 1985). That both Rhodes's and Wistrich's essential works have generally been ignored by scholars of National Socialism, and in fact are more often cited by nonhistorians or by historians, sociologists, and psychologists studying millennialism, points to what Richard Landes has termed the "rooster and owl" problem in the historiography of millennial studies. Briefly put, Landes contrasts those he terms roosters, including apocalyptic prophets, messianic wannabes, and doomsday date setters, who crow at dawn (the imminent apocalypse), attempting to rouse the other animals into action, and the owls, night creatures that loathe light and noise, that attempt to hush the roosters by claiming they are wrong about the imminent dawn (apocalypse) and dangerous to believe. Most chroniclers and historians, Landes argues, are owls, dismissing, ignoring, and even deliberately obscuring the work of the roosters. As a result, the owls have left large gaps in the history of world civilization as it regards all things millennial. This also is the case with the historiography of Nazism, which has largely marginalized the readily apparent millennial beliefs of the Nazis, the very beliefs that are essential to understanding both Nazism and the Holocaust. See Richard Landes, "On Owls, Roosters, and Apocalyptic Time: A Historical Method for Reading a Refractory Documentation," *Union Seminary Quarterly Review* 49 (1996): 165–85.

31. Michael Ley, *Genozid und Heilserwartung: zum nationalsozialistischen Mord am europäischen Jundentum* (Vienna: Picus, 1993), and his more recent collection of essays, *Apokalypse und Moderne: Aufsätze zu politischen Religionen* (Vienna: Sonderzal, 1997); Claus-Ekkehard Bärsch's study of Goebbels's messianism, *Erlösung und Vernichtung: Dr. phil. Joseph Goebbels: zur Psyche und Ideologie eines jungen Nationalsozialisten 1923–1927* (Munich: Boer, 1987), and especially his *Die politische Religion des Nationalsozialismus: die religiöse Dimension der NS-Ideologie in den Schriften von Dietrich Eckart, Joseph Goebbels, Alfred Rosenberg und Adolf Hitler* (Munich: W. Fink, 1998). Another important collection of essays along these lines is Ley and Schoeps, eds., *Der Nationalsozialismus als politische Religion.*

32. For instance, is the Iranian Revolution of 1979, millennial to the core, secular because the clerics who provided its spiritual and ideological impetus assumed political power?

33. See Arthur P. Mendel's *Vision and Violence* (Ann Arbor: University of Michigan Press, 1992) and *Michael Bakunin: Roots of Apocalypse* (New York: Praeger, 1981), both of which properly place Marxism and anarchism within a millennial and apocalyptic construct. See also the published dissertation of Mendel's student, David G. Rowley, *Millenarian Bolshevism, 1900 to 1920* (New York: Garland, 1987). The essential difference here is that while Marxist-derived movements often utilized millennial and messianic themes in their rhetoric and ideology, such as conceiving the coming worker's utopia as the third

and final stage of historical development, much like Joachim of Fiore's millennial third *stasus* or third Reich, which inspired the Nazi conception, they categorically rejected religion as a component of that utopia. Nazism never rejected spirituality, only certain aspects of what it considered impure Pauline Christianity (meaning aspects of Christianity supposedly tainted by Jewish thought).

34. To be applauded in this regard is Richard Landes and the Center for Millennial Studies at Boston University, which held an annual multidisciplinary conference on millennial studies from 1996 to 2002. A number of the essays presented there will be published as part of Equinox Publishing's Millennialism and Society series (London: 2004–2005), including Brenda Brasher and Lee Quinby, eds., *Gender and Apocalyptic Desire*; Glen McGhee and Stephen O'Leary, eds., *War in Heaven/Heaven on Earth: Theories of the Apocalyptic*; Cathy Gutierrez and Hillel Schwartz, eds., *The End that Does: Art, Science and Millennial Accomplishment*.

Notes to Chapter 1

1. Detlev J. K. Peukert, *The Weimar Republic: The Crisis of Classical Modernity*, trans. Richard Deveson (New York: Hill & Wang, 1993), xii. This work is crucial for an understanding of the total and radical nature of the change that exemplifies the Weimar era. In this chapter I follow Peukert's brilliant analysis closely. My goal is to elucidate the depth of the change, as well as its convergent nature, and to link this rapid and radical change to its apocalyptic interpretation by many of those who became Nazis.

2. I should note, however, that while not hit by earthquakes and floods, Germany during the early postwar years did experience long periods of hunger and starvation, which at times were endemic and epidemic. A series of unusually harsh winters only added to the overwhelming sense of chaos.

3. The concepts of modernization and modernity are not without their critics. See Hans-Ulrich Wehler, *Modernisierungstheorie und Geschichte* (Göttingen: Vandenhoeck und Ruprecht, 1975), and Gerald Feldman, "The Weimar Republic: A Problem of Modernization?" *Archiv für Sozialgeschichte* 26 (1986): 1–26. However, as general concepts that encompass the process of, and structural elements inherent in, the changes that we experience as modern life, they are certainly useful.

4. The best general history of Weimar Germany is Eberhard Kolb, *The Weimar Republic*, trans. P. S. Falla (New York: Routledge, 1988). Also useful is A. J. Nicholls, *Weimar and the Rise of Hitler*, 3rd ed. (New York: St. Martin's Press, 1991); Helmut Heiber, *The Weimar Republic*, trans. W. E. Yuill (Oxford: Blackwell, 1993); Hagen Schulze, *Weimar: Deutschland 1917–1933* (Berlin: Severin und Siedler, 1982).

5. Historians of Weimar Germany most often speak of "crisis" when describ-

ing the prevailing mood. The titles of articles and books on the subject are re-plete with the word. However, crisis implies a turning point, a decisive period in the development or progress of something (for better or worse). While this is cer-tainly true to an extent, a bit of historical hindsight is evident here. The histo-rian's notion of progress often betrays a belief in a natural development from au-thoritarianism to democracy, a development that, in historians' minds, went awry with the return to authoritarianism under Hitler after Weimar democracy failed to meet the crisis of modernity (as is Peukert's major point). While there may be some truth to this, for those who experienced Weimar, the word "crisis" is rarely used. Rather, they refer to their experience of radical change almost without variation as a time of chaos, as a time when existence itself was on the line. Progress, then, was not thought to be *in* crisis; rather, it was itself thought to be a major factor in the formation *of* chaos. Therefore, I will respect the expe-riences of many who lived through Weimar and use the word chaos.

6. These quotations are from the Theodore Abel Collection, at the Hoover In-stitute on War, Revolution and Peace, Stanford, California. This collection con-tains 580 short biographies of early Nazis first gathered by Abel for his book *Why Hitler Came to Power* (New York: Harvard University Press, 1938). I will cite these autobiographies by Abel number, followed by my own pagination, numbering page sides consecutively, as many of the originals lack pagination. These quotations come from Abel #263, 3; #546, 1; #284, 3; #199, 1. For an-other description of death in war as a "holy obligation," see Abel #321, 1.

7. Abel #50, 1.

8. Found in *Die alte Garde spricht,* a four-volume collection of short biogra-phies of early Nazis commissioned by Rudolf Hess in 1936. Two sets of this col-lection are housed at the Library of Congress (Washington, D.C.). This quota-tion is from vol. 1, Roman Pornschlegel, p. 1. Hereafter citations to this collec-tion appear as *DAGS,* volume #, author, page #.

9. *DAGS*, vol. 1, Adam Nickel, 1. The generally poor view of the so-called system (the Weimar Republic) will be discussed shortly.

10. *DAGS*, vol. 1, August Reise, 1.

11. Abel #62, p. 4.

12. *DAGS*, vol. 2, Hans Neff, 1.

13. *DAGS*, vol. 3, Friedrich Heinrich Schott, 1. The "stab-in-the-back" (*Dolchstoss*) myth refers to the lie, promulgated most notably by Erich Luden-dorff (chief of staff to Hindenburg), that the socialist-dominated provisional government ended the war with Germany deep in enemy territory and poised for victory. The truth was that it was Ludendorff who told the socialist government that the war was lost. However, the lie was widely believed. Since the provisional government was wrongly considered by many Germans as Jewish led, the myth played into the further myth of the international Jewish conspiracy to annihilate Germany. I return to the latter theme in the next chapter.

14. Abel #3, 2.

15. *DAGS,* vol. 2, Hans Otto, 3–4.

16. *DAGS,* vol. 1, Heinrich Völker, 1.

17. Abel #35, 1. The Spartacists were one of the leading German communist groups. Many were former sailors who had mutinied or had been dismissed from service and still wore their uniforms during protests.

18. Abel #33, 1. Many future Nazis such as this man were drawn to Hitler because he revealed the power allegedly behind the "unknown forces," the Jews. Conspiricism, a profound belief in the reality of conspiracy, helps make sense of chaos by attributing its appearance to hidden forces deliberately generating the disorder. If one reveals and eliminates that force, order will surely return. The "Noske-troops" reference is to the moderate socialist Defense Minister Gustav Noske, who employed volunteers (*Freikorps*) to attempt to put down "communist rebels," many of whom were simply protesting workers.

19. Abel #245, 1. Schulz speaks of Major von Lützow, whom he calls "leader of the *Freikorps.*" Interestingly, the Lützow *Freikorps* advertised in the Juni-Klub's journal *Gewissen,* an antidemocratic conservative and volkish journal led by Moeller van den Bruck, whose book *Das Dritte Reich,* gave the Nazis the name of their millennial Reich.

20. *DAGS,* vol. 4, Hans Haster, 4.

21. Abel #579, 19.

22. *DAGS,* vol. 2, Wilhelm Schuchman, 2. Other future Nazis found hope in Hitler's failed putsch. See *DAGS,* vol. 1, Paul Bierwirth, 2; Karl Schmidt, 2; vol. 2, Hans Neff, 1; Hermann Möser, 1.

23. Abel #583, 3.

24. Abel #43, 2–3.

25. Abel #582, 1.

26. *DAGS,* vol. 1, Roman Pornschlegel, 1–2.

27. Abel #35, 1.

28. *DAGS,* vol. 2, Jakob Buscher, 42.

29. *DAGS,* vol. 3, Walter Gerwein, 1.

30. Abel #70, 2. Similarly, see Abel #4, 2; Abel #16, 3; Abel #2, 1; *DAGS,* vol. 3, Wilhelm Meder, 2; vol. 4, L. Eifert, 2.

31. *DAGS,* vol. 2, Hans Otto, 4.

32. Abel #24, 8.

33. Abel #3, 2.

34. Abel #583, 3. By Black *Reichswehr* he means the paramilitary groups like the various *Freikorps* or voluntary armies that sprang up after the war to allegedly support the restricted official army of the Republic, especially in its dealings with the Red (communist) paramilitary groups that also appeared at this time.

35. *DAGS,* vol. 4, Heinrich Wick, 1.

36. *DAGS,* vol. 2, Ludwig Nöll, 2; Gustav Bonn, 3; Dr. Daum, 1.

37. Abel #245, 4.

38. Abel #3, 2–3. Albert Leo Schlageter, war veteran and *Freikorps* member turned Nazi, was executed by firing squad by the French in 1923 for his part in what they considered a terrorist bombing. He became a national hero and martyr.

39. Heinersdorf and Kötter are quoted in Jay W. Baird, *To Die for Germany: Heroes in the Nazi Pantheon* (Bloomington: Indiana University Press, 1990), 26, 32. While he does not discuss its millennial significance, the linkage of sacrificial death, rebirth, and immortality appears throughout Baird's materials.

40. Statistics from Jackson J. Spielvogel, *Hitler and Nazi Germany: A History* (Upper Saddle River, N.J.: Pearson Prentice Hall, 2005), 16. Written originally as a textbook, this is one of the best short introductions to the subject.

41. Abel #17, 4.

42. *DAGS,* vol. 1, Heinrich Wilkenlon, 1.

43. Abel #495, 2; *DAGS,* vol. 2, Willi Martin, 14; vol. 3, Werner Goerendt, 2–3. The repetition of the word "orgy" throughout the Nazi testimonials is interesting. The linkage of sexual frenzy and loss of control with Weimar chaos, be it political, economic, social, or cultural, points to German's fear that humanity in times of chaos succumbs to baser instincts at a time when they believed that only the noblest virtues could provide the needed salvation. That many Nazis viewed Weimar as a time of sexual licence approaching a Sodom and Gomorrah is also pertinent here. For an interesting psychological analysis of the sexual preoccupations of *Freikorps* members, many of whom became Nazis, see Klaus Theweleit, *Male Fantasies,* trans., Stephen Conway et al., 2 vols. (Minneapolis: University of Minnesota Press, 1987–89).

44. Abel #468, 2.

45. Peukert, *Weimar,* part 4, "Deceptive Stability," 193–246, esp. chapter 11, "The Illusion of Domestic Stability," 209–21. See also Heinrich August Winkler, *Der Schein der Normalität: Arbeiter und Arbeiterbewegung in der Weimarer Republik, 1924 bis 1930* (Berlin: J. H. W. Dietz, 1985); Nicholls, *Weimar,* chapter 9, "The Semblance of Stability: 1924–1929," 105–19.

46. Abel #244, 7.

47. The statistics and analysis that follow are from Peukert, *Weimar,* 88ff.

48. See, for instance, the near-messianic sense of self-importance promoted in Ernst Günther Gründel, *Der Sendung der jungen Generation: Versuch einer umfassenden revolutionären Sinndeutung der Krise* (Munich: Beck, 1932). On the sense of apocalypse and the dynamism of youth see Klaus Vondung, "Apokalyptische Erwartung: Zur Jungendrevolte in der deutschen Literatur zwischen 1910 und 1930," in Thomas Koebner et al., *"Mit uns zieht die neue Zeit": Der Mythos Jugend* (Frankfurt am Main: Suhrkamp, 1985), 519–44.

49. Peukert, *Weimar,* 95–101.

50. Ibid., 96. The largest category of female workers, those in family businesses, remained relatively constant at 36 percent.

51. A rejection and a fear reflected in the near-obsession of male Weimar artists with depicting the violated female corpse. See Maria Tatar, *Lustmord: Sexual Murder in Weimar Germany* (Princeton: Princeton University Press, 1995).

52. Abel #58, 2.

53. Abel #24, 7; Abel #18, 1; Abel #4, 2.

54. Abel #477, 1. The Nazis would provide this man with the necessary Evil Other, the Jewish Bolsheviks, to explain those forces "from without" that supposedly fomented the social strife. Once again, conspiricism within the context of the apocalypse complex helps create a sense of order by providing a root cause for the chaos.

55. *DAGS,* vol. 3, Emil Hofmann, 1–2.

56. Abel #579, 11.

57. Abel #579, 14–15.

58. As Eberhard Kolb described the tensions, in *Weimar,* 84.

59. Wilhelm Hausenstein, "Die Kunst in diesem Augenblick," *Die neue Merkur* (1919–20), as found in Anton Kaes, Martin Jay, and Edward Dimendberg, eds., *The Weimar Republic Sourcebook* (Berkeley: University of California Press, 1994), 480. This is a highly useful collection of primary sources. Though not the intention of the editors, the material collected here, while only a fraction of that available, clearly reflects the prevalence of the contemporary apocalyptic interpretation of the rapid and radical change of Weimar culture.

60. Quoted in Peukert, *Weimar,* 168.

61. Paul Schultze-Naumberg, *Kunst und Rasse,* 2nd ed. (Munich: J. F. Lehmanns, 1935), 104, 119. The Hitler quotation is found in Otto Wagener, *Hitler: Memoirs of a Confidant,* ed. Henry Ashby Turner, Jr., trans. Ruth Hein (New Haven: Yale University Press, 1985), 309.

62. The same can be said of the emerging film industry. In Weimar, a few artists used film to achieve highly original works, including expressionist masterpieces such as Robert Wienes's *The Cabinet of Dr. Caligari* (1920), Paul Wegener's *The Golem* (1920), Friedrich Wilhelm Murnaus's *Nosferatu* (1922), and Fritz Lang's *Metropolis* (1927). The subject matter of insane asylums, monsters, vampires, and science fiction dystopia certainly lent itself to an expressionist approach. Yet it also reflected the medium's often uneasy mix of technology and visual illusion, speed and motion, epitomizing the fleeting and hyperkinetic modern world that existed on the streets outside the darkened cinema.

63. Alice Gerstel, "Jazzband," *Die Aktion* 12 (February 4, 1922): 90–91, as found in Kaes et al., *Weimar Sourcebook,* 554.

64. Ivan Goll, "Die Neger erobern Europa," *Die literarische Welt* 2 (January 15, 1926): 3–4, as found in Kaes et al., *Weimar Sourcebook,* 559–60.

65. Abel #100A, 4.

66. Discussed in Reinhard Klooss and Thomas Reuter, *Körperbilder: Menschenornamente in Revuetheater und Revuefilm* (Frankfurt am Main: Syndikat, 1980). The same might be said of modern dance during Weimar. The mix of modern music, especially jazz, and scantily clad dancers, moving in "primitivistic" and "sexual" gyrations, appeared in the eyes of many to reflect not only an unwelcome imposition of American and black culture into a pure German culture but also the moral decay of society in general. See Valerie Preston-Dunlop and Susanne Lahusen, eds., *Schrifttanz: A View of German Dance in the Weimar Republic* (London: Pennington, 1990); Susan A. Manning, *Ecstasy and the Demon: Feminism and Nationalism in the Dances of Mary Wigman* (Berkeley: University of California Press, 1993).

67. Erich Kästner, "Kabarett der Namenlosen," *Magdeburger General-Anzeiger* (April 7, 1920), as found in Kaes et al., *Weimar Sourcebook*, 562.

68. *DAGS*, vol. 3, Robert Rohde, 2. The actual percentage of Berlin theater owners who were Jewish was less than 15 percent. While statistically significant, considering that Berlin's Jewish population was less than 5 percent, it leaves 85 percent of the theaters in non-Jewish hands. Not surprising then, Rohde's blaming of Jews for his personal difficulties in the Berlin theater is unwarranted.

69. Joseph Goebbels, "Rund um die Gedächtsniskirche," *Der Angriff: Aufsätze aus der Kampfzeit* (Munich: Eher, 1939), 338–40. The "Piscator" mentioned here is Erwin Piscator, who created multimedia political theater on topical issues like abortion, juvenile delinquency, and judicial bias. See David Bathrick, "Closing the Gaps: Erwin Piscator's Theater of the Spectacle," *Journal of Communication Inquiry*, 13 (1989): 70–79.

70. *DAGS*, vol. 3, Georg Heinzebecker, 2.

71. *DAGS*, vol. 2, Hans Neff, 1.

72. Abel #20, 1. That Hitler's soteriology of race drew this man to Nazism, and alleviated his apocalyptic fears, is telling. I return to this process in subsequent chapters.

73. Abel #4, 2.

74. Peukert, *Weimar*, 66. This is at least partially true. However, many criminals ignored old values because of a simple but pervasive factor called hunger. Peukert and other German scholars who stress the unseemly drive for status and wealth may be buying into the fears of an "Americanization" of German culture that they themselves have critiqued. Hitler, too, saw the inversion of values as symptomatic of a world gone wrong. But can one change the world by changing the values, or must the world be changed to allow such "higher" morals to survive?

75. Abel #24, 7.

76. Abel #70, 1–2.

77. Abel, *Why Hitler*, 123–24. See also ibid., 257, for a similar observation.

78. *DAGS*, vol. 3, Wilhelm Scherer, 5.

79. Abel #3, 5.

80. *DAGS*, vol. 2, Gustav Bonn, 1; Albert Barnscheidt, 3.

81. Gregor Strasser, "Gedanken über Aufgaben der Zukunft," originally *NS-Briefe*, June 15, 1926, here as found in his *Kampf um Deutschland: Reden und Aufsätze eines Nationalsozialisten* (Munich: Eher, 1932), 137. Strasser, as with a number of the Berlin Nazis, interpreted the "socialism" of National Socialism in a more traditional economic way than Hitler ever intended. For Hitler, socialism meant a racial communalism of a millennial sort. Strasser was later killed in the infamous "Night of the Long Knives," accused of plotting a second revolution.

82. Adolf Hitler, *Ein Jahr Nationalsozialismus in Deutschland: Rede des Reichskanzlers Adolf Hitler vor dem Reichstag am 30. Januar 1934* (Berlin: Liebheit & Thiessen, 1934), 5–6.

83. In time, Hitler realized that the politics of religion in Germany required backing off on the anti-Catholic position. It was for this reason above all else that Erich Ludendorff and Artur Dinter, ardent anti-Catholics, broke with the Nazis. Rosenberg and Himmler would keep up the anti-Jesuit rhetoric, but in a less public way. Hitler, too, continued the stance privately, as his monologues demonstrate.

Notes to Chapter 2

1. Édouard Calic, *Secret Conversations with Hitler: Two Newly Discovered 1931 Interviews*, trans. Richard Barry (New York: John Day, 1971), 21.

2. Alfred Rosenberg, *Der völkischer Staatsgedanke: Untergang und Neugeburt* (Munich: Eher, 1924), 3, 21–34.

3. *DAGS*, vol. 2, Jakob Hoffmann, 1.

4. *DAGS*, vol. 2, Wilhelm Scherer, 12.

5. *DAGS*, vol. 3, Heinrich Maxeiner, 10.

6. Abel #468, 1; Abel #20, 1.

7. Abel #33, 1.

8. Quoted in Otto Wagener, *Hitler: Memoirs of a Confidant*, ed. Henry Ashby Turner, Jr., trans. Ruth Hein (New Haven: Yale University Press, 1985), 44–45. This important source is discussed in the appendix.

9. Quoted in Hermann Rauschning, *The Voice of Destruction* (New York: Putnam, 1940), 80.

10. On Wagner's notion of regeneration and redemption through annihilation see the work of Helmut Zelinsky, especially "Die 'feuerkur' des Richard Wagner oder die 'neue religion' der 'Erlösung' durch 'Vernichtung,'" in Heinz-Klaus Metzger and Rainer Riehen, eds., *Richard Wagner: Wie antisemitisch darf ein Künstler sein?* (Munich: Edition + Text, 1981): 79–112; "Der 'Plenipotentarius des Untergangs,'" *Neohelicon* 9 (1982): 145–76; "Verfall, Vernichtung, Wel-

tentrückung: Richard Wagner's antisemitische Werk-Idee als Kunstreligion und Zivilisationskritik und ihre Verbreitung bis 1933," in Saul Friedländer and Jörn Rüsen, eds., *Richard Wagner im Dritten Reich: ein Schloss Elmau-Symposion* (Munich: Verlag C. H. Beck, 2000), 309–41. Also instructive is Paul Lawrence Rose, "Wagner, Hitler und historische Prophetie: Der geschichtliche Kontext von 'Untergang', 'Vernichtung' und 'Ausrottung,' in Friedländer and Rüsen, 283–308.

11. *DAGS,* vol. 3, Jakob Heist, 2.

12. *DAGS,* vol. 1, Paul Bierwirth, 2.

13. *DAGS,* vol. 2, Robert Mayer, 1.

14. Abel #528, 1.

15. Abel #8, 4.

16. After achieving power, the Nazis would continue to use pageantry to stimulate the rebirth of the millennial community. See Robert A. Pois, "The National Socialist *Volksgemeinschaft* Fantasy and the Drama of National Rebirth," in Glen W. Gadberry, ed., *Theatre in the Third Reich, the Prewar Years: Essays on Theatre in Nazi Germany* (Westport, Conn.: Greenwood Press, 1995): 17–32.

17. Quotations found in James Rhodes, *The Hitler Movement: A Modern Millenarian Revolution* (Stanford: Hoover Institution Press, 1980), 59.

18. Rosenberg, *Der völkischer Staatsgedanke,* 21.

19. Quoted in Rhodes, *The Hitler Movement,* 59.

20. *DAGS,* vol. 1, Karl Hepp, 2.

21. Abel #62, 9.

22. Theodore Abel, *Why Hitler Came to Power* (New York: Harvard University Press, 1938), 179, 244.

23. Abel #60, 24–25.

24. *DAGS,* vol. 1, Willi Altenbrandt, 18.

25. I return to Hitler's role as prophet and messiah and to the relationship of leader and his disciples in chapters 4 and 5.

26. Abel #10, 8. The song is, of course, the German national anthem, *Deutschland über Alles.*

27. *DAGS,* vol. 1, Johannes Zehfuss, 6.

28. Abel #49, 2.

29. Quoted in Josef Wulf, *Literatur und Dichtung im Dritten Reich: Eine Dokumentation* (Gutersich: Sigbert Mohn, 1963), 55.

30. *DAGS,* vol. 3, August Eckart, 1. Similarly, see *DAGS,* vol. 1, Johann Uhrig, 1; vol. 3, Wilhelm Kumpf, 1; vol. 3, Heinrich Wider, 1.

31. *DAGS,* vol. 1, Friedrich Neuber, 1–2.

32. *DAGS,* vol. 3, Philipp Balthaser Ripper zu Pfaffen-Beerfurth, 1.

33. Abel #4, 2.

34. Abel #2, 1–2.

35. Abel #60, 10.

36. *DAGS,* vol. 2, Georg Schorbach, 5–6.

37. Abel #4, 3.

38. The most complete work on the Thule Society is Hermann Gilbhard, *Die Thule Gesellschaft: Vom okkulten Mummenschanz zum Hakenkreuz* (Munich: Kiessling 1994). The word "Thule" refers to the mythical northern homeland of the ancient Aryans that, like Atlantis, sank into the sea. The Aryans then purportedly migrated around the Eurasia continent, creating wondrous civilizations from India to Greece to Rome to Germanic Europe. For many volkish and occult thinkers, Thule came to represent both an ideal past where Aryans, perfect in body and soul, ruled a Golden Age and a ideal future, a New Age that would see a resurrection of the Aryan god-men of old. See the essay by Jost Hermand, "Ultima Thule: Völkische und faschistische Zukunftsvisionen," in his collection *Orte, irgendwo: Formen utopischen Denkens* (Königstein: Athenäum, 1981), 61–86.

39. By far the best work on the ariosophists is Nicholas Goodrick-Clarke, *The Occult Roots of Nazism* (New York: New York University Press, 1992).

40. On the fusion of Social Darwinism and occultism see Helmut Zander, "Sozialdarwinistische Rassentheorie aus dem okkulten Untergrund des Kaiserreich," in Uwe Puschner et al., eds., *Handbuch zur 'Völkisch Bewegung' 1871–1918* (Munich: K. G. Saur, 1996): 224–51.

41. On the *Germanenorden* see Reginal H. Phelps, "'Before Hitler Came': Thule Society and Germanen Orden," *Journal of Modern History* 25 (1963): 245–61.

42. For brief accounts on Fritsch see Reginal H. Phelps, "Theodor Fritsch und der Antisemitismus," *Deutsche Rundschau* 87 (1961): 442–49 and Goodrick-Clarke, *Occult Roots of Nazism,* 123–28. On the Hammer movement see Michael Bönisch, "Die 'Hammer' Bewegung,'" in Puschner et al, *Handbuch zum 'Völkisch Bewegung,'* 341–65.

43. Quoted in Goodrick-Clarke, *Occult Roots of Nazism,* 145.

44. Gottfried zur Beek, ed., *Die Geheimnesse der Weisen von Zion* (Charlottenberg: Verlag "Auf Vorposten," 1919). Beek/Müller had received a copy of the *Protocols* from Fyodor Vinberg, a Russian refugee who also published a Russian version of the work in *Luch Sveta* (Ray of Light), a yearbook that presented the combat against the Jewish Elders as a religious mission. According to Vinberg, if the Germans and Russians joined together to defeat the Jews, there would be peace on earth. For more on this and other aspects of the *Protocols* see Norman Cohn, *Warrant for Genocide: The Myth of the Jewish World Conspiracy and Protocols of the Elders of Zion* (London: Serif, 1996).

45. An English translation by Victor Marsden continues to be sold today as a true document. I was able to purchase a copy through Amazon.com, which used a vendor that specializes in conspiratorial nonsense. Reader comments at that

time showed that purchasers found themselves "enlightened" by the "facts" found therein. Editions continue to appear around the world, and Egyptian television recently ran a multipart dramatic series that used the *Protocols* as if they were true. On some of the modern uses of this pernicious forgery see Dina Porat, "*The Protocols of the Elders of Zion: New Uses of an Old Myth*," in Robert S. Wistrich, ed., *Demonizing the Other* (Amsterdam: Harwood Academic, 1999), 322–34. This is a useful collection for understanding the construction of Jews as an Evil Other in its multifarious expressions.

46. Maurice Joly, *Dialogue aux enfers entre Machiavel et Montesquieu ou La politique de Machiavel au XIXe siècle, par un contemporain* (Brussels: A. Mertens, 1864). Gödische's book, written under the name Sir John Retcliffe the Younger, was titled *Biarittz* (Berlin: C. S. Liebrecht, 1868).

47. Quotations from *The Rabbi's Speech* as found in appendix 1 of Cohn, *Warrant for Genocide*, 279–84.

48. Ibid., 99–100.

49. Quoted in Claus Ekkehard-Bärsch, "Der Jude als Antichrist in der NS-Ideologie," *Zeitschrift für Religions und Geistesgeschichte* 47 (1995): 171.

50. Quoted in Cohn, *Warrant for Genocide*, 216–17.

51. Quoted in Ekkehard-Bärsch, "Der Jude als Antichrist," 166.

52. For an analysis of Hitler's early speeches and their indebtedness to the *Protocols*, see Günter Schubert, *Anfänge nationalsozialistischer Außenpolitik* (Köln: Verlag Wissenschaft und Politik, 1963), esp. 27ff.

53. Adolf Hitler, *Adolf Hitlers Reden*, ed. Ernst Boepple (Munich: Deutscher Volksverlag, 1925), 71. Interestingly, Sergi Nilius earlier had interpreted the Jewish star as the sign of the anti-Christ.

54. Adolf Hitler, *Mein Kampf*, trans. Ralph Manheim (Boston: Houghton-Mifflin, 1971), 307–8.

55. Dietrich Eckart, *Der Bolschewismus von Moses bis Lenin. Zwiegespräch zwischen Adolf Hitler und mir* (Munich: Hoheneichen-Verlag, 1924). Hereafter cited as Eckart, *BML*. For the sake of clarity, I will ascribe quotations from *BML* to Eckart and Hitler respectively, although they should be understood, as with other examples of what I call the Hitler gospels, as Eckart's rendering of Hitler's sentiments as expressed in many conversations and discussions. On more background on Eckart see Margarete Plewnia, *Auf dem Weg zu Hitler: Der völkische Publizist Dietrich Eckart* (Bremen: Schünemann, 1970), and Ralph Max Engelman, "Dietrich Eckart and the Genesis of Nazism," Ph.D. dissertation, University of Michigan, Ann Arbor, 1971.

56. Hitler later said of Eckart, "He shone in our eyes like the polar star. . . . At the time, I was intellectually a child still on the bottle." Adolf Hitler, *Hitler's Secret Conversations, 1941–1944*, trans. Norman Cameron and R. H. Stevens (New York: Signet, 1961), 222.

57. These include classical writers such as Strabo and Cicero and early

Church fathers such as Aquinas and Chrysostom, as well as later religious and philosophical thinkers such as Martin Luther, Giordano Bruno, Schopenhauer, and many others. The citations attributed to Hitler reflect more the reading habits of Eckart or Rosenberg than those of the pamphlet-loving Führer.

58. This propaganda technique built on the work of Alfred Rosenberg, who in the pages of Eckart's *Auf Gut Deutsch* and in his *Die Spur des Juden im Wandel der Zeiten* (Munich: Deutscher Volksverlag, 1920) attempted to fuse the Talmud and the notorious forgery *The Protocols of the Elders of Zion* in order to "expose" the Jews. This tendency to use Jewish sources to "reveal" their true nature continued after the Nazis assumed power. Discussed by Paul Lawrence Rose in "Talmudic Scholarship in the Stab-Rosenberg's Institute for Research into the Jewish Question," paper delivered at the 113th annual meeting of the American Historical Association, Washington, D.C., January 7–10, 1999.

59. Eckart, *BML,* 7–8.

60. Ibid., 9. The reference is to Joshua 6:21, "Then they utterly destroyed all in the city, both men and women, young and old, oxen, sheep and asses, with the edge of the sword." Interestingly, a modern partial translation of *BML,* which appeared in *National Socialist World* (fall 1966): 13–33, translates the original text's *Massenmorden* (mass murder) with the modern post-Holocaust word "genocide," a not-so-subtle attempt to shift the blame for the Nazi genocide of Jews back to the Jews themselves by perpetuating the Nazi myth that Jewish genocidal tendencies forced the Nazis to act first.

61. Ibid., 4. The reference is to John 8:43. By the time of the writing of the Gospel of John, the distinction between Christian and Jew (increasingly portrayed as a dreaded Other) began to shape the developing Christian anti-Jewish narrative. It is not surprising that the Gospel of John is reported to have been Hitler's favorite Gospel. For background on the Christian myth of the satanic Jew see Joshua Trachtenberg, *The Devil and the Jews: The Medieval Conception of the Jew and Its Relation to Modern Antisemitism* (New York: Harper & Row, 1943), and Andrew Gow, *The Red Jews: Antisemitism in an Apocalyptic Age, 1200–1600* (New York: E. J. Brill, 1995). Not surprisingly, John 8:43 was used after the Nazis came to power by both Catholic and Protestant anti-Semites. See Doris L. Bergen, "Catholics, Protestants, and Christian Anti-Semitism in Nazi Germany," *Central European History* 27 (1994): 331. It was used in German classrooms, as well. A 1936 children's book included a poem with the line "The Devil is the father of the Jew. When God created the world, He invented the races: the Indians, the Negroes, the Chinese and also the wicked creature called the Jews." Quoted in Christa Kamenetsky, *Children's Literature in Hitler's Germany: The Cultural Policy of National Socialism* (Athens: Ohio University Press, 1984), 166.

62. Eckart, *BML,* 30. The massacre of the innocents in the Children's Crusade is likewise transformed into a Jewish-designed massacre, rather than a

Turkish victory. It also conveniently ignores the thousands of Jews killed by millennially obsessed crusaders.

63. Ibid., 31. The cited source is *Spaccio della bestis trionfante* [The Expulsion of the Triumphant Beast] (1584).

64. Eckart, *BML*, 49–50.

65. Hitler, *Mein Kampf*, 64, 313, 452.

66. Ibid., 65.

67. Adolf Hitler, *Hitler's Second Book: The Unpublished Sequel to* Mein Kampf, trans. Krista Smith (New York: Enigma Books, 2003), 231. For a detailed discussion of the origins of this book and why it was not published earlier, see the introduction by the book's editor, Gerhard L. Weinberg.

68. Otto Wagener, *Hitler: Memoirs of a Confidant*, 64–65. On the Nazi idea of Jews as parasites see Alexander Bein, "'Der Jüdische Parasit,' Bemerkungen zur Semantik der Judenfrage," *Vierteljahrshefte für Zeitsgeschichte* 2 (1963): 121–49. On animalization in general see Philippe Burrin, "Nazi Antisemitism: Animalization and Demonization," in Wistrich, *Demonizing the Other*, 223–35.

69. The intellectual origins of Nazi millennialism is a subject so vast I plan on devoting an entire subsequent volume to it. However, since my main concern in the present volume is how millennialism affected the Old Guard, most of whom knew little of these origins, I focus here on the general ideas that they as disciples received and accepted.

70. Hitler, *Mein Kampf*, 533.

71. Ibid., 346.

72. *DAGS*, vol. 3, Wilhelm Scherer, 12.

73. *NSDAP Hauptarchiv*, Hoover Institution microfilm, roll #4, folder #107, Vogel, "Was Ist und Was Will die Hitlerbewegung" (1931), 4.

74. Calic, *Secret Conversations with Hitler*, 68.

75. Hitler, *Mein Kampf*, 338–39.

76. Ibid., 382.

77. Adolf Hitler, *Die Rede Adolf Hitlers in der ersten grossen Massenversammlung bei Wiederausrichtung der Nationalsozialistischen Deutschen Arbeiter Partei* (Munich: Ehrer, 1925), 8.

78. Louis L. Snyder, *Hitler's Third Reich: A Documentary History* (Chicago: Nelson-Hall, 1981), 51–52.

79. Hitler, *Mein Kampf*, 324. This is in line with the thinking expressed in Eckart's *Bolshevism from Moses to Lenin*, which again validates the usefulness of this source.

80. Quoted in Ekkehard-Bärsch, "Der Jude als Antichrist," 172.

81. As found in Leon Poliakov and Josef Wulf, eds., *Das Dritte Reich und die Juden: Dokumente und Aufsätze* (Berlin: Arani, 1955), 91–92.

82. *DAGS*, vol. 4, Paul Schneider, 35.

83. Rauschning, *Voice of Destruction,* 241.

84. Ibid., 384, 65; see also Snyder, *Hitler's Third Reich,* 29, in which Hitler refers to himself as a "Fighter for my Lord and Savior."

85. Hitler, *Adolf Hitlers Reden,* 17.

86. Discussed at length in Wistrich, *Hitler's Apocalypse: Jews and the Nazi Legacy* (New York: St. Martins Press, 1985), 27–47. This book is essential for understanding the apocalyptic nature of Nazi anti-Semitism, as well as its continuing appeal.

87. Josef Hell, "Wie mich Adolf Hitler über sich belehrte. Und für immer mich von seinem Ich bekehrte," ZS 640, p. 5, Institut für Zeitgeschichte, Munich. I would like to thank the Institute for providing me with a copy of this document.

88. Hitler, *Mein Kampf,* 214, 397, 497, 214.

89. Ibid., 530.

90. Ibid., 383–84.

91. *DAGS,* vol. 3, Heinrich Grebe, 2. The *Verbotenzeit* (forbidden period) refers to the time after the Hitler putsch during which the party was officially banished from Weimar politics.

92. Abel #70, 3.

93. *DAGS,* vol. 3, Balzer, 2.

94. *DAGS,* vol. 3, Heinrich Götz, 1.

95. *DAGS,* vol. 2, Willi Martin, 17.

96. *NDSAP Hauptarchiv,* roll #4, folder #100, Martin Reihl, 8. Reihl is discussing his company's role in the putsch. Many of the reminiscences in this folder recall the putsch in apocalyptic terms. Again, the construction of a group memory via apocalyptic symbolism applies here.

97. *NSDAP Hauptarchiv,* roll #4, folder #99. Bavarian State Ministry report on the Nazi party (1922), 5–6.

98. *NSDAP Hauptarchiv,* roll #4, folder #100. Theodor Schwindel, 4.

99. Abel #526, 3–4.

100. Abel #3, 4.

101. Abel #60, 26.

102. Abel #244, 7.

103. Abel #163, 6.

104. *DAGS,* vol. 2, Johannes Christ, 14. As Adam Pfeiffer explained, in regard to spreading the word: "I had the mission to convince the yet still unconverted *Volksgenossen* of the idea of our revered Führer Adolf Hitler, and to win them for our cause." *DAGS,* vol. 3, Adam Pfeiffer, 1. The importance of canvassing for the idea of Hitler is taken up in the next chapter.

105. Ibid., 15.

106. Abel #524, 3.

107. Abel #67, 3.

108. *DAGS*, vol. 4, Paul Schneider, 36.

109. *DAGS*, vol. 1, Lange, 1. That this individual experienced the sense of mission as being "seized" by a "holy fire," and that he felt "dragged" with "elemental force to its spell," reveals the profound psychological power of millennial rhetoric for the converted.

110. Quoted in Rauschning, *Voice of Destruction*, 40.

111. Hitler, *Mein Kampf*, 107.

112. "Hitler Source Book," (Washington, D.C.: National Archives, Records of the Office of Strategic Services, 1943), RG 226, p. 142.

113. Ibid., 413.

114. *DAGS*, vol. 1, Otto Besenbruch, 3.

115. Quoted in Rhodes, *The Hitler Movement*, 60.

116. Gregor Strasser, *Kampf um Deutschland: Reden und Aufsätze eines Nationalsozialisten* (Munich: Ehrer, 1932), 139.

117. Quoted in Barbara Miller Lane and Leila J. Rupp, *Nazi Ideology before 1933: A Documentation* (Austin: University of Texas Press, 1978), 110. It was Otto Strasser who most likely brought Moeller van den Bruck's millennial conception of the Third Reich, expressed in his book *Das Dritte Reich* to the Nazis. Otto Strasser eventually lost faith in the Nazis as the chosen elite and subsequently formed his own group, the Black Front. After his brother Gregor's murder at the hands of Hitler's thugs, Otto emigrated from Germany and became an even more vocal opponent of Hitler. See Karl O. Paetel, "Otto Strasser und 'Schwarze Front' des wahren Nationalsozialismus," *Politische Studien*, 92 (1957): 269–82.

118. Abel #50, 1.

NOTES TO CHAPTER 3

1. Alfred Rosenberg, *Der völkisch Staatsgedanke: Untergang und Neugeburt* (Munich: Eher, 1924), 31.

2. The *Kampfzeit*, the time of struggle or struggle-time, is the term used by the Nazis to designate the period from the founding of the movement in 1919, to the assumption of power, in 1933. Almost uniformly, the struggle-time is described using the rhetoric of the apocalypse: "chaos," "turning point," "New Age," "mission," "salvation," "savior," "redeemer," and so on.

3. Quoted in Ernest K. Bramstead, *Goebbels and National Socialist Propaganda, 1925–1945* (East Lansing: Michigan State University Press, 1965), 129–30, 163–64.

4. Albert Speer, *Spandau: The Secret Diaries*, trans. Richard Winston and Clara Winston (London: Collins, 1976), 81–82.

5. Kurt G. W. Lüdecke, *I Knew Hitler: The Story of a Nazi Who Escaped the Blood Purge* (New York: Scribner, 1937), 128–37; see also 22–23. On the gen-

eral reliability of Lüdecke's memoirs see Roland V. Layton, "Kurt Lüdecke and I Knew Hitler: An Evaluation," *Central European History* 12 (1979): 372–86. Hitler reportedly told Rauschning something similar; "Our spirit is so strong, and the power of our magnificent movement to transform souls so elemental, that men are remodeled against their will." Hermann Rauschning, *The Voice of Destruction* (New York: Putnam, 1940), 131.

6. Otto Wagener, *Hitler: Memoirs of a Confidant*, ed. Henry Ashby Turner, Jr., trans. Ruth Hein (New Haven: Yale University Press, 1985), 55–57.

7. As Lewis Rambo notes, some crisis, whether religious, political, cultural, or psychological, usually precedes the conversion process. See his *Understanding Religious Conversion* (New Haven: Yale University Press, 1993), 44–55. See also William B. Bankson, H. Hugh Floyd Jr., and Craig J. Forsyth, "Toward a General Model of the Process of Radical Conversion: An Interactionist Perspective on the Transformation of Self-Identity," *Qualitative Sociology* 4 (1981): 279–97.

8. *DAGS*, vol. 2, Adalbert Gimbel, 2; vol. 1, Otto Leinweber, 1; Abel #20, 1; *DAGS*, vol. 2, Gustav Bonn, 2; vol. 1, Karl Aldinger, 2–3; Abel #563, 1.

9. See, for instance, Abel #531, 1; Abel #245, 1.

10. Abel #579, 12.

11. Abel #50, 4.

12. *DAGS*, vol. 1, Emil Schlitz, 1.

13. *DAGS*, vol. 1, Karl Hepp, 2.

14. John Lofland and Rodney Stark, in "Becoming a World Saver: A Theory of Conversion to a Deviant Perspective," *American Sociological Review* 30 (1965): 862–75, noted that the stress and tension generated by crisis are essential catalysts for conversion. While this is a salient point, stress and tension are insufficient in themselves to cause the dramatic transformation of a conversion experience. It is the rapid and radical change that brings about the crisis state, and conversion is the psyche's attempt to elevate the crisis by constructing a new perception of order.

15. Abel #13, 6–9.

16. Rambo, *Understanding Religious Conversion*, 133.

17. Ibid., 57–65.

18. Discussed in John Lofland and Norman Skonovd, "Conversion Motifs," *Journal for the Scientific Study of Religion* 20 (1981): 373–85.

19. *DAGS*, vol. 3, Johannes Zehfuss, 1; Georg Konrad Klinger, 2–3; Heinrich Maxeiner, 1; Wilhelm Reuter, 2; Walter Gerwien, 1–2; Emil Hofmann, 2. Similarly, see Abel #10, 8. The importance of community as being symbolically reflective of order, and the subsequent postconversion desire to canvass or proselytize the new world view, will be discussed shortly.

20. The German word *weg* can be defined as both "path" and "way." Psychologically and religiously speaking, both senses are important. For one searches for the one right path to salvation, but that *path* is also the *way*, the

means to salvation. It is the new way of perceiving reality. Interestingly, many respondents to Abel and in *DAGS* gave their pieces such titles as "The Path of a German to National Socialism," "The Path from the Old to the New German Men," "My Path to the NSDAP," and, most often, "My Path to Adolf Hitler."

21. Abel #43, 1–2.

22. Abel #20, 2.

23. *DAGS*, vol. 3, Otto Glas, 1. He also noted that Hitler had only revealed the path, that it must be struggled through in order to achieve liberation: "For us it was only the path that the Führer had shown us, and, indeed, we must fight for freedom."

24. *DAGS*, vol. 3, Wilhelm Fleck, 5.

25. Abel #20, 2.

26. Abel #194, 5.

27. *DAGS*, vol. 4, L. Eifert, 11.

28. *DAGS*, vol. 1, Josef Schimmel, 2.

29. *DAGS*, vol. 4, Paul Schneider, 14.

30. *DAGS*, vol. 2, Johannes Christ, 3.

31. In sociology, this is referred to as network theory. The most influential study is Lofland and Stark, "'Becoming a World Saver.'" See also John Lofland, "Becoming a World Saver' Revisited," *American Behavioral Scientist* 20 (1977): 805–18; Rodney Stark and William Bainbridge, "Networks of Faith: Interpersonal Bonds and Recruitment to Cults and Sects," *American Journal of Sociology* 85 (1980): 1376–95; David A. Snow, Louis A. Zurcher Jr., and Sheldon Ekland-Olson, "Further Thoughts on Social Networks and Movement Recruitment," *Sociology* 17 (1983): 112–20.

32. *DAGS*, vol. 1, Karoline Leinweber, 3.

33. *DAGS*, vol. 1, Heini Bickendorf, 9.

34. *DAGS*, vol. 2, Eduard Hohbein, 3.

35. Rambo, *Understanding Religious Conversion*, 50–51. According to Walter Conn, an expert on Christian conversion, the desire for self-transcendence is the primary motivational factor behind conversions. See his *Christian Conversion: A Developmental Interpretation of Autonomy and Surrender* (New York: Paulist Press, 1986) and "Pastoral Counseling for Self-Transcendence: The Integration of Psychology and Theology," *Pastoral Psychology* 36 (1987): 29–48.

36. Old Guard Nazis, like their Führer and other anti-Semites, almost uniformly blamed the Jews for the perceived materialism and egoism of modern life. Rejecting the materialism that seemed to define modernity was deemed essential in order to achieve the Nazi millennium and to thwart the alleged conspiratorial machinations of the materialistic and temporal Jews.

37. *DAGS*, vol. 3, Ludwig Heck I, 2.

38. Abel #545, 2.

39. Abel #179, 1. As we will see in the next chapter, Hitler likewise claimed

to follow a transcendent "inner voice." Hitler's inner voice would become the voice of millions.

40. *DAGS,* vol. 3, Peter Weber, 1. The sudden nature of this individual's conversion is not uncommon and will be discussed at length shortly.

41. *DAGS,* vol. 4, Franz Madre, 1.

42. Abel #163, 6.

43. Abel #207, 6.

44. Quoted in Theodore Abel, *Why Hitler Came to Power* (New York: Harvard University Press, 1938), 244.

45. Abel #10, 6; Abel #199, 1.

46. Abel #3, 1.

47. Abel #71, 3.

48. Abel, *Why Hitler,* 116–17.

49. Abel #526, 3.

50. Abel #570, 1.

51. *DAGS,* vol. 3, Rudolf Bergmann, 1.

52. *DAGS,* vol. 1, Hermann Hirth, 2.

53. Abel #526, 4; *DAGS,* vol. 3, Georg Schönberger, 3.

54. Abel #477, 1; Abel #245, 7; *DAGS,* vol. 3, Valentin Schwöbel, 6; *DAGS,* vol. 2, Heinrich Berwig, 1; *DAGS,* vol. 1, Heini Bickendorf, 8.

55. *DAGS,* vol. 1, Willi Altenbrandt, 21.

56. Rambo, *Understanding Religious Conversion,* 1.

57. *DAGS,* vol. 3, Wilhelm Scherer, 4.

58. *DAGS,* vol. 4, Otto Schroeder, 9.

59. Abel #586, 1.

60. Abel #172, 3.

61. Abel #9, 2.

62. Abel #44, 3; Abel #36, 1; Abel #265, 7; *DAGS,* vol. 1, Otto Besenbruch, 3.

63. However, as I discuss in the following chapters, the significance of Hitler's symbolic role as both prophet and savior, combined with his noted oratorical gift, cannot be disparaged, either. Moreover, Hitler was present symbolically in the speeches of other Nazis, almost always referred to in his role as "savior," "redeemer," or "prophet."

64. Abel, *Why Hitler,* 117. Abel's conclusion was based on some of the same material used in the present study. I concur with his analysis, and my examination of similar sources such as *Die alte Garte Spricht* corroborates and extends it.

65. *DAGS,* vol. 4, L. Eifert, 3–4.

66. *DAGS,* vol. 3, Elisabeth Kranz, 26.

67. *DAGS,* vol. 2, Emil Schneider, 2. He also noted that "in this gathering I had learned about the inner division and disunity of the German Volk." Once

again, psychological division and disunity generate a perception of chaos, and reestablishing psychic unity elicits a sense of salvation.

68. *DAGS,* vol. 2, Johannes Christ, 12.

69. *DAGS,* vol. 2, Hans Grün, 1.

70. *DAGS,* vol. 1, Paul Hainbach, 25.

71. Abel #23, 3.

72. *DAGS,* vol. 4, Heinrich Wick, 2.

73. Abel #33, 2.

74. *DAGS,* vol. 2, Robert Mayer, 2.

75. *DAGS,* vol. 1, Dora Sott, 2.

76. See George L. Mosse, *Fallen Soldiers: Reshaping the Memory of the World Wars* (New York: Oxford University Press , 1990).

77. Abel #50, 4.

78. This oneness was, of course, limited to those of Aryan blood. All others were excluded from the Nazi "community." The dualism inherent in Nazi apocalyptic cosmology necessitated an anticommunity, a group whose separation from the Aryan community was a key element in "restoring" that community and, ultimately, in creating the Nazi millennium. The limited nature of this oneness, the Nazi *Volksgenossen,* is a crucial factor leading to the Holocaust.

79. Quoted in Wagener, *Memoirs of a Confidant,* 212.

80. Abel #24, 9.

81. *DAGS,* vol. 3, Georg Konrad Klinger, 2; Abel #477, 1; *DAGS,* vol. 4, Paul Schneider, 2; Abel #369, 1.

82. Abel, *Why Hitler,* 179, 138.

83. Abel #10, 7; *DAGS,* vol. 1, Hermann Jung, 25; vol. 4, Franz Madre, 6.

84. Abel #60, 26.

85. Abel #43, 6.

86. *DAGS,* vol. 3, Elisabeth Kranz, 27.

87. On the infusion of a sense of power after conversion see Rambo, *Understanding Religious Conversion,* 85–86.

88. *DAGS,* vol. 2, M. Hetzel, 2; Abel #41, 1; *DAGS,* vol. 2, Karl Dörr, 5.

89. Abel, *Why Hitler,* 145.

90. *DAGS,* vol. 1, Heinrich Oesterling, 6; Roman Pornschlegel, 3; Wilhelm Schneider, 2; Abel #10, 6; *DAGS,* vol. 3, Anne Heilmann, 2. Heilmann's perception of invincibility is not uncommon among converts to apocalyptic faiths.

91. For a discussion of the importance of ritual, pre- and postconversion, see Rambo, *Understanding Religious Conversion,* 113–18.

92. From a technical standpoint, the Party Day experiences of individuals who were already Nazis could be termed intensifications, rather than conversions. However, it is clear from the experiences described later that the psychological effects of conversion occurred, and therefore the distinction between intensification and conversion may be more academic then real. From a psycholog-

ical standpoint, it is not so much a change of affiliation that marks the conversion but the profound inner experience of having the old self die and the new self be reborn.

93. *DAGS,* vol. 3, Karl Baumann, 3; vol. 1, Hans Schmidt, 6; vol. 2, Johannes Christ, 14–15. Christ further explained that he soon won over eight "sports comrades." The desire to spread the word and extend the conversion experience to others is common.

94. *DAGS,* vol. 3, Emil Sauer, 12.

95. *DAGS,* vol. 1, Karl Müller, 2; vol. 2, Jakob Tritsch, 4; Abel #44, 2.

96. Adolf Hitler, *Mein Kampf,* trans. Ralph Manheim (Boston: Houghton Mifflin, 1971), 533.

97. Ibid., 346.

98. *DAGS,* vol. 3, Wilhelm Scherer, 12.

99. Rauschning, *Voice of Destruction,* 290; see also ibid., 291–92.

100. Abel #60, 10.

101. *DAGS,* vol. 3, Ludwig Heck I, 2. He then began intensive "man to man canvassing" (ibid., 3). He perceptively noted that "parallel with the rising propaganda activity went the economic decline of Germany" (ibid., 4). Canvassing at work, however, was not always so easy. Another Nazi was told by his fellow workers "to keep his politics in the streets, not the shop." See *DAGS,* vol. 2, Fritz Günther Stroh, 2.

102. Abel #1, 2; *DAGS,* vol. 3, Emil Hofmann, 2.

103. *DAGS,* vol. 2, Hans Otto, 6.

104. *DAGS,* vol. 1, Roman Pornschlegel, 4. This is a common statement. See also ibid., vol. 1, Hermann Möser, 1; G. V. Porembsky, 2; vol. 2, Dr. Daum, 2; Karl Carrier, 1; Heinrich Oesterling, 1; Freiherr von Lynker, 2; vol. 3, Ludwig Heck I, 3; Karl Baumann, 1.

105. Abel, *Why Hitler,* 118, 146, 142.

106. *DAGS,* vol. 4, L. Eifert, 11.

107. *DAGS,* vol. 1, Emil Wiesemann, 1; Hermann Eberhardt, 2.

108. *DAGS,* vol. 1, Adalbert Gimbel, 3.

109. *DAGS,* vol. 2, Georg Dingeldein, 3. Others noted the propaganda activity "evening to evening, house to house." See ibid., vol. 2, Albert Barnscheidt, 3; W. R. Möckel, 2; Otto Erb I, 1.

110. *DAGS,* vol. 2, Stroh, 2; Josef Schneider, 3.

111. Abel, *Why Hitler,* 146.

112. *DAGS,* vol. 1, Emil Schlitz, 2.

113. *DAGS,* vol. 2, Adam Schneider, 2.

114. On sacrifice as a form of surrendering see Rambo, *Understanding Religious Conversion,* 132–37.

115. *DAGS,* vol. 1, Mages, 5; vol. 2, Georg Schorbach, 10; Abel #9, 3.

116. Abel, *Why Hitler,* 278. Hitler said much the same thing in private,

telling Wagener, "who will ever know how much quiet sacrifice, heroism, and greatness have been expended on behalf of Germany and her salvation." Quoted in Wagener, *Memoirs of a Confidant*, 23.

117. Abel, *Why Hitler*, 278, 293. He is, of course, speaking of those who died in the failed putsch attempt of 1923.

118. *DAGS*, vol. 3, Wilhelm Schnabel, 4. On the willingness to make "blood-sacrifice" see also ibid., vol. 1, Leonhard Fleck, 1.

119. *DAGS*, vol. 3, Wilhelm Jockel, 3.

120. Quoted in *DAGS*, vol. 2, Jakob Buscher, 9.

121. Abel #22, 5.

122. Abel #10, 7. The best study of the importance of martyrdom in Nazism is Jay W. Baird, *To Die for Hitler* (Bloomington: Indiana University Press, 1990). Though he is not explicit in this regard, Baird demonstrates that the Nazi conception of martyrdom was thoroughly millennial, with accompanying songs, poems, and ceremonies referring to death and resurrection/rebirth, purity and regeneration, and so on. The millennialism is more clearly evident in Sabine Behrenbeck, *Der Kult um die toten Helden* (Vierow: SH-Verlag, 1996).

123. *DAGS*, vol. 1, Julius Stehl, 2–3, 8; Rudolf Manz, 10; Abel #522, 1.

124. Quoted in *DAGS*, vol. 2, Stroh, 5. The young man was killed when he yelled out, at a communist meeting, "I am a Hitlerian!"

125. Both the Abel Collection and the *Die alte Garte spricht* autobiographies presented an opportunity for Old Guard Nazis to demonstrate their commitment to Hitler and his movement. The litany of sacrifices that many include in their writings does just that.

126. *DAGS*, vol. 1, Ernst Hass, 1. Similarly see ibid., vol. 2, Georg Weiss, 3.

127. *DAGS*, vol. 3, Walter Gerwien, 7; ibid., vol. 1, Willi Altenbrandt, 19.

128. *DAGS*, vol. 3, Walter Gerwien, 7.

129. *DAGS*, vol. 3, Peter Hartmann I, 2; ibid., vol. 2, Albert Barnschadt, 3. The boycotts, almost uniformly and falsely blamed on Jews, figure prominently in many stories. This may explain the relish with which many of the Old Guard participated in the Nazi boycott of Jewish businesses shortly after the Nazis took power.

130. *DAGS*, vol. 2, Hans Wagner, 48.

131. *DAGS*, vol. 2, Georg Weiss, 2.

132. *DAGS*, vol. 2, Retired Major Strelow, 2. Not exactly sacrificing one's life, but horrid nonetheless. One man's sacrifice is, I suppose, another's luxury.

NOTES TO CHAPTER 4

1. On Hitler's childhood see Bradley F. Smith, *Adolf Hitler: His Family, Childhood, and Youth* (Stanford: Hoover Institution on War, Revolution, and Peace, 1967); Franz Jetzinger, *Hitlers Jugend* (Vienna: Europa-Verlag, 1956).

2. Hitler's own version of his childhood, which must be taken as just that, his version, part imagined, part historical, can be found in the first chapter of *Mein Kampf*. The quotation here is from *Mein Kampf*, trans. Ralph Manheim (Boston: Houghton Mifflin, 1971), 17.

3. This episode is discussed in Jetzinger, *Hitlers Jugend*, 148–51 and Smith, *Adolf Hitler*, 97–98. A recent psychological and medical analysis of Hitler can be found in Fritz Redlich, *Hitler: Diagnosis of a Destructive Prophet* (New York: Oxford University Press, 1999), 17.

4. August Kubizek, *The Young Hitler I Knew*, trans. E. V. Anderson (Boston: Houghton Mifflin, 1955). I agree with Ian Kershaw that Kubizek, despite his occasional factual mistakes and literary embellishments, is more reliable than previously thought. See Kershaw, *Hitler, 1889–1936: Hubris* (New York: W. W. Norton, 1999), 20–21. Brigitte Hamann makes this point as well in *Hitler's Vienna* (New York: Oxford University Press, 1998), 52–59.

5. Kubizek, *Young Hitler I Knew*, 22. I discuss Hitler's penchant for nondirected thinking in the next chapter.

6. Quoted in Charles Bracelen Flood, *Hitler, the Path to Power* (Boston: Houghton Mifflin, 1989), 432. Thirteen years later, Hitler said much the same thing, telling associates, "I have built up my religion out of *Parsifal*. Divine worship in solemn form." Quoted in Joachim C. Fest, *Hitler*, trans. Richard Winston and Clara Winston (New York: Harcourt Brace Jovanovich, 1974), 519.

7. As described by John Deathridge in *Wagner's Rienzi: A Reappraisal Based on a Study of the Sketches and Drafts* (Oxford: Clarendon Press, 1977), 22–23. Interestingly, Rienzi utilizes what can be loosely termed mass propaganda to gain public support. His rule collapses because of the intrigues and machinations of those around him. Ibid., 35–36.

8. Quoted in Hamann, *Hitler's Vienna*, 24.

9. Kubizek, *Young Hitler I Knew*, 99–100.

10. Ibid., 290.

11. While generally supportive of Kubizek as a source, Ian Kershaw regards his account of the Rienzi incident as "highly fanciful, reading in mystical fashion back into the episode an early prophetic vision of Hitler's own future." He concludes that Kubizek's account is a "melodramatically absurd claim." Kershaw, while not denying that some incident took place, feels that the "vision" should not be taken seriously. Kershaw, *Hitler: Hubris*, 610, note 128.

I disagree for a number of reasons. First, it is highly unlikely that Kubizek could have manufactured such a convincing description of a revelatory experience, one that is so psychologically consistent with visionary experiences of other would-be messiahs. Again, a visionary experience is a psychological phenomenon and need not be taken as evidence of divine intervention or genuine messianic calling. Kershaw takes a exceedingly narrow approach, arguing that it is impossible for Hitler to have made such a claim as a young man and then for it to subsequently to have come true. But there is nothing "absurd" in this at all. That a prophecy comes true does not mean that Hitler was prophetic, any more than it means that he was in fact Germany's messianic Rienzi incarnate. By chance, some prophecies do come true. Hitler likewise envisioned one day rebuilding Linz and Vienna to conform to his own fantasy reconstructions. This indeed began to occur after the *Anschluss* some thirty years later. Is Kubizek's recollection of Hitler's teenage reconstruction plans likewise absurd? Throughout his career, Hitler made many prophecies and made political gambles based on his so-called inner voice, which he took to be the voice of Providence. Some of these prophecies came true, and some did not. The question of the legitimacy of the prophecy is moot, anyway, as it is not a question of whether it came true but whether a preponderance of the evidence points to Hitler's believing that it was a true prophecy or vision. And in this we can respond in the positive.

12. Otto Wagener, *Hitler: Memoirs of a Confidant*, ed. Henry Ashby Turner, Jr., trans. Ruth Hein (New Haven: Yale University Press, 1985), 217.

13. Deathridge, *Wagner's Rienzi*, 2.

14. Albert Speer, *Spandau: The Secret Diaries*, trans. Richard Winston and Clara Winston (London: Collins, 1976), 88. According to Speer, during a subsequent visit to the Linz theater Hitler became visibly emotional and asked to be left alone (ibid., 173).

15. On his formative teenage years see William Jenks, *Vienna and the Young Hitler* (New York: Columbia University Press, 1960); Anton Joachimsthaler, *Korrektur einer Bibliographie: Adolf Hitler, 1908–1920* (Munich: Herbig, 1989), corrects some of the mistakes of earlier biographies of this historically difficult-to-document time in Hitler's life. Most recently see Hamann, *Hitler's Vienna*.

16. Discussed in Kubizek, *Young Hitler I Knew*, 164–65.

17. Ibid., 109.

18. The cultural contrasts are illustrated in Carl Schorske's classic study *Fin-de-Siècle Vienna: Politics and Culture* (New York: Knopf, 1980). Hamann's *Hitler in Vienna* is likewise highly illustrative of this culture in transition.

19. Peter Pulzer's *The Rise of Political Anti-Semitism in Germany and Austria*, rev. ed. (Cambridge, Mass.: Harvard University Press, 1988), is indispensable here.

20. Hitler, *Mein Kampf*, 161.

21. Ibid., 163. Hitler's belief in his "inner voice," which directed him to participate in the war, was a component of his growing messianism. I return to the notion of the inner voice in the next chapter.

22. Ibid.

23. Ian Kershaw finds the notion that Hitler had a second visionary experience "highly unlikely" and believes that the "quasi-religious" nature of the experience was solely "part of the mystification of his own person which Hitler encouraged as a key component of the Führer myth." However, that an individual

with prior messianic tendencies, under great physical and psychological distress, could have a messianic visionary experience is far from being "highly unlikely" but rather is quite typical of individuals with such propensities. The idea that Hitler's visionary experiences were all part of some grand "mystification," a scheme to make Hitler appear messianic, misses the point. The more important question is whether there is evidence for the significance of this experience for Hitler and whether *he* interpreted it messianically. The answer certainly is yes. The alternative, that it was a calculated story for propaganda purposes only (which is not to say that it could not be and was used in such a way) is simply not supported by the evidence. Kershaw rejects the "colorful" account of a hallucination tied to Hitler's sense of mission, but he has no real factual basis for that rejection. Evidence and common sense suggest that Hitler, and many others, believed that some experience had in fact occurred. Kershaw's interpretation can be found in *Hitler: Hubris,* 103–5.

24. The diagnosis of Hitler's second blindness as psychosomatic is discussed in an OSS Intelligence report (#31963, March 21, 1943), now at the National Archives. Titled "Adolf Hitler's Blindness: A Psychological Study," it details the reminiscences of Dr. Karl Kronor, who purportedly participated with Dr. Edmund Forster when he treated Hitler. Kronor's analysis is extremely superficial and highly vindictive. He believed, perhaps correctly, that the SS killed Forster to silence him, although his death, after he was forced into retirement by the Nazis, in 1933, was ruled a suicide. It should be noted, as well, that the reliability rating of the report was downgraded from B-3 to F-3. The status of Forster's treatment is also in doubt. On this see Redlich, *Hitler,* 42–43. However, other sources appear to verify Hitler's belief in his visionary experience, as well as its psychosomatic basis.

25. R. G. L. Waite, *The Psychopathic God: Adolf Hitler* (New York: Basic Books, 1977), 27.

26. Quoted in Rudolf Binion, *Hitler among the Germans* (New York: Elsevier, 1976), 136.

27. Ludwell Denny, "France and the German Counter-Revolution," *The Nation* 116 (February 1923): 295.

28. "Hitler Source Book," (Washington, D.C.: National Archives, Records of the Office of Strategic Services, 1943), RG 226, 901.

29. Karl von Wiegand, "Hitler Foresees His End," *Cosmopolitan* (April 1939), 28, in "Hitler Source Book," 490.

30. Quoted in Alan Bullock, *Hitler: A Study in Tyranny* (New York: Harper & Row, 1964), 109.

31. Hitler, *Mein Kampf,* 206.

32. Max Domarus, ed., *Hitler: Reden und Proklamationen, 1932–1945: Kommentiert von einem deutschen Zeitgenossen* (Neustadt: a. d. Aisch, Schmidt, 1962), vol. I, 704.

33. Kershaw, *Hitler: Hubris,* 105, says this claim by Hitler must be false since Hitler had no connections or means of entering politics in 1919, so he could not have envisioned it. This is beside the point, for what Hitler envisioned himself doing need not be tied to any realistic estimate of whether it was possible at that time. Many significant figures in history saw themselves as being great in the future, even though at the time they seemingly had no real prospects for achieving greatness. Of course, many more individuals envision greatness for themselves and never achieve it. That few such dreams come true does not mean that the original dream is absurd or never happened. Hitler's visionary experiences would not have provided any clear image of how he would achieve greatness and save Germany, only that he would somehow, someway, someday, do so.

34. Kubizek, *Young Hitler I Knew,* 140.

35. Ibid., 188, 192.

36. "Hitler Source Book," 647.

37. Quoted in Heinz A. Heinz, *Germany's Hitler* (London: Hurst & Blackett, 1934), 103.

38. "Hitler Source Book," 895.

39. George E. Atwood, "On the Origins and Dynamics of Messianic Salvation Fantasies," *International Review of Psycho-Analysis* 5 (1978): 85. For a different take on patients with delusions of having been chosen for a messianic mission see John Weir Perry, *The Far Side of Madness* (Englewood Cliffs, N.J.: Prentice Hall, 1974), esp. 20, 96.

40. Further examples of messianic visions obtained during trance states can be found in B. G. Burton-Bradley, "The New Guinea Prophet: Is the Cultist Always Normal?" *Medical Journal of Australia* (January 17, 1970): 126; W. W. Meissner, "The Cult Phenomenon: Psychoanalytic Perspective," *Psychoanalytic Study of Society* 10 (1984): 91–111; John Weir Perry, "The Messianic Hero," *Journal of Analytic Psychology* 17 (1972): 192–93; Leon Perez, "The Messianic Psychotic Patient," *Israel: Annals of Psychiatry and Related Disciplines* 15 (1977): 364; Hue-Tam Ho Tai, *Millenarianism and Peasant Politics in Vietnam* (Cambridge: Cambridge University Press, 1983), 84–85.

41. *NSDAP Hauptarchiv,* Hoover Institution microfilm, roll #4, folder #107, Vogel, "Was Ist und Was Will die Hitlerbewegung," 2.

42. Ibid.

43. The Taiping millenarian leader Hung Hsiu-Ch'uan (Hong Xiuquan) had his primary vision after a complete physical and emotional breakdown. See P. M. Yap, "The Mental Illness of Hung Hsiu-Ch'uan, Leader of the Taiping Rebellion," *Far Eastern Quarterly* 13 (November 1953–August 1954): 287–304. The Seneca prophet Handsome Lake had his visions after a near-death experience brought on by extreme alcoholism, discussed in Anthony F. C. Wallace's sociopsychological study *The Death and Rebirth of the Seneca* (New York: Vintage, 1972). The Maori prophet Te Ua Haumene had his visions during a time of

extreme illness that may have been psychosomatic. See Michael Adas, *Prophets of Rebellion: Millenarian Protest Movements against the European Colonial Order* (Chapel Hill: University of North Carolina, 1979), 109–10.

44. Such a messianic visionary experience may not even be unique to Hitler among the Nazis. Eduard Hohbein claimed that "when I laid on the Festung sick bed at Saint Sauveur in Lille, on January 5, 1918 at 8 o'clock in the evening, with a fever from the amputation, I was ready to go before my Lord (though I still wanted to live), a light-form appeared in my room and transmitted to me that I would not die yet, because I had a mission yet to fulfill!" While Hitler's chosen mission was that of messiah, Hohbein's would be that of devoted disciple. In *DAGS,* vol. 2, Eduard Hohbein, 6–7.

45. Hitler, *Mein Kampf,* 346–47.

46. Albrecht Tyrell, *Vom "Trommler" zum "Führer": der Wandel von Hitlers Selbstverständnis Zwischen 1919 u. 1924 u. d. Entwicklung d. NSDAP* (Munich: Fink, 1975). Kershaw, *Hitler: Hubris,* largely follows Tyrell for this portion of his biography. While I agree that a transformation took place, I do not believe the chronology of the personality change is as clearcut as either Tyrell or Kershaw present it.

47. Otto Strasser, *Hitler and I,* trans. Gwenda David and Eric Mosbacher (Boston: Houghton Mifflin, 1940), 66–67.

48. Eberhard Jäckel and Axel Kuhn, eds., *Hitler: Sämtliche Aufzeichnungen 1905–1924* (Stuttgart: Deutsche Verlags-Anstalt, 1980), 924. Of course, Hitler may have simply been waiting for the populace to acclaim him as the "coming man," which, in time, many did.

49. Quoted in Ian Kershaw, *The Hitler Myth: Image and Reality in the Third Reich* (New York: Oxford University Press, 1987), 23.

50. "Hitler Source Book," 901.

51. Quoted in Georg Schott, *Das Volksbuch vom Hitler* (Munich: Hermann A. Wiechmann, 1924), 55. This early work presents Hitler as a prophet and genius, and his movement as salvational. Joachim Fest similarly quotes Hitler as calling himself "a very small sort of St. John." In Fest, *Hitler,* 162

52. This according to the conservative publisher Rudolf Pechel in his postwar *Deutscher Widerstand* (Zurich: Rentsch, 1947), 280.

53. Quoted in Helmuth Auerbach, "Hitlers politische Lehrjahre," *Vierteljahrshefte für Zeitgeschichte* 25 (1977): 29.

54. Kershaw, *Hitler: Hubris,* 165.

55. On the postwar Munich political scene see David Clay Large, *Where Ghosts Walked: Munich's Road to the Third Reich* (New York: Norton, 1997). Although lacking in historical analysis, Charles Bracelen Flood, in *Hitler, The Path to Power* (Boston: Houghton Mifflin, 1989), brings a novelist's skill to the accurate recreation of a sense of the truly apocalyptic nature of Munich society after the war.

56. For important documents and insight into this sometimes obscure period of Hitler's life see Joachimsthaler, *Korrektur einer Bibliographie*, esp. 184, 188, 200–204, 211.

57. Captain Mayr would later claim that Hitler at this time was like a "stray dog" looking for a master to treat him well, "totally unconcerned about the German people and their destinies." Quoted in his anonymously published "I Was Hitler's Boss," *Current History* 1 (November, 1941): 193. This statement should be treated with caution, since by the Second World War Mayr had long since worked against Hitler and in fact wrote this piece while in exile. To portray Hitler as a selfish opportunist unconcerned with the fate of Germany was a well-established anti-Nazi propaganda technique. Mayr was later captured by the Nazis in France and died in Buchenwald in 1945.

58. Karl Alexander von Müller, *Mars und Venus: Erinnerungen, 1914–1919* (Stuttgart: G. Kilpper, 1954), 338.

59. Hitler, *Mein Kampf*, 215–16.

60. Cited in Ernst Deuerlein, "Hitlers Eintritt in die Politik und die Reichswehr," *Vierteljahrshefte für Zeitgeschichte* 7 (1959): 200.

61. Ibid., 198–99. Hitler was becoming increasingly known for his "Jewish agitation." Hitler was even told to tone it down by one superior.

62. Michael Lotter, "Der Beginn meines politischen Denkens!" Typescript from 1935, in *NSDAP Hauptarchiv*, roll #3, folder #78, 6. Lotter noted that Drexler spoke "of the will to annihilation of everything German by Jewry and Freemasonic lodges" (3). As we saw earlier, the belief in the Jewish will to exterminate would be a major thesis of Eckart and Hitler and later a justification for the Final Solution.

63. The speech took place on November 3, 1922, and was reported in the *Völkischer Beobachter* on November 8. Esser was responding to Mussolini's March on Rome on October 28, 1922. Cited in Kershaw, *Hitler: Hubris*, 180.

64. Reginald Phelps, "Die Hitler Bibliotek," *Deutsche Rundschau* 80 (1954): 925. Phelps argued that this is the earliest dedication to Hitler as "Führer."

65. Cited in Kershaw, *Hitler: Hubris*, 182.

66. Kershaw notes in this regard that at no time did Hitler "unambiguously claim those qualities [that of the coming great leader] for himself." But of course he would not have at this point. Hitler's messianic self-perception needed to be legitimated. He needed disciples, growing public adulation, continued successes as speaker, the national publicity of the putsch trial, and finally the triumphs of the early years of the seizure of power to feel fully legitimated as messiah.

67. Quoted in Tyrell, *Vom "Trommler" zum "Führer,"* 63.

68. Quoted in Kershaw, *Hitler: Hubris*, 185. I agree with Kershaw and Tyrell that 1923 reveals a process of change, but it is in the intensification and legitimization of pre-existing messianism, not a sudden change to messianism.

69. Siegfried was not so impressed, seeing in Hitler only "a fraud and an up-

start." Both quoted in Friedeland Wagner, *The Royal Family of Bayreuth* (London: Eyre & Spottiswoode, 1948): 8–9.

70. Quoted in Flood, *Hitler,* 433.

71. Cited in Kershaw, *Hitler: Hubris,* 192–93.

72. Ludwell Denny, "France and the German Counter-Revolution," *The Nation* 116 (March 14, 1923), 295.

73. Paul Gierasch, "The Bavarian Menace to German Unity," *Current History Magazine* 223 (1923): 226. Interestingly, Gierasch calls Hitler a machinist. That Denny thought Hitler to be a locksmith and Gierasch a machinist most likely reflects the desire by some Nazis to portray Hitler as, or to believe that he was, a working-class man of the people.

74. From the trial report reproduced in Jäckel and Kuhn, *Hitler: Sämtliche und Aufzeichnungen,* 1117.

75. Quoted in Kershaw, *Hitler: Hubris,* 214.

76. Hitler's discussion of this can be found in Jäckel and Kuhn, *Hitler: Sämtliche und Aufzeichnungen,* 1188.

77. Ibid., 1210.

78. Quoted in Fest, *Hitler,* 210. For more on Goebbel's quest for salvation see Claus-Ekkehard Bärsch, *Der junge Goebbels: Erlösung und Vernichtung* (Munich: Boar, 1995).

79. Quoted, respectively, in Flood, *Hitler,* 190, and Ernst Hanfstängl, *Hitler: The Missing Years* (London: Eyre & Spottiswoode, 1957), 83.

80. Quoted in Robert Cecil, *Myth of the Master Race: Alfred Rosenberg and Nazi Ideology* (New York: Dodd, Mead, 1972), 221.

81. "Hitler Source Book," 901. Max Rothe (604) noted similarly that after the putsch "he was no longer the 'drummer' . . . he made himself into the 'coming Man.'"

82. Quoted in Wagener, *Memoirs of a Confidant,* 170, 172. Hitler's Aryanized Christian socialism, perhaps inspired by the work of Houston Stewart Chamberlain or Lanz von Liebenfels, was determined not by shared faith but by shared racial characteristics, a racial community of Aryan nations, led by Germany.

83. Baldur von Schirach, *Ich Glaubte an Hitler* (Hamburg: Mosaik Verlag, 1967), 160. A good source for the messianic devotion of Hitler's inner circle is Claus-Ekkehard Bärsch, *Die politische Religion des Nationalsozialismus* (Munich: W. Fink, 1998), 136–78.

84. Ludwig Wagner, *Hitler: Man of Strife* (New York: W. W. Norton, 1942), 320–21. During the morning of the putsch Eckart exclaimed, "Let it happen as it will and must, but I believe in Hitler; above him there hovers a star." Quoted in Cecil, *Myth of the Master Race,* 41.

85. Quoted in Flood, *Hitler,* 141.

86. Rudolf Hess, "Wie wird der Mann beschaffen sein, der Deutschland

wieder zur Höhe führt," typescript in *NSDAP Hauptarchiv*, roll #35, folder #689.

87. Ibid., 1.

88. Ibid., 2.

89. Ibid., 3.

90. Ibid., 5.

91. Ibid., 6.

92. Quoted in Kershaw, *Hitler: Hubris*, 165.

93. Letter 342, *Rudolf Hess Briefe 1908–1933*, ed. Wolf Rüdiger Hess (Munich: Langen Müller, 1987), 338.

94. On one occasion Hess wrote, "At the core the Tribune is deeply religious." Ibid., letter 353, 155.

95. Discussed in John Toland, *Adolf Hitler* (New York: Doubleday, 1976), 64, 67–68.

96. According to Ernst Schmidt and Ignaz Westenkirchner, in Heinz A. Heinz, *Germany's Hitler* (London: Hurst & Blackett, 1934), 67–68, 82, 96.

97. Hans Mend, *Adolf Hitler im Felde, 1914–1918* (Munich: J. C. Huber, 1931), 172. One could, of course, once again look at this as Mend reading back into history, seeing in Hitler another prophecy fulfilled. But why continue to jump through hoops to explain away the obvious, that Hitler, before, during, and after the war, had a pronounced messianic self-perception, one that continued to ebb and flow until the time of the putsch when Hitler finally became convinced that his earlier visions were real, or, put another way, when external reality seemed to catch up to his internal reality. Besides, Mend's account is not exactly flattering to Hitler. In fact, he ended up in Dachau. There seems little reason for Mend to help build the Hitler myth.

98. Quoted in George Ward Price, *I Know These Dictators* (London: Harrap, 1937), 39–40. Konrad Heiden, in *Adolf Hitler: A Biography* (New York: A. A. Knopf, 1936), 319–20, reports Hitler's saying, on another occasion, "I was seated over a meal at the front with several comrades. Suddenly an inner voice bade me: 'Stand up and seat yourself at that spot over there!' I obeyed; the spot was about twenty yards distant. Hardly had I reached it before a shell burst among my comrades. Not one escaped." I will return to Hitler's belief in his "inner voice," and its providential implications, shortly. Regarding stories of this episode, Ian Kershaw, *Hitler: Hubris*, 634, note 111, refers to Hitler's "characteristic embellishment of the story," implying that Hitler's interpretation of the incident is to be dismissed as simply another example of Hitler's hubris, and part of the post-facto mythification. Once again, this misses entirely the point that Hitler's "embellishment" is a mode of interpreting, or reinterpreting, as the case may be, his personal history in messianic terms; the incident is seen and reseen as proof that he is indeed the heaven-sent Führer saved by Providence in order that he might one day fulfill his mission. Autobiograph-

ical reconstructions to legitimate one's messianism are typical of individuals who assume the mantle of savior, and they should not be dismissed lightly. It is central to the psychology of messianism and, thus, to the individual's motivation.

99. Quoted in Wagener, *Memoirs of a Confidant*, 174.

100. Quoted in Heinz Assmann, "Some Personal Recollections of Adolf Hitler," *Proceedings, U.S. Naval Institute* 79 (July 1953): 1290–91. Regarding the same incident, he told his valet, "that is new proof that I have been selected from among other men by Providence to lead greater Germany to victory." To another, he stated, "because I have been saved while others had to die, it is clearer than ever that the fate of Germany lies in my hands." Quoted in Waite, *Psychopathic God,* 28. Himmler seems to have agreed with Hitler's analysis, telling his masseur, Felix Kersten, "By preserving the Führer Providence has given us a sign. The Führer lives, invulnerable—Providence has spared him to us so that we may bring the war to a triumphant conclusion under his leadership." Quoted in Felix Kersten, *The Kersten Memoirs, 1940–1945* (London: Hutchinson, 1956), 201. Hitler reportedly referred to the conspirators as "traitors against Divine Providence." Quoted in Hugh Trevor-Roper, *Last Days of Hitler* (London: Pan Books, 1968), 94.

101. Quoted in Price, *I Know These Dictators, 25.*

102. Quoted in Heiden, *Hitler,* 274.

103. Quoted in Price, *I Know These Dictators,* 119–20.

104. Albert Speer, *Inside the Third Reich: Memoirs* (New York: Bonanza Books, 1982), 357.

105. Walter Schellenberg, *The Labyrinth: Memoirs of Walter Schellenberg* (New York: Harper, 1956), 93.

106. Hermann Rauschning, *The Voice of Destruction* (New York: Putnam, 1940), 201.

107. Domarus, *Reden und Proklamation,* vol. I, 817, 849.

108. Ibid., 849.

109. Ibid., 606.

110. Quoted in Wagener, *Memoirs of a Confidant,* 100.

111. Quoted in Rauschning, *Voice of Destruction,* 181. That Rauschning and Wagener both recall Hitler making similar statements about his inner voice and its role in his decision making goes a long way to validating both sources. On Hitler's inner voice, see also ibid., 184, 224, 260; Speer, *Inside the Third Reich,* 85, 165. As one individual explained, "Hitler considers himself essentially an artist who brings the resources of his intuition into the realities of life and succeeds because he perceived things which are hidden from the sight of the specialists" ("Hitler Source Book," 599).

112. Quoted in Wagener, *Memoirs of a Confidant,* 150–51.

113. Hitler's physical response reflects the somatic aspect of the apocalypse

complex, such as glossolalia, trembling, and sensations of an inner fire or of being touched by God. The importance of following the "inner voice" became part of the Nazi worldview. One minor ideologue explained that the instinctual aversion to race mixing was nothing other than the voice of God. As he explained, "we call instinct the still soul or the voice of God." That voice demanded Germans to keep their blood (soul) pure, for "God wants his people to be of pure blood and thereby maintain its fitness for life." Explaining further, he defined soul as "the godliness in us . . . the soul is the union of us and God. So it is a piece of God Himself, the voice of God in us. Never will the harmony between God and us be destroyed, if we listen to the commands and admonitions of our soul." Quoted in Dr. Zilcher, "Deutsche Sozialismus," 2–5, *NSDAP Hauptarchiv,* roll #4, folder #107.

114. Quoted in Wagener, *Memoirs of a Confidant,* 153.

NOTES TO CHAPTER 5

1. Ulrich Linser, *Barfüßige Propheten: Erlöser der zwanziger Jahre* (Berlin: Siedler, 1983). Most of these "barefoot prophets," as Linser demonstrates, were more akin to New Age gurus than to political redeemers and unlikely to ever attract more than a small group of followers. Hitler did his best to avoid the label of volkish crackpot and probably for this reason kept many of his own eccentric beliefs from the public. While Hitler had his cult and allowed it to flourish, he also wanted to avoid looking politically suspect. For more on the postwar messianic atmosphere see Klaus Schreiner, "Messianism in the Political Culture of the Weimar Republic," in Peter Schäfer and Mark Cohen, eds., *Toward the Millennium: Messianic Expectations from the Bible to Waco* (Leiden: Brill, 1998): 311–61.

2. Alfons Heck, *A Child of Hitler: Germany in the Days When God Wore a Swastika* (Frederick: Renaissance House, 1985), 22.

3. Otto Strasser, *Hitler and I,* trans. Gwenda David and Eric Mosbacher (Boston: Houghton Mifflin, 1940), 62–65.

4. Ernst Hanfstängl, "My Leader," *Collier's* 94 (1934): 7–9.

5. Quoted in Kershaw, *Hitler, 1889–1936: Hubris* (New York: W. W. Norton, 1999), 187.

6. Kurt G. W. Lüdecke, *I Knew Hitler* (New York: Scribner, 1937), 22–23.

7. Francis Yeats-Brown, "A Tory Looks at Hitler," *Living Age* 354 (1938): 512. This man also noted the "intense mystical fervor" of the performance. Again, while Yeats-Brown was attempting to sell Hitler to his countrymen, this fact does not detract from the value of his subjective perception of the Hitler experience, one that others much less enamored of, if not openly hostile, to Hitler likewise reported. That the reaction of Hitler's audiences as portrayed here is reminiscent of the later experiences of pop idols from Elvis to the Beatles and be-

yond is perhaps not coincidence but symptomatic of larger issues of identity in an age of mass media and mass audience.

8. Walter Schellenberg, *The Labyrinth: Memoirs of Walter Schellenberg* (New York: Harper, 1956), 94–95. In an interview with John Toland, Hanfstängl reported that Hitler told him that, "The mass, the Volk, is for me a wife." Quoted in Charles Bracelen Flood, in *Hitler, The Path to Power* (Boston: Houghton Mifflin, 1989), 615, note 28.

9. Karl Alexander von Müller, *Im Wandel einer Welt: Erinnerungen, 1919–1932* (Munich: Süddeutscher Verlag, 1966), 149. Sometimes the experience was mutually stimulating. Müller remembered that "after one such frenetic cascade of words . . . Dietrich Eckart sprang upon a table with a red-hot face and with the appearance of a raving madman, screamed his song 'Deutschland Erwache!' to the multitude as a booming brass band took it up as in a paroxysm: it was the image of a madman unleashed as in a frenzy." Ibid.

10. Lüdecke, *I Knew Hitler*, 489.

11. George Ward Price, *I Know These Dictators* (London: Harrap, 1937), 39.

12. Sisley Huddleston, *In My Time: An Observer's Record of War and Peace* (New York: E. P. Dutton, 1938), 302. This believer also noted that "flames leaped out of his large luminous eyes: and when he talked he was transformed." Hyperbole to be sure, but film of Hitler speaking attests to the emotional transformation that took place when Hitler spoke before the mass audience, for both Hitler and his disciples.

13. Stanley High, "Hitler and the New Germany," *Literary Digest* 116 (October 7, 1933): 42. Hitler had himself photographed practicing such gestures to see which were the most effective. See Joachim C. Fest, *Hitler,* trans. Richard Winston and Clara Winston (New York: Harcourt Brace Jovanovich, 1974), for some examples. Its been claimed that Hitler learned some of his oral and gesticular techniques for "mass hypnosis" or persuasion from the psychic entertainer Hanussen. However, Hitler's skills as a speaker seemed to have come naturally, despite his later efforts to make improvements. They certainly predate his contact with Hanussen.

14. "Hitler Source Book," (Washington, D.C.: National Archives, Records of the Office of Strategic Services, 1943), RG 226, pp. 642, 644.

15. Egon Larson, *Weimar Eyewitness* (London: Bachman & Turner, 1976), 147.

16. Quoted in Heinrich Hoffmann, *Hitler Was My Friend,* (London: Burke, 1955), 47. The wedding was Hermann Esser's. Interestingly, Hoffmann reports that the wedding cake had a likeness of Hitler in the middle. Everyone cut around the effigy, not wanting to desecrate the image of the sacred Führer.

17. Bella Fromm, *Blood and Banquets: A Berlin Social Diary* (New York: Harper, 1942), 96–97; Ernst Rüdiger and Fürst von Starhemberg, *Between*

Hitler and Mussolini: The Jews and the Italian Authorities in France and Tunisia (New York: Harper & Brothers, 1942), 78; Dorothy Thompson, *I Saw Hitler* (New York: Farrar & Rinehart, 1932), 16; Louis P. Lochner, *What about Germany?* (New York: Dodd, Mead, 1942), 111.

18. H. R. Knickerbocker, *Is Tomorrow Hitler's?: 200 Questions on the Battle of Mankind* (New York: Reynal & Hitchcock, 1941), 11.

19. T. R. Ybarra, *Collier's* (July 1, 1933), 17.

20. Frederick Oechsner, *This Is the Enemy* (Boston: Little, Brown, 1944), 69.

21. Lothrop Stoddard, *Into the Darkness: Nazi Germany Today* (New York: Duell, Sloan and Pearce, 1940), 292.

22. Although he had not yet coined the term, possibly his best discussion of the concept can be found in C. G. Jung, "The Transcendent Function," *The Collected Works of C. G. Jung* (New York: Pantheon Books, 1953), vol. 8, paras. 166–75.

23. Lochner, *What about Germany?* 112.

24. Interview with Adolf Zeissler in Hollywood, California, June 24, 1943, in "Hitler Source Book," 921.

25. Müller, *Im Wandel einer Welt*, 162–63.

26. Quoted in St. Clair McKelway, "Who Was Hitler?" *Saturday Evening Post* 213 (1940): 12.

27. Lochner, *What about Germany?* 102. Lochner noted that after the speech, Hitler "was still in a trance." Ibid., 103.

28. Quoted in Leo Lania, *Today We Are Brothers: The Biography of a Generation* (Boston: Houghton Mifflin, 1942), 234.

29. Strasser, *Hitler and I,* 65–66.

30. Quoted in Janet Flanner, *An American in Paris: Profile of an Interlude between Two Wars* (New York: Simon & Schuster, 1940), 414.

31. Otto Strasser and Michael Stern, *Flight from Terror* (New York: R. M. McBride, 1943), 24–25; Lochner, *What about Germany?* 109–10.

32. Cyril Brown, "New Popular Idol Rises in Bavaria," *New York Times,* November, 21, 1922: 18.

33. Klaus Vondung, *Magie und Manipulation: ideologischer Kult und politische Religion des Nationalsozialismus* (Göttingen: Vandenhoeck and Ruprecht, 1971). A brief explanation of these ideas in English can be found in Vondung, "Spiritual Revolution and Magic: Speculation and Political Action in National Socialism," *Modern Age* 23 (1979): 394–402.

34. Hanns Johst, *Ich glaube!: Bekenntnisse* (Munich: Albert Langen, 1928), 75, as quoted in Vondung, "Spiritual Revolution and Magic," 400.

35. Heck, *A Child of Hitler,* 18, 23.

36. Otto Wagener, *Hitler: Memoirs of a Confidant,* ed. Henry Ashby Turner, Jr., trans. Ruth Hein (New Haven: Yale University Press, 1985), 4.

37. Quoted in Gilmer W. Blackburn, *Education in the Third Reich: A Study*

of Race and History in Nazi Textbooks (Albany: State University of New York Press, 1985), 4.

38. Jean-Pierre Sironneau, *Sécularisation et religions politiques* (The Hague: Mouton, 1982), 581–82.

39. Ibid., 582–83.

40. Hermann Rauschning, *The Voice of Destruction* (New York: Putnam, 1940), 192.

41. Rudolf Hess, "Wie wird der Mann beschaffen sein, der Deutschland wieder zur Höhe führt," typescript in *NSDAP Hauptarchiv*, roll #35, folder #689, 3.

42. Müller, *Im Wandel einer Welt*, 144–45.

43. Ibid.; Denny, "France and the German Counter-Revolution," 295.

44. Theodore Abel, *Why Hitler Came to Power* (New York: Harvard University Press, 1938), 298.

45. Lochner, *What about Germany?* 99.

46. Flanner, *An American in Paris*, 403.

47. Karl von Wiegand, "Hitler Foresees His End," *Cosmopolitan* 4 (1939): 28.

48. "Hitler at Fifty," *Living Age* 7 (1939), 453. This article is signed simply G. H. It appeared originally in German in the Basel newspaper *National-Zeitung*, no date.

49. Knickerbocker, *Is Tomorrow Hitler's*, 45–47. I would add to Jung's analysis only a slight caveat. And that is that Hitler's magic was not effective solely on the Germans (there were numerous British, American, and other converts). By giving voice to the apocalypse complex, Hitler struck a responsive chord that still resonants for many neo-Nazis today. See the many examples found in Nicholas Goodrick-Clarke's two books, *Hitler's Priestess: Savitri Devi, the Hindu-Aryan Myth, and Neo-Nazism* (New York: New York University Press, 1998), and *Black Sun: Aryan Cults, Esoteric Nazism and the Politics of Identity* (New York: New York University Press, 2002).

50. Joseph Nyomarkay applied Weber's concept of charisma to Hitler and his followers in *Charisma and Factionalism in the Nazi Party* (Minneapolis: University of Minnesota Press, 1967).

51. "When Hitler Hit the Ceiling," *Literary Digest* 115 (1933): 30.

52. Rauschning, *Voice of Destruction*, 258.

53. Wagener, *Memoirs of a Confidant*, 151.

54. Ibid., 75. On another occasion, Wagener noted that ideas "bubbled out of him, so that I hardly felt that he was speaking on the basis of thought; rather, the words seemed to come from him by themselves." Ibid., 319. This description is strikingly similar to Kubizek's account of Hitler's visionary diatribe after the *Rienzi* performance, lending credence to both Kubizek's and Wagener's interpretations.

55. Ibid., 325.

56. William L. Shirer, *Berlin Diary: The Journal of a Foreign Correspondent, 1934–1941* (New York: Knopf, 1941), 588; Sebastian Haffner, *Germany: Jekyll and Hyde* (New York: E. P. Dutton, 1941), 31–32; Stoddard, *Into the Darkness,* 294.

57. "Hitler Source Book," 795; Heiden, *Adolf Hitler,* 93.

58. Albert Speer, *Inside the Third Reich* (New York: Bonanza Books, 1982), 471.

59. Quoted in Lüdecke, *I Knew Hitler,* 419.

60. Rauschning, *Voice of Destruction,* 60.

61. Ibid., 82, 255.

62. Quoted in Hugh Trevor-Roper, *The Last Days of Hitler* (New York: Macmillan, 1947), 72.

63. Thompson, *I Saw Hitler,* 13–14.

64. C. G. Jung, "After the Catastrophe," *The Collected Works of C. G. Jung* (New York: Pantheon Books, 1953), vol. 10, para. 419.

65. Strasser and Stern, *Flight from Terror,* 112.

66. Strasser, *Hitler and I,* 52.

67. Abel, *Why Hitler,* 118, 120.

68. *NSDAP Hauptarchiv,* Roll #4, Folder #100, Otto Schiedermaier, 1.

69. Ernst Hanfstängl, *Unheard Witness* (Philadelphia: Lippincott, 1957), 70–71.

70. Quoted in Heinz A. Heinz, *Germany's Hitler* (London: Hurst & Blackett, 1934), 218–19.

71. Rauschning, *Voice of Destruction,* 259.

72. Abel #395, 2.

73. *DAGS,* vol. 3, Johannes Zehfuss, 2.

74. Abel #10, 7.

75. Abel #50, 5.

76. Abel #533, 4–5.

77. *NSDAP Hauptarchiv,* roll #4, folder #100, Josef Richter, 1.

78. Abel #5, 5.

79. Abel #579, 16.

80. *DAGS,* vol. 1, Paul Then, 4–5.

81. *DAGS,* vol. 2, Georg Schorbach, 4.

82. *DAGS,* vol. 4, Heinz Hermann Horn, 20.

83. *DAGS,* vol. 1, Willi Schondorff, 3.

84. *DAGS,* vol. 1, Adalbert Gimbel, 9; F. Zimpelmann, 4; M. Gläser, 2; Heinz Schmidt, 5; Hermann Jung, 13–14.

85. *DAGS,* vol. 2, Andreas Dees, 2.

86. Quoted in Blackburn, *Education in the Third Reich,* 11.

87. Ibid.

88. Georg Schott, *Das Volksbuch vom Hitler* (Munich: H. A. Wiechmann, 1924), 18. Pointedly, Schott also stated that the "Volk soul" was "conscious in him." There is a certain psychological truth in that statement. Hitler's unconscious often intruded into his waking life.

89. *Völkisch Beobachter,* April, 21–22, 1935.

90. Heinz Haake, *Das Ehrenbuch des Führers: Der Weg zur Volksgemeinschaft* (Düsseldorf: F. Floeder, 1933), 32. This book was designed for youth and stressed that Hitler was "Germany's savior." Its chapter titles included "Adolf Hitler's German Mission," "Germany's Awakener from Shame and Servitude," "A New Age Begins," "We Become One Volk under Adolf Hitler's Leadership," and, "I Belong to You and You Belong to Me."

NOTES TO CHAPTER 6

1. Lucy Dawidowicz, *The War against the Jews 1933–1945* (New York: Holt, Rinehart & Winston, 1975), xxii.

2. Saul Friedländer's brilliant discussion of what he termed redemptive anti-Semitism can be found in *Nazi Germany and the Jews* (New York: Harper-Collins, 1997), esp. 73–112.

3. Hitler's 1919 typescript letter to Adolf Gemlich can be found in *NSDAP Hauptarchiv* roll #4, folder #96. It is reproduced in Eberhard Jäckel and Axel Kuhn, eds., *Hitler: Sämtliche und Aufzeichnungen, 1905–1924* (Stuttgart: Deutsche Verlags-Anstalt, 1980), 88–90. Josef Hell, "Wie mich Adolf Hitler über sich belehrte und für immer mich von seinem Ich bekehrte," Typescript, 5. Institute for Contemporary History, Munich.

4. Adolf Hitler, *Adolf Hitler Reden,* ed. Ernst Boepple (Munich: Deutscher Volksverlag, 1925), 17.

5. It was the historian Karl Schleunes, in *The Twisted Road to Auschwitz: Nazi Policy toward German Jews, 1933–1939* (Urbana: University of Illinois Press, 1970), who argued that the road to the Final Solution was twisted and not straight. This brings us to the intentionalist/functionalist debate, which has ebbed and flowed over the years. Historians deemed intentionalists argue that the Nazi leadership always aimed to exterminate the Jews, usually pointing to the Nazis' own words, as I have, to make their point. Those termed functionalist or structuralist historians argue, rather, that the decision to exterminate all the Jews of Europe occurred only after World War II had started and that the process of extermination happened rather haphazardly. They tend to emphasis the role of broader structures within the Nazi state that made extermination possible. It was not so much Hitler and the inner circle that conceived and directed the Final Solution but the thousands of petty careerists within the immense Nazi

bureaucracy who turned a murderous fantasy into a horrifying reality. I return to this important discussion at the end of this chapter, noting how an understanding of Nazi millennialism informs this debate.

6. As found in Kurt Pätzold, ed., *Verfolgung, Vertreibung, Vernichtung: Dokumente des faschistischen Antisemitismus 1933 bis 1942* (Frankfurt am Main: Röderberg-Verlag, 1984), 111.

7. Joseph Goebbels, "Der Bolschewismus in Theorie und Praxis," in *Der Parteitag der Ehre: Vom 8 bis 14 September 1936* (Munich: F. Eher, 1936), 97, 99, 101. According to Goebbels, the goal of Bolshevik propaganda "is the destruction of the world [*Weltzerstörung*]." Ibid., 103.

8. Joseph Goebbels, "Die Wahrheit in Spanien," *Der Parteitag der Arbeit vom 6 bis 13 September 1937: Offizeller Bericht über den Verlauf des Reichsparteitages mit sämtlichen Kongressreden* (Munich: F. Eher, 1938), 140, 144, 156, 157. Goebbels is paraphrasing a host of famous anti-Semitic sayings by the likes of Theodor Mommsen and Richard Wagner, among others.

9. Heinrich Himmler, *Geheimreden 1933 bis 1945 und andere Ansprachen,* ed. Bradley F. Smith and Agnes F. Peterson (Frankfurt on Main: Proyläen Verlag, 1974), 37.

10. *Das Schwarze Korps* (November 24, 1938), in Friedländer, *Nazi Germany and the Jews,* 312.

11. Quoted in Pätzold, *Verfolgung, Vertreibung, Vernichtung,* 158. This is a frightening presentiment of the "just atonement" order of Wehrmacht General von Reichenau, to be discussed shortly.

12. Quoted in ibid., 212–13.

13. Max Domarus, ed., *Hitler: Reden und Proklamationen, 1932–1945* (Neustadt: a. d. Aisch, Schmidt, 1962), vol. 2, 1058.

14. Historians are increasingly arguing this fact. For instance see Doris L. Bergen, *War and Genocide: A Concise History of the Holocaust* (Lanham: Roman & Littlefield, 2003); Donald M. McKale, *Hitler's Shadow War: The Holocaust and World War II* (New York: Cooper Square Press, 2002).

15. Domarus, *Hitler: Reden und Proklamationen,* vol. 2, 1663.

16. For recent literature on the *vernichtstungkrieg,* variously translated as "war of extermination" or "war of annihilation," see Hannes Heer and Klaus Naumann, eds., *War of Extermination: The German Military in World War II, 1941–1944* (New York: Berghahn Books, 2000). For literature on the interrelationship of ideology and annihilation see Gerd R. Ueberschär, "The Ideologically Motivated War of Annihilation in the East," in Rolf-Dieter Müller and Gerd R. Ueberschär, eds., *Hitler's War in the East, 1941–1945: A Critical Assessment* (New York: Berghahn Books, 2002), 209–80. The notion of the war of annihilation is an old one, but it gained new impetus during World War II and was expanded on in subsequent years. See, in the volume cited, Jan Philipp Reemtsma,

"The Concept of the War of Annihilation: Clausewitz, Ludendorff, Hitler," 13–35.

17. Quoted in Jürgen Förster, "Hitler Turns East: German War Policy in 1940 and 1941," in Bernd Wegner, ed., *From Peace to War: Germany, Soviet Russia, and the World, 1939–1941* (Providence: Berghahn Books, 1997), 129. Four years earlier Himmler had said much the same thing, telling leaders of the SS that "wars of the future will not be a skirmish, but a life and death settlement of peoples." *Geheimreden*, 48.

18. Michael Geyer, "German Strategy in the Age of Machine Warfare, 1914–1945," in Peter Paret, ed., *Makers of Modern Strategy: From Machiavelli to the Nuclear Age* (New York: Oxford University Press, 1991), 546.

19. Ibid., 551.

20. Ibid., 574. The important work of Omer Bartov, which studies the conceptualizations of German officers and soldiers involved in the Eastern war, bears this out. See Bartov, *The Eastern War, 1941–45* (New York: St. Martin's Press, 1986) and *Hitler's Army: Soldiers, Nazis, and War in the Third Reich* (New York: Oxford University Press, 1992).

21. Percy Ernst Schramm, ed., *Kriegstagebuch des Oberkommando der Wehrmacht (Wehrmachtführungstab) 1940–1945,* (Frankfurt am Main: Bernard & Graefe, 1961–1965), vol. 2, 336–37.

22. Quoted in "Deutschland zum Endkampf mit dem jüdisch-bolschewistisch Mordsystem angetreten." National Archives Microfilm Collection, Records of the National Socialist German Labor Party, T81, serial 890, roll 672, pages 5, 34, 22 of this document. The pamphlet further notes that Bolshevism is not an "idea" or "Weltanschauung" but rather "organized criminality" (22).

23. *Mitteilungen für die Truppe* no. 116, "Rettung aus schwester Gefahr," as found in Manfred Messerschmidt, *Die Wehrmacht im NS-Staat: Zeit der Indoktrination* (Hamburg: R.v. Decker, 1969), 326–27.

24. Quoted in Bartov, *Hitler's Army*, 129.

25. Quoted in Christian Streit, *Keine Kameraden: Die Wehrmacht und die sowjetischen Kriegsgefangenen, 1941–1945* (Stuttgart: Deutsche Verlags-Anstalt, 1978), 115. Reichenau further argued that "Draconian measures" should be taken against civilians who harbored "partisans." Streit's main concern is the factors that elicited mistreatment of Soviet POWs. The same forces, in part conceptualized in millennial and apocalyptic terms, also propelled atrocities against Russian civilians and Jews.

26. Ibid., 115. As Streit notes, this order quickly became known to other units throughout the eastern front. Far from meeting with disapproval, it became a model for other commanders.

27. Ibid., 116.

28. Ibid., 116–17.

29. Joseph Goebbels, *Die Tagebücher von Joseph Goebbels*, ed., Elke Fröhlich (Munich: K. G. Saur, 1996), part 1, vol. 9, 379. Entry June 16, 1941.

30. Quoted in Daniel Jonah Goldhagen, *Hitler's Willing Executioners: Ordinary Germans and the Holocaust* (New York: Knopf, 1996), 404. Goldhagen is certainly correct when he states that many German soldiers believed that they were engaged in an apocalyptic war for existence with Jewry, one that necessitated, if not demanded, the extermination of all Jews. However, whether the "Germans" as a collective body believed this, which Goldhagen argues, is not at all clear.

31. Quoted in ibid., 442.

32. Ibid., 593, note 50. That *Einsatzgruppen* commandos believed they were engaged in an apocalyptic battle with Jewish-Bolsheviks was argued even by their postwar criminal defender. See Dr. Reinhard Maurach, "Expert Legal Opinion Presented on Behalf of the Defense," "U.S. v. Ohlendorf et al.," *Trials of the Major War Criminals Before the International Military Tribunal, Nuremberg, 14 November 1945–October 1946* (Nuremberg: S. N., 1947–1949), vol. 4., 339–55. Ohlendorf, who commanded *Einsatzgruppe* D, continued to argue after the war that Jewry "has continued to sow hate; and it reaps hate again. What else could we have done when confronted with demons at work, engaged in a struggle against us?" Quoted in Goldhagen, *Hitler's Willing Executioners,* 393–94. Jewish victims were well aware that many perpetrators had come to accept the demonization of the Jews. Chaim Kaplan, in his Warsaw ghetto diary, explained that

> The masses have absorbed this sort of qualitative hatred. . . . They have absorbed their masters' teachings in a concrete, corporeal form. The Jew is filthy; the Jew is a swindler and an evildoer; the Jew is the enemy of Germany, who undermines its existence; the Jew was the prime mover in the Versaille Treaty, which reduced Germany to nothing; the Jew is Satan, who sows dissension between one nation and another, arousing them to bloodshed in order to profit from their destruction. These are easily understood concepts whose effect in day-to-day life can be felt immediately.

See Kaplan, *The Warsaw Diary of Chaim A. Kaplan* (New York: Collier Books, 1973), 130.

33. Quoted in *Deutsche Soldaten sehen die Sowjet-Union,* collected and edited by Wolfgang Diewerge (Berlin: W. Limpert, 1941), 49. The letters found in this source were clearly chosen by the Nazis for propagandistic reasons. However, I agree with Omer Bartov, *Hitler's Army,* note 145, 212–13, that, used in combination with other collections of letters from the front, they provide invaluable insight into the mental conceptions of the German soldier.

34. Ibid., 41, 43.

35. Wilhelm Prüller, *Diary of a German Soldier* (London: Faber & Faber, 1963), 166.

36. Letter of August 4, 1941, in Horst Fuchs Richardson, ed., *Sieg Heil! War Letters of Tank Gunner Karl Fuchs, 1937–1941* (Hamden: Archon Book, 1987), 124.

37. Letter 351, in Ortwin Buchbender and Reinhold Sterz, eds., *Das andere Gesicht des Krieges: Deutsche Feldpostbriefe, 1939–1945* (Munich: C. H. Beck, 1982), 171.

38. Arno J. Mayer, *Why Did the Heavens Not Darken? The "Final Solution" in History* (New York: Pantheon, 1988). The title reference is to Solomon bar Simon's lament referring to the Jewish massacre of 1096, "Why did the heavens not darken and the stars not withhold their radiance, why did not the sun and moon turn dark?" (Ibid., 26–27). Mayer unfortunately missed the millennial aspects of both the medieval crusades and the Nazi push to destroy Jewish Bolshevism and to colonize the East. For a critique of Mayer's book see John K. Roth, "Review of Holocaust Revision, by Arno Mayer," *Holocaust and Genocide Studies* 5 (1990): 217–21.

39. See for instance the evidence put forward by Peter Longerich, "From Mass Murder to the 'Final Solution': The Shooting of Jewish Civilians during the First Months of the Eastern Campaign within the Context of Nazi Jewish Genocide," in Wegner, *From Peace to War*, 253–75.

40. On the notion of the eastern war as a crusade and its usefulness for generating volunteers see Jürgen Förster, "The Crusade Aspect," in *Germany and the Second World War. Vol. 4: The Attack on the Soviet Union*. Ed. by Research Institute for Military History (New York: Oxford University Press, 1998), 1049–80. See also Wolfram Wette, "Die propagandistische Begleitmusik zum deutschen Überfall auf die Sowjetunion am 22. Juni 1941," in *"Unternehmen Barbarossa" Der deutsche Überfall auf die Sowjetunion, 1941: Berichte, Analysen, Dokumente* ed. Gerd R. Ueberschär and Wolfram Wette (Paderborn: F. Schöningh, 1984), 111–29, especially pages 122–23.

41. See Gerald Reitlinger, *The Final Solution: An Attempt to Exterminate the Jews of Europe, 1939–1945* (South Brunswick: T. Yoseloff, 1968), 89ff; Helmut Krausnick, "Die Einsatzgruppen vom Anschluß Österreichs bis zum Feldz ug gegen die Sowjetunion," in Helmut Krausnick and Hans-Heinrich Wilhelm, *Die Truppe des Weltanschauungskriegs: Die Einsatzgruppen der Sicherheitspolizei und des SD, 1939–1941* (Stuttgart: Deutsche Verlags-Anstalt, 1981), 107ff, 150ff; Raul Hilberg, *The Destruction of the European Jews* (Chicago: Quadrangle Books, 1961). In later editions Hilberg put the date to shortly before June 22, 1941, when Operation Barbarossa began.

42. Richard Breitman, "Plans for the Final Solution in Early 1941," *German Studies Review* 17 (1994): 483–93.

43. Originally put forth in Christopher Browning, "The Euphoria of Victory and the Final Solution: Summer–Fall 1941," *German Studies Review* 17 (1994): 473–81. Browning's analysis is greatly expanded in his *The Origins of the Final*

Solution: The Evolution of Nazi Jewish Policy, September 1939–March 1942 (Lincoln: University of Nebraska Press, 2004).

44. Ralf Ogorreck, *Die Einsatzgruppen und die "Genesis der Endlösung"* (Berlin: Metropol, 1996); Philippe Burrin, *Hitler and the Jews: The Genesis of the Holocaust* (New York: Edward Arnold, 1994), esp. 133ff.

45. Reproduced in Kurt Pätzold and Erika Schwarz, *Tagesordnung, Judenmord: Die Wannsee-Konferenz am 20. Januar 1942: eine Dokumentation zur Organisation der "Endlösung,"* 2nd ed., (Berlin: Metropol, 1992), 79. Longerich, "From Mass Murder to the 'Final Solution,'" 272, argues that this order does in fact point to the universal order. Christian Gerlach argues the opposite in "The Wannsee Conference, the Fate of German Jews and Hitler's Decision in Principle to Exterminate all European Jews," in Omer Bartov, ed., *The Holocaust: Origins, Implementation, Aftermath* (New York: Routledge, 2000), 106–61. Longerich points out the Auschwitz commandant Hoss wrote in his autobiography that Himmler informed him of Hitler's order to exterminate all Jews in "the summer of 1941." The reason he was informed was that the "existing death camps in the east are unable to carry out the planned large-scale campaigns," implying that the "large-scale campaign" was to exterminate all Jews. By December 8 the first Polish Jews died in the gas chambers.

46. Gerlach, "The Wannsee Conference," 118. I will return to Gerlach's counter argument shortly.

47. Quoted in Longerich, "From Mass Murder to the 'Final Solution,'" 270.

48. See the documentation in Czeslaw Madajczyk, "Besteht ein Synchronismus zwischen dem 'Generalplan Ost' und der Endlösung der Judenfrage?" in Wolfgang Michalka, ed., *Der Zweite Weltkrieg. Analysen, Grundzüge, Forschungsbilanz,* 2nd ed. (Munich: Piper, 1990): 858–73.

49. Adolf Hitler, *Hitler's Secret Conversations, 1941–1944,* trans. Norman Cameron and R. H. Stevens (New York: Signet, 1961), 108

50. Quoted in Gerlach, "The Wannsee Conference," 136. Gerlach concludes that this referred only to a "slow process of annihilation" to occur in the distant future. He provides no documentation for why he has come to this conclusion.

51. Quoted in Hermann Graml, *Antisemitism in the Third Reich,* trans. Tim Kirk (Cambridge: Blackwell, 1992), 186.

52. Discussed in Gerlach, "The Wannsee Conference," esp. 120–27.

53. Ibid., 123. Gerlach, I think rightly, rejects Browning's argument, cited earlier, that Hitler made the decision to extermination in the "euphoria" of victory, thinking the war was over and that he was invincible (although the latter does fit with Hitler's messianic self-perception).

54. Heinrich Himmler, *Der Dienstkalender Heinrich Himmlers 1941/1942,* ed. Peter Witte et al. (Hamburg: Hans Christians Verlag, 1999), 292–94. A photocopy of the handwritten notation can be found on page 294.

55. Trial of the Major War Criminals, vol. 27, PS-1517, 270.

56. Goebbels, *Tagebücher*, pt. 2, vol. 2, 498–99. Entry December 13, 1941.

57. Hans Frank, *Das Diensttagebuch des deutschen Generalgouverneurs in Polen 1939–1945* (Stuttgart: Deutsche Verlags-Anstalt, 1975), ed. Werner Präg and Wolfgang Jacobmeyer, 457–58.

58. The minutes of the meeting demonstrate that there was little resistance to the idea of extermination, only some disagreement over how to define part-Jews and the like. Broadening the definition not only met Hitler's desires but, as Gerlach, "The Wannsee Conference," 118, notes, the broader definition sped up the process by diminishing the number of cases forwarded to Hitler for possible exclusion from deportation and eventual extermination.

59. Quoted in Gerlach, "The Wannsee Conference," note 142, page 153.

60. Dormarus, *Hitler: Reden und Proklamationen, 1932–1945,* vol. 2, 1828–29.

61. Quoted in Gerlach, "The Wannsee Conference," 132.

62. Himmler, *Geheimreden*, 200. In a speech of 1944, one that was sparked by God "saving" Hitler from the July 20 assassination attempt, and one that justified the killing of innocent Jewish women and children by comparing it to the result of Allied bombing raids then being made on Germany, Himmler concluded that if Germany had not removed the Jews from Germany the raids would not have happened. Himmler then returned to the prophecy, tying the atrocities committed by the Nazis and the Allied carpet bombing to alleged Jewish machinations. Himmler also tied the world-historical turning point of the war and the Holocaust repeatedly to Hitler's life, telling his men again and again that Hitler was a once-in-two-thousand-year savior sent by God. Ibid., 238–39.

63. Quoted in Diewerge, *Deutsche Soldaten sehen die Sowjet-Union,* 38.

64. Quoted in Norman Cohn, *Warrant for Genocide: The Myth of the Jewish World Conspiracy and Protocols of Zion* (London: Serif, 1996), 240.

65. Speech excerpted in Jeremy Nokes and Geoffrey Pridham, eds., *Nazism 1919–1945: A Documentary Reader,* vol. 3 (Exeter: University of Exeter, 1988), 1200.

66. Quoted in Cohn, *Warrant for Genocide,* 211.

NOTES TO THE APPENDIX

1. Ian Kershaw, *Hitler, 1889–1936: Hubris* (New York: W. W. Norton, 1999), xiv. *Hitler Speaks* is the title of the British edition of Rauschning's *Gespräche mit Hitler* (New York: Europa Verlag, 1940), which was published in the United States as *The Voice of Destruction* (New York: Putnam, 1940).

2. Hitler can, however, be compared to Jesus in his self-perception as a prophet and messiah figure, as well as in his acceptance in this role by many of his followers. I explore this messianic identification in chapters 4 and 5. Besides,

it is not for the historian to decide who is a genuine messiah and who is false. That is a religious decision not an academic one.

3. Indeed, many of the world's great religious writings come to us second-hand, often reconstructed many years after the fact. This is true of the *Koran* and the *Hadith*, the attributed utterances of Mohammed, both compiled many years after the fact. The same is true of the *Avesta*, the "authoritative utterances" of Zoroaster/Zarathustra, the Iranian apocalyptic prophet whose words were passed down orally for centuries before being composed as a text. Similarly, the words of the Gautama Siddhartha, the historical Buddha, were written down decades after his death. If we applied the harsh historiographic criteria of historians of Nazism to these sources, all would be rendered suspect and consequently useless. The history of religion would be difficult, if not impossible, to reconstruct. If the Nazi movement is essentially religious in nature, as I argue it is, then we must treat the sources accordingly.

4. I address the nature of this speaking style in more detail in chapter 5.

5. Besides the Eckart, Rauschning, Wagener, and Table Talk sources described later, accounts by individuals who witnessed such performances can be found in the "Hitler Source Book," (Washington, D.C.: National Archives, Records of the Office of Strategic Services, 1943), RG226 pp. 141, 292, 307, 343, 369, 420, 668.

6. Dietrich Eckart, *Der Bolschewismus von Moses bis Lenin: Zwiegespräch zwischen Adolf Hitler and mir* (Munich: Hoheneichen-Verlag, 1924).

7. This portion of Himmler's recommended reading list can be found in Manfred Messerschmidt, *Die Wehrmacht im NS-Staat: Zeit der Indoktrination* (Hamburg: R.v. Decker, 1969), 241.

8. Ernst Nolte, "Eine früher Quelle zu Hitlers Antisemitische," *Historische Zeitschrift* 192 (1961): 584–606. Hitler's wartime monologues, compiled from notes taken by party secretary Martin Bormann, have most recently appeared as *Hitler's Table Talk, 1941–44: His Private Conversations*, 3rd ed., trans. Norman Cameron and R. H. Stevens (New York: Enigma Books, 2000).

9. Margarete Plewnia, *Auf dem Weg zu Hitler: Der völkische Publizist Dietrich Eckart* (Bremen: Schüneman, 1970), esp. 94–112, and Shaul Esh, "Eine neue literarische Quelle Hitlers? Eine methodologische Überlegung," *Geschichte in Wissenshaft und Unterricht* 15 (1964): 487–93.

10. Ralph Max Engelman, in his unpublished but essential "Dietrich Eckart and the Genesis of Nazism," Ph.D. dissertation, University of Michigan, 1971, 233–38, noted that Eckart's correspondence from the time of the work's composition makes it clear that Eckart is in fact the sole author. However, he adds, I believe correctly, that "everything we know about Eckart and Hitler lends credence to the document as a representation of the relationship and ideas they shared" (236).

11. Hitler ended the second volume of *Mein Kampf* with reference to the

putsch martyrs who "sacrificed themselves for us all" and who took fulfillment of their chosen duty "to its final consequence." He then wrote, "And among them I want also to count that man, one of the best, who devoted his life to the awakening of his, our people, in his writings and his thoughts and finally in his deeds" (687). Ian Kershaw, in a rather weak attempt to dismiss Eckart's importance, states that the dedication was "pro forma—directed at the many who knew full well Hitler's early indebtedness to Eckart." Here Kershaw is echoing Albrecht Tyrell's equally unsubstantiated refutation of Eckart's importance. See Kershaw, *Hitler, 1889–1936: Hubris* (New York: W. W. Norton, 1995), 651, note 119, and Albrecht Tyrell, *Vom 'Trommler' zum 'Führer': der Wandel von Hitlers Selbstverständnis Zwischen 1919 u. 1924 u. d. Entwicklung d. NSDAP* (Munich: Fink, 1975), 190–91, note 49, and 194, note 70. Kershaw allows Hitler some "indebtedness" to Eckart, but only for his ability to connect Hitler with politically and financially powerful individuals; he thus ignores Eckart's intellectual influence on Hitler. However, everything we know of Hitler points to the sincerity of his feelings for Eckart. In fact, even nearly twenty years after his death, with Germany entangled in world war, Hitler referred to Eckart more than any other individual. Kershaw, not surprisingly, largely dismisses the table talk, as well.

12. Rauschning, *Voice of Destruction*.

13. Rauschning utilized accounts of personal contacts and published speeches and other Nazi publications. His notes have never surfaced.

14. Theodor Schieder, *Hermann Rauschnings "Gespräche mit Hitler" als Geschichtsquelle* (Opladen: Westdeutscher, 1972), 62. It has since come out that Schieder was complicit in the Nazi coordination of higher education and remained silent about this fact for years after the war. However, his analysis of Rauschning is judicious, and certainly not the work of a crypto-Nazi, as some have recently claimed.

15. Ibid., 62. As translated by Henry A. Turner in his edition of Otto Wagener's *Hitler: Memoirs of a Confidant* (New Haven: Yale University Press, 1985), xv–xvi.

16. Wolfgang Hänel, *Hermann Rauschnings "Gespräche mit Hitler"—Eine Geschichtsfälschung* (Ingolstadt: Zeitgesch. Forschungsstelle Ingolstadt, 1984). Interestingly, the Nazis themselves used a similar argument to down play what they considered to be a very dangerous book. A document found in the German Federal Archives reports the following discussion between Nazi propaganda leaders at a weekly conference that took place in Goebbels's office in February 1940: "Mr. Böhme pointed out the great dangerousness of the new Rauschning book. He maintains that it is essential to take the position in the Foreign Office, that is possible by the demonstrable observation, that Rauschning was near the Führer altogether but a few times, and in no way, as he asserts, [freely] came and went." Found in a Goebbels Conference folder, *Bundesarchiv* R5/20.001. I

would like to thank Kerstin Stutterheim, who found this document, for bringing it to my attention.

17. Eckhard Jesse, "Herman Rauschning—Der fragwürdige Kronzeuge," in Ronald Smelser, Enrico Syring and Rainer Zitelmann, eds., *Die braune Elite II: 21 weitere biographische Skizzen* (Darmstadt: Wissenschaftliche Buchgesellschaft, 1993), 193–205; Fritz Tobias, "Auch Fälschungen haben lange Beine: Des Senatespräsidenten Rauschnings 'Gespräche mit Hitler,'" in Karl Corino, ed., *Gefälscht!: Betrug in Politik, Literatur, Wissenschaft, Kunst und Musik* (Nördlingen: Greno, 1988), 91–105.

18. Martin Broszat, "Enthüllung? Die Rauschning-Kontroverse," in his *Nach Hitler: Der Schwierige Umgang mit unserer Geschichte* (Munich: R. Oldenbourg, 1986), 249–51.

19. Eberhard Jäckel, *Hitler's World View: A Blueprint for Power* (Cambridge, Mass.: Harvard University Press, 1981), 124–25.

20. It should be noted that *Mein Kampf* was not actually composed by Hitler alone but originated as notes taken from Hitler's dictations while he was in Landsberg and was later compiled with the help of others as a semicoherent book. Hitler's unpublished second book was compiled in much the same way.

21. Published in German as *Hitler aus nächster Nähe: Aufzeichn. e. Vertrauten: 1929–1932* (Kiel: Arndt, 1987), then in English as *Hitler: Memoirs of a Confidant*. Editor Henry A. Turner's analysis of the historiographic importance of the work is balanced and well thought out. See ibid., ix–xxvi. The original notebooks are at the Institut für Zeitgeschichte, Munich, as part of the collection "Aufzeichnungen des Gen. Maj a.D. Dr.h.c. Otto Wagener." For background on Wagener see Henry A. Turner, "Otto Wagener—Der vergessene Vertraute Hitlers," in Smelser et al, *Die Braune Elite II*, 243–53.

22. Turner's introduction to Wagener, *Memoirs of a Confidant*, xvi.

23. Ibid., xv.

24. This is perhaps because of their obvious similarity to the now ostracized Rauschning work. It also reflects a general historiographic trend in Hitler studies away from any subjective source, whether police battalion postwar interrogations or Holocaust survivor testimonials, deemed suspect by their subjectivity (including the vagaries of memory and questions of motive), and to objective sources such as voting records and the like. This is unfortunate, for history is as much about reconstructing how historical actors subjectively conceptualized their experiences as it is about who did what when. It is interesting that while historians in general, and in particular historians who study ethnic, religious, and gender identities, have embraced subject constructions of history as valid and crucial sources, historians of Hitler studies have gone the other direction, rejecting most such sources as "tainted," hoping to find answers instead in impersonal collective databases of voting records and the like, or in the mountains of bureaucratic memos gathering dust in German archives. It is time, I be-

lieve, for new approaches to historiography to be applied to study of the Nazi period.

25. According to Schieder, Rauschning met with Hitler some thirteen times, perhaps half of these alone. Wagener had an office in the Brown house and was in the inner circle around Hitler and had many more opportunities to have personal contact with Hitler than did Rauschning, perhaps hundreds of times. Fact checking has proven Rauschning to have had an unusually good memory, though his dating is unreliable and he appears to have invented statistics. Once again, however, it is the subjective imagery that is important for this study, and not so much the objective chronological and statistical material.

26. For a fine discussion of the postconversion reconstruction of self see Charles Strozier, *Apocalypse: On the Psychology of Fundamentalism in America* (Boston: Beacon Press, 1994).

27. The Theodore Abel Collection is housed at the archives of the Hoover Institute on War, Revolution, and Peace at Stanford University. Two sets of *Die alte Garte sprichts* can be found as part of the Third Reich Collection in the manuscript section of the Library of Congress, Washington, D.C. The sets are nearly identical. Set 1 includes reproductions of letters to the editor Adalbert Gimbel from Nazi luminaries such as Goebbels. Part of the materials originally intended for this set, but not included (perhaps because of the war), can be found in the *NSDAP Hauptarchiv*, roll 26, available on microfilm from the Hoover Institute. The *"Kampfberichte"* collected by the regional leaders of Hessen-Nassau are also of interest. This can be found in *NSDAP Hauptarchiv*, roll 27, folders 528–31.

28. Theodore Abel, *Why Hitler Came to Power*, reprint edition (Cambridge: Harvard University Press, 1986), 3. The Nazis certified announcement further made it clear to the prospective essayists that the contest was "organized under the tutelage of the sociology department of Columbia University" and that "the purpose of the contest is the collection of material on the history of National Socialism, so that the American public may be informed about it on the basis of factual, personal documents." To limit hyperbole and flights of fancy, Abel noted that the judges were looking for the essays that offered "the most detailed and trustworthy accounts. Style, spelling, or dramatic story value will not be considered. Completeness and frankness are the sole criteria." Ibid. The style found in the Abel Collection does in fact run the gamut, from barely literate accounts of brawls by some less educated SA men to well-written, if a bit overly dramatic, accounts by well-educated respondents. Despite the differences in education and writing style among the writers, the millennial and messianic imagery in the essays is remarkably consistent, a testament to the power of millennial myth. I would add that Abel decided to ignore those essayists who wrote with the most flair and hyperbole, but if the imagery is largely consistent, I see no need to follow this example. Indeed, the more picturesque writers often put into words bet-

ter the millennial impulse apparent even among the lesser or more mundane essayists. Again, it is the imagery that I am most interested in, as it is a window into the subjective emotional world of the Old Guard. Abel also left out the forty-eight women writers as constituting too small a sampling to be relevant. However, their narrative is important, and, regarding millennial and messianic content, largely consistent.

29. Moreover, Abel's project reflected the Nazis' own desires to reconstruct party history with the development of the NSDAP *Hauptarchiv*. After their assumption of power, the Nazis began to acquire original documents pertaining to, and to solicit accounts by participants in, the early party history. Interestingly, these accounts, such as the history of the Hitler putsch and the now sacralized blood flag, are similarly remembered in millennial terms. The party's reconstruction of its history, therefore, is millennial in content and interpretation.

30. Thomas Childers, foreword to Theodore Abel, *Why Hitler Came to Power* (Cambridge: Harvard University Press, 1986), xvii.

31. Thomas Childers, *The Nazi Voter: The Social Foundations of Fascism in Germany, 1919–1933* (Chapel Hill: University of North Carolina Press, 1983), 12.

32. Childers, *The Nazi Voter;* Merkl, *Political Violence under the Swastika* (Princeton: Princeton University Press, 1975); and Claudia Koonz, "Nazi Women before 1933: Rebels against Emancipation," *Social Science Quarterly* (1976): 553–63. See James Rhodes, *The Hitler Movement: A Modern Millenarian Revolution* (Stanford: Hoover Institution Press, 1980). With the exception of Rhodes, all these scholars miss the apocalypticism, millennialism, and messianism found in the collection.

33. Childers, foreword to Abel's *Why Hitler,* xix.

34. Ludwell Denny, "France and the German Counter-Revolution," *The Nation* 116 (February 1923): 295.

Index

About the Author

David Redles is Assistant Professor of History at Cuyahoga Community College in Ohio and Research Associate of the Center for Millennial Studies at Boston University.